The Mythology of Work

The Mythology of Work

How Capitalism Persists Despite Itself

Peter Fleming

PlutoPress
www.plutobooks.com

First published 2015 by Pluto Press
345 Archway Road, London N6 5AA

www.plutobooks.com

Copyright © Peter Fleming 2015

The right of Peter Fleming to be identified as the author of this work has been
asserted by him in accordance with the Copyright, Designs and Patents Act 1988.

British Library Cataloguing in Publication Data
A catalogue record for this book is available from the British Library

ISBN   978 0 7453 3487 5   Hardback
ISBN   978 0 7453 3486 8   Paperback
ISBN   978 1 7837 1299 1   PDF eBook
ISBN   978 1 7837 1301 1   Kindle eBook
ISBN   978 1 7837 1300 4   EPUB eBook

10   9   8   7   6   5   4   3   2   1

Typeset by Stanford DTP Services, Northampton, England
Text design by Melanie Patrick
Simultaneously printed by CPI Antony Rowe, Chippenham, UK
and Edwards Bros in the United States of America

Contents

Introduction
Once Upon a Time,
Man Invented Work ...

Once upon a time, in some faraway corner of that universe which is dispersed into countless solar systems, there was a planet upon which clever animals invented 'work'. Slowly, work lost its association with survival and self-preservation and became a painful and meaningless ritual acted out for its own sake. Taking on a hue of endlessness and inescapability, this curious invention consumed almost every part of the clever beast's lives. Its constant presence kept the order; held certain divisions in place; lavished the few at the top with untold riches. Wonderful discoveries that might have made life easier for its inhabitants – like a device called 'email' – were twisted into the opposite, scattering dread and unhappiness everywhere. Life-support conditions on the planet became increasingly intolerable as the availability of actual work began to disappear. Strangely, this made the leaders celebrate it even more. The situation was clearly out of hand. Would these poor creatures ever rebel?

Readers of Nietzsche will recognize the paragraph above, echoing his attempt to temper the self-centredness of modern man and the arrogant belief in eternal 'knowledge'. The parable places this conceit in proper historical context and demonstrates the limited specificity of a system that appears universal. This book represents my attempt to do the same with the notion of work. But if 'man' was difficult to dislodge from the throne of infinity then doing the same with 'work' in the present era feels an almost impossible task. And I suggest that this bearing of impossibility is only a recent achievement. Following the postmodern historization of everything during the 1980s and 1990s, work strangely remained one of the few concepts that retained a sense of preordained immutableness – perhaps more so *following* the postmodern turn. This may have something to do with the close sympathies that postmodern relativism enjoyed with the neoliberal capitalist project. Whilst gender, race, sexuality and all other manner of identity positions were deemed 'up for grabs', capitalism was silently ushered in as the ultimate ontological horizon of social life. It was not that work was beyond question. Rather it was not worthy of questioning. After all, is it not a rather boring notion to be excessively concerned with? And let's face it, don't we actually *need* work in order to remain distinct from the dark lands of economic backwardness and cultural stasis?

It is no exaggeration to suggest that work has become one of the new false universals of our time. This book seeks to understand why this is so and what we might do about it, since this is by no means a natural state of affairs. But it is easy to forget that given the way work has been implicated in so many social activities we engage in today (from paying the bills to education, to family matters, to choosing a life-long romantic partner for some, and so forth). Work and 'living' more generally are so inextricably entwined that it might seem that questioning the idea of work is a little like questioning 'life itself'. For don't we all have to work to live? No, not really. It is a social construct like any other – but the ubiquity it has attained over the last 20 years is quite astonishing. The patent dysfunctions of building a world around our jobs (or lack thereof if we are unemployed) are now becoming clear: not only permanent existential dread, which we have crafted as a way of life in order to tolerate the intolerable, but also the psychical and social damage that so much work has precipitated. Moreover, this trend is not contradicted by the fact that over half the global population eligible for work are currently unemployed. I shall argue that neoliberal rationality has created a neat ideological symbiosis between this strict 'no alternative' attitude we have towards paid employment and its manufactured scarcity (i.e. unemployment). And this serves an important class function under conditions of extreme inequality.

So how and why do many jobs feel so all-encompassing? To put it crudely, why are we working so much today and having difficulty in seeing a life beyond work in both personal and political terms? Of course, the bills have to be paid. But conventional wisdom presents a number of other answers, all of which I suggest are problematic. For example, perhaps the desire to make more money is to blame. Where this explanation falls down is that many organizations don't increase our rewards if we spend more time in the office. And once a certain level of material wealth is obtained, we tend to work for other reasons. What about the fear of unemployment, especially in times of economic crisis and uncertainty? There might be something to this. But marathon-like displays of work are also observed in occupations that are relatively secure and unthreatened by cuts. Perhaps we work so much because we simply love our jobs. Unfortunately, 'love' is not a word used by most of the global workforce when describing their occupations. A recent survey (discussed further in Chapter 1) reveals that only about 13 per cent of the global workforce considered themselves 'engaged' by their jobs. The remaining 87 per cent feel deeply alienated. What about iPhones and email? Mobile technology comes closer to accounting for our work-obsessed culture. Smart phones and laptops mean that we are always contactable and this facilities the creeping encroachment of work over our lives. But this explanation is not completely convincing since there is nothing inherent in mobile technology that *forces* us to check our emails at 5 a.m. There must be some other social pressure behind it.

These typical accounts of contemporary work tend to overlook its fetishistic character. When we focus on the notion of work, we ought to see it as being only the concrete personification of a broader process. That process is, of course, capitalism. The accumulation of capital – in all its variants, including financial or fictitious capital – involves the use of a labour process that takes a variety of organizational forms. That labour process is in turn built around exploitation and class relations (i.e. who owns and controls the means of production). What we call work is the social embodiment and ritualistic calculus of that exploitation process. One reason that the ideology of work has got away with its recent exponential growth, becoming a 'way of life', is that it is still confused with survival and ineluctable necessity. This is one of the great ruses of neoliberal reason: it is able to impose an artificial regime based upon the pretext of organic self-preservation. And who can argue with that? I hope to demonstrate in the following pages that our workers' society has little to do with material subsistence, although that doesn't mean our jobs are any less real in terms of the influence and sway work holds over vast numbers of people around the world.

The way work exploits us in post-industrial societies has taken on some specific attributes that this book aims to explore in more depth. Neoliberal class relations are distinct in that they transform exploitation into something that strongly resembles *subsidization*. We work, pay taxes, take care of the bills and commuting costs for one single reason: not to 'survive' but so that the governing elite gains its privileges for nothing. Our labour is designed to provide freedom to the rich. Our work exists in order to subsidize the costs of their existence. For example, when I pay my taxes as a middle-class worker (which, counter to the neoliberal ideology of a minimalist state, is more oppressive than ever under this system), the state is able to provide 'tax relief' to the corporate oligarchy. When I pay exorbitant fees for my education, this frees up cash for the ruling class to enjoy their world gratis. And so on. In this sense, work is no longer about 'earning' an income but closer to a rentier logic of extraction, whereby our struggle to make ends meet forms an outward payment structure that has no return benefit. And that structure is class based, of course. The more the neoliberal elite desires complete exemption from the social systems we are forced to participate in, the more we have to work. And because neoliberal capitalism entails such extreme inequalities of wealth distribution, work must become an inexorable way of life for most of us, rather than something we do among other things.

It has recently been stated that almost half of working people are economically insecure in Western capitalist societies. In the large cities of the world, the first hour of the working day is simply paying for that day's commute. All of this might sound like a banal fact, but it is actually quite shocking since work was once promoted as an exclusive vehicle for avoiding insecurity. Today it is the chief method for promulgating precarity. Full-time employment is one of the few things about you that predicts the likelihood that you will someday face true impoverishment. Big banks have an algorithm that uses the proxy of work to make these predictions on a daily basis since overdraft and financial indebtedness is their central source of profit. The calculation goes like this: if you work, then you probably need to commute; that means you must expend a specified proportion of your income on the capacity to work itself, which will often require some kind of credit, and this credit can be correlated with accommodation costs (since it is less expensive to commute than to live close to the workplace). That relationship allows the bank to make a rough calculation of the type of mortgage or rental arrangement in place, and from there they can delineate your family status, number of children, and future education costs. And so on. The neoliberal state adores this situation because workers are its prime source of economic subsidization (i.e. the transfer of wealth from you to the rich, and also to the underclass who would rebel without your cash) and the raw material of a different kind of ideological self-vindication. Insecurity itself becomes an *ideology*; let's call this the ideology of work, a class-tale that exceeds its own concrete social consequences. And this is why the negative is now integral to the new propaganda. Your enemy outsider status is the norm – everyone's exception is the norm. This is the only way it could ever be in a society that actively advocates the freedoms of socialism for an elite and nasty dog-eat-dog capitalism for the rest. Perhaps this also highlights the underlying meaning of a society in which it looks as if work is done simply for the sake of it. This mythological status means that work is experienced as a sort of cultural ritual that is ultimately pointless. But it actually fulfils a specific class relation that is not accidental, but economically strategic and intentional. In short, we are no longer living in the 1950s. Nor the 1990s. Or the 2000s. Welcome to the desert of a rebirthed *pre-modernity*, the new social constellation of advanced capitalism.

Two interesting implications follow. First, the universalization of the ideology of work makes it difficult to challenge. This has been an extremely effective weapon for the ruling class, because the notion of work takes on near ontological qualities. And as I mentioned above, how can we question or reject that? It would be like rebuffing 'life itself'. This allows the subsidization process to be firmly entrenched and difficult to avoid. It is for this reason too that neoliberal apologists despise the social common – be it shareware, cooperatives and so forth – since it short-circuits the cross-subsidization structure of the late-capitalist order. When we engage in self-help another world emerges which is eminently milder, more realistic and happier. And secondly, much of the work we conduct comes to look rather purposeless and without objective merit. We feel trapped in a self-referential malaise of 'empty labour' (Paulsen, 2014). This ritualistic purposelessness is not orchestrated merely for ideological reasons. It also plays an important economic or class function. The future becomes a reflection of the broken present that everyone can see but do little about. The false totality of capitalist relations morphs into a fetish of its own apparent irreplaceability. Of course, this is all imaginary, but a *concrete imaginary* nevertheless with very real effects and consequences.

The labour of subsidization that has become the key motif of exploitation under neoliberal capitalism has both a vertical and a horizontal trajectory. Our productive labour – and given work's ritualistic aspect described already, a good deal of it isn't 'productive' – follows an upward movement of subsidization to the ruling elite. However, this also necessitates a horizontal and closely related form of exploitation. We not only pay for the neoliberal oligarchy directly but also indirectly as the template of work spreads out across the social body. For example, as the neoliberal state cuts housing welfare, working families and loved ones pick up the bill instead. The social commons stands in to cushion the blow caused by the subsidization economy, which today often takes the form of a massive reservoir of personal debt. Indeed, debt is the ultimate instrument of horizontal subsidization, for it frees dominant groups from the direct social costs of their predatory activities.

Perhaps this structure also accounts for why the boundaries between work and non-work once so important for the reproduction of capitalism have slowly been dismantled over the last 20 years. Many of us no longer check in and out as our parents and grandparents once did. Work is a way of life, not only for symbolic (or cultural) reasons but also for practical reasons. With the streamlining of organizations (to save costs) and the increasingly chaotic nature of many jobs that are structured around 'free market' principles (e.g., competitive individualism, performance incentives, etc.), we begin to bear the full material costs of an employment system that is totally dysfunctional. And much of this occurs outside formal office hours: preparing for a meeting at the weekend, receiving a call from the boss at 11 p.m., paying for things vital to the job (uniforms, dental care, etc.) off our own bat. The neoliberal dream of turning us all into our own individual micro-enterprises – or what I will call in this book the 'I, Job' function – appears to have succeeded. But of course, here is the downside. Taking on capitalism's structural weaknesses as our own entails a serious price. The crisis of economic reason is lived as an internal social/ existential crisis.

This facet of the post-industrial subsidization economy is wonderfully captured in the British TV comedy, *Peep Show*, starring David Mitchell and Robert Webb as Mark and 'Jez'. The comedy conveys the post-Blair years of social dejection and pointless work, all with a touch of absurdity added to the mix. In one episode, the otherwise happily unemployed Jez lands what he thinks might be his dream job when he meets Ben, an arrogant geek who sells music merchandize on the Web. Jez is rewarded with the job after sitting by Ben's side as he lies in a deep coma in hospital (Jez was really only there because he had designs on Ben's beautiful girlfriend). What is interesting about Jez is that he displays a healthy feat of work. But this time it is different. Because Ben is so relaxed and unconcerned about when the workday begins and the job is free from the clocking-in system typical of his previous forays into paid employment, Jez boasts that in his new role, 'work never starts'. The boundaries between labour and private life are fluid and almost non-existent. Jez aims to relish this informality. However, things turn out very differently:

Mark: Jez, It's 12 p.m. on a Saturday and you're up, you've been out. Are you tripping?

Jez: Ben rang at 7 a.m. and wanted me to go into the office.

Mark: But I thought 'work never starts'?

Jez: Yeah, well, apparently work never starts and work never stops [holds up mobile phone]: it's got me by the blackberries! Turning it off is a sackable offense. If I go to a funeral, I can switch it on to vibrate. Plus, it turns out that the website is only really about the 'merch'.

Mark: The 'merch'?

Jez: Merchandize. Ben says I am all about the 'merch'. Cut me and I bleed 'merch'. I can't believe I had him at my mercy in the hospital and I let him go. If I'd known he was such an arsehole I would have given his tube a waggle ... there was not even anyone at the office. Just me and the servers. After a while I started to pretend to be a robot and then ... I sort of couldn't remember if I was a robot or not and so I had to get out of there.

Humour aside, this exchange nicely expresses some interesting dynamics concerning the 'social factory' of neoliberal capitalism. So-called non-work time is a resource to be used up, especially with the help of mobile technology. This is what gives late capitalism a strange sense of permanence – we are never not at work. Even if we are not being formally paid, that is no longer an excuse for deserting one's role. The time of labour curves back on itself, with only the happy occasion of a funeral partially exempting you from the injunction always to be on call. Moreover, this relationship to one's job functions to transform the body into an observable commodity form. As Jez points out, he is the 'merch' and he must fully identify with the product; not only in terms of liking or living it – this is nothing to do with commitment – but of sacrificing oneself for it. The metaphor of blood is very significant here. Your personal fortunes are but a mirror image of how much you are willing to be taken over by the immaterial labour process.

It is also telling that when Jez arrived at the office, he just sat there surrounded by mainframe servers. The intent of Ben's order was not related to productivity, but to obedience. This is the real cause of the 'empty labour' that defines so many jobs today – not mindless boredom but egregious displays of subordination that have little bearing on actual economic output. Moreover, we can observe that the authority relationship between Jez and Ben has a very strong informal flavour. Popular management pundits would like us to believe that this makes work more pleasant.

They even suggest that organizations ought to design their offices after warehouse apartments, to mimic the creativity, comradery and ethos of people driven by a labour of love. But workplace informality has a dark side; namely, the potential for authoritarianism to take on a rather sadistic and perverse quality. Informality and power do not go well together. Under such circumstances we are not only paying for the elite's freedoms, but being callously toyed with to boot. Hence Jez's rancour.

And herein lies the problem with anti-work arguments that evoke Parkinson's Law. The idea behind the law is simple. If we are given eight hours to perform a task, it usually takes eight hours to do so successfully. If we are only given three hours to do *the same* task, it typically takes three hours to do so successfully. Therefore, we could spend much less time on the job whilst maintaining the same level of productivity achieved by the 40-hour work week. But there is hitch with this rationale. Capitalism doesn't operate by presenting us with finite tasks. Instead, many jobs are characterized by forever multiplying demands – this is why we are never 'done' with our work. Now we are getting to the heart of Jez's complaint. The time spent at work is structured by a certain type of display, particularly one's protracted submission. The neoliberal theatre of subordination is only partially interested in measurable productiveness. The informalization of the employment relationship reveals this quite clearly.

Other criticisms of contemporary management, including my own, have pointed out how neoliberalism aims to enlist the entire subjective personality of the worker, warts and all. Hence the recent focus on 'authenticity' and the 'just be yourself' philosophy in contemporary corporate jargon, whereby managers seek to tap the vast wealth of social knowhow and vested intuition that isn't easy to prescribe in formal workplace settings. In doing so, creativity and innovation are successfully wedded to self-exploitation. The evidence suggests that this trend has certainly been important, especially regarding self-managing teams, autonomy and so forth. But I would say that the focus on 'the subject' actually camouflages a more significant force indicative of capitalism today: namely, *rationalization*. For all the talk about individuality, difference, personal authenticity and plural identities, late capitalism is extremely one-dimensional, revolving almost singularly around questions of efficiency, utility and input–output effectiveness. And society doesn't function very well when organized exclusively on these principles: it bends and groans under the pressure as faceless technocrats further rationalize our worlds so that our bodies absorb the costs of an unworkable system.

Such rationalization does not contradict my earlier point concerning the primacy of gratuitous obedience over real economic efficiency. Indeed, the two trends operate in tandem, with some rather bizarre consequences.

Financialization and shareholder capitalism perhaps represents the apogee of rationalized capitalism. Here, the numerical monetary logic of pure accumulation truly creates an inversion of ends and means that is shocking. Whatever it takes to increase shareholder value – firing staff, plundering the natural environment, creating extremely volatile property-market bubbles – must be pursued in a single-minded fashion, even if it *harms* the organization in question. Like all forms of hyper-rationalization, shareholder capitalism fosters a mentality that is generally antisocial and sometimes diabolical when observed from an outside perspective. For example, a large funeral home corporation in the United Kingdom recently had to break some bad news to its shareholders. Dividends will be less than expected because the winter was rather mild. Therefore, fewer elderly people died. The valuable ends of providing funeral home services now become a mere means for profit maximization. The more deaths, the more money made, which is now the end that matters. One may even imagine the firm's managing directors eventually hoping for a harsh winter (as energy firms clearly do), perhaps even encouraging a speculative market around future weather patterns (as Enron notoriously did) and so forth.

We can observe a similar shareholder rationalism depleting city accommodation in the large centres of the capitalist West, something that is directly linked to the reproduction of the global workforce. Affordable and decent housing ought to be a basic entitlement. But it is not in a city like London, which is caught in an out-of-control frenzy of corporatization. Now property is a mere means to enhance the profits of large construction firms. As a result, it is no surprise that London is now considered one of the least liveable cities in Europe according to a recent 'liveability index' (see Economist Intelligence Unit, 2014), especially for a workforce that is dwelling in almost Victorian levels of deprivation (the 1800s blight of 'rickets' has recently made a return in England). For most of its citizens, a small plastic rectangle that we 'never leave home without' is the only thing that stands between them and the burgeoning under-proletariat. For sure, bankers need to be forever banished for (a) causing the current mess we are in and (b) having the audacity to continue to make excessive profits from the very socio-economic crisis they created. But construction firms are not far behind them in this respect.

This peculiar money-only focus entails a cultural logic too. All forms of rationality invariably seep into the biosphere and contaminate the way we appreciate the world. We are truly Weber's heirs. If we went back only 20 or 30 years, we would be astounded by the sheer non-utility that made up good parts of society, which to us today look incomprehensibly wasteful, irrational and non-transparent: tariffs in automobile industries that were never profitable in a 'free market' sense; jobs maintained to keep people in employment, and for no other reason; national sports teams that were still amateur and unremunerated; universities free of league tables and regimented performance assessment exercises. Even at the level of everyday culture and aesthetics, our currently conditioned perspective would view the formalities of the early 1970s as alien, meandering and uneconomical. Neoliberalism represents the reign of technocrats, and this has changed the way we see ourselves and others. In Marcuse's brilliant 1941 essay, 'Some Social Implications of Modern Technology', he focuses on this ideological aspect of rationalization, which has been amplified to the nth degree today. According to him, 'efficiency here called for integral unification and simplification, and for the removal of all "waste", the avoidance of all detours, it called for radical coordination' (Marcuse, 1941/1982: 65).

This is an important facet of how our overly contractualized lives around work are organized today and why it seems so inevitable and inescapable. Our very perceptions have been colonized by the technocrat – the fascist inside us. For some, even their own redundancy appears 'reasonable' if the economy is slowing down. They understand that this fate must be so. More importantly, this rationalization makes any other activity that does not fit the template of strict efficiency seem bizarre, especially behaviour that signals a degree of deviation or non-observance:

> The decisive point is that this attitude – which dissolves all actions into a sequence of semi-spontaneous reactions to prescribed mechanical norms – is not only perfectly rational but also perfectly reasonable. All protest is senseless, and the individual who would insist in his freedom of action would become a crank … It is a rational apparatus, combining utmost expediency with utmost convenience, saving time and energy, removing waste, adapting all means to ends. (Marcuse, 1941/1982: 66)

So, we have the worst of both worlds. Sadistic informality and punitive rationalization. For this reason, the tattle about 'play', 'well-being' and 'authenticity' in recent discussions of the modern workplace, even among radical critiques of capitalism, seems out of place. The rise of zero-hour contracts (whereby workers are paid only for the hours they work, and must wait until called upon by their employer) is a perfect exemplar of neoliberal employment systems in this respect. Extremely personal – we now know our bosses, they have our personal phone numbers, acknowledge our problems, etc. – but also ruthlessly rational. For these employers, would it not simply be a 'waste' to pay a worker for an extra hour when they technically didn't do anything? Ultimately, this is a cruel form of employment (low real wages, unpaid 'waiting time', no guarantee of work, employees bearing the negative externalities of business, etc.). But it makes perfect rational sense from a myopic economic perspective because it more effectively facilitates the subsidization process. Who will carry the real price that underlies the cost-saving and profit-maximizing employment policies of fast-food restaurants and online book stores? Perhaps family, more reluctantly the now emasculated welfare state, but ultimately the working class itself.

We must place this rationalization process once more in the context of class relations defined by subsidization. In the thought experiment above, we travelled back to that alien world 20 or 30 years ago and noted an unfathomable abundance of 'waste'. What exactly is this ostensible waste? Of course, we know the answer: a more equal distribution of wealth and life chances, and in some cases the rich subsidizing the poor and less fortunate – which is the complete opposite of the trend we observe today in which the recipients of subsidization are the ultra-super-rich. Rationalization is thus a question of perspective or standpoint rather than numerical formulation, and that standpoint is completely determined by class politics. The 'waste' that managerialism so meticulously identifies is often simply our freedom to act in concert to achieve self-determined ends. Or, our freedom to do nothing (although it should be remembered that, unlike Bertrand Russell, most successful anti-work advocates hate 'doing nothing' per se, which is more akin to life in the post-industrial office than anything else). But most importantly, neo-capitalism views the freedoms of worker democracy as the clearest manifestation of wastefulness. Workplace democracy is technocratic capitalism's greatest fear and enemy for obvious reasons. The computer says 'no'.

Private corporations, in tandem with the neoliberal state, play a powerful part in shaping the nature of modern work patterns today. However, the reader will note that I do not spend too much time discussing the corporation, as I have done this elsewhere in much more detail. But there is another reason for my lack of interest in the corporate form here. I believe that critical theory's concentration on the corporation is vital, but we must realize it for what it is: a symptomatic vehicle for class regulation, and one that is increasingly driven by labour divestment rather than inclusion or direct exploitation. My argument here has three parts. First, most people in the West (and the global economy) who have jobs are employed in small- or medium-sized businesses. The image of a vast throng toiling in the colossal firm does not really apply to the majority of workers. Secondly, the ideology of work is something detached from its organizational epitome – the private enterprise. As I hope to show in the following pages, we are compelled to produce via a diagrammatic mode of influence. This virtual articulation ironically makes the ideology of work even more concrete and material. Criticisms of the corporation are still crucially important, but they do not engage very well with this register of power. And thirdly, the multinational enterprise functions more as an easily identifiable (and divestible) front for class interests than as a seat of domination in itself. What lies precisely *behind* the large firm ought to be the true target of our criticism. But identifying this target is no easy task. Let me give an example.

At 3.44 p.m. on 19 November 2010, the Pike River Coal mine in New Zealand exploded. Dangerous levels of methane gas had been accumulating for some time. Some miners managed to escape, but 29 were trapped 1.5 kilometres underground as management alerted the local authorities and emergency services. Another major explosion rocked the mine on 24 November and then a third on 26 November. After a final explosion on the 28th all hope was lost. The miners' bodies were never recovered. Pike River Coal was an exemplar of neoliberal ideology in almost every respect. Established in the early 1980s when New Zealand underwent an unprecedented level of capitalist deregulation almost overnight, New Zealand Oil and Gas (NZOG) later purchased 31 per cent of the firm and two Indian firms 18.5 per cent. Then came investor demands to extract coal productively. The problem was obvious from the start. Extraction was an extremely difficult task given the geological setting. Moreover, the company cut corners on safety, having only one entrance to the mine rather than the two which are mandatory in most other counties. Subcontractors were also used, which put pressure on workers to bypass safety protocols (MacFie, 2013). And the New Zealand government significantly downsized the health and safety inspectorate to render it all but useless (self-regulation was the watchword of the day).

Following the disaster, Pike River Coal was put into receivership. Many of its governmental and corporate creditors were paid out. But the subcontractors were unsecured creditors right from the start. No compensation was paid to their families. As for the other workers, a court order was issued following an investigation. Given their negligence in breeching safety regulations, Pike River Coal was order to pay NZ$3.41 million to the workers' families. However, the firm simply stated that it had no money. The CEO of Pike River Coal, Peter Witthall, was then charged with health and safety crimes. He was found not guilty. An Australian contractor was also charged with negligence and found guilty. The penalty? NZ$46,800. The corporate form was no doubt an important factor for facilitating this disaster. But let's put this another way. Following the tragedy, who are we going to hold accountable? Pike River Coal? No, they were swiftly wound down as a going concern. The New Zealand government? Technically unaccountable – they didn't own the firm and had presented basic health and safety guidelines. What about the major investor NZOG? Technically unaccountable. They were only a shareholder. And trying to discover who actually owns a publicly listed firm like NZOG takes us ever closer to a murky world of multilayered subsidiaries and silent shareholders. What about the two Indian corporate shareholders? Saurashtra Fuels is a co-venture between Agarwalla and B.D. Sinha Group. And Gujarat NRE is a holding company, with many subsidiaries and investment layers, making it almost impossible to discern who exactly the key players are.

So, as you can see, the corporation is an impersonal house of mirrors, serving as a veiling anterior for a class coalition that would like to remain anonymous. Partially at least, we ought to analytically bypass the corporate form. This will typically lead back (after many levels of subsidiaries and holding companies) to a small group of individuals, members of the global ruling class who are often closely aligned with the state. We must speak of individuals rather than the corporation if we are to fight neoliberal capitalism successfully. Whereas work is an ideological abstraction or scripted structural position which has a universal tendency, ownership can often be traced back to a *real* individual or family. These two dimensions of capitalism form the texture of neoliberal reason. Plaintively focusing on an immediate, branded corporation (e.g. Pike River Coal) – especially when things go wrong and men die in a bottomless mine – often misses how domination functions through a Russian-doll-like rationale of displacement and potential divestment.

And finally, to come to grips with the debasement of work today, we must figure a theory of the state into the equation. This too is often forgotten, with many commentators overly concentrating on the corporate or private business as the fundamental expression of capitalist domination. The state has become a curious institutional form during the present phase of capitalist development. When neoliberal politicians extol the virtues of a minimal governmental apparatus, they are really calling on us to decide something quite specific about our economic subordination: how might our subsidization of the rich most effectively be facilitated? Which method works best for you? To prompt us to choose, the state initially withdraws from the provision of public services, which are either privatized (e.g. healthcare) or simply abandoned. The real message is, 'You're on your own.' Couple this with stagnating real wages and the aggressive taxation of working people and the state inevitably becomes a key agent of capitalist class oppression. Taxation policy is indicative in this regard. In the United Kingdom, for example, we now have a scenario in which an ordinary 25-year-old worker will be heavily taxed to pay for services he/she cannot access (e.g. dental care and transport). So they pay for it (again) in the private sector, which is another example of how the subsidization economy functions. And as the neoliberal state withdraws in this manner, it proliferates on an unprecedented level in the area of policing, surveillance and security (which is perhaps where our taxes are really spent). Moreover, the management of the process of wealth transfer from workers to the ruling elite requires a lot of red tape and bureaucracy, so we see a considerable extension of punitive governmental technocracy in that regard too.

Despite all the rhetoric about being against 'big government', it is really through punishing taxation policies that the working people are hit hard. This is where the rich are able both to have their cake (low taxes) and eat it (the majority being taxed to subsidize the 1 per cent's luxurious existence). We saw this most clearly in the United States and the United Kingdom when public funds (derived from income tax) were used to bail out the banks following the 2008 crisis. This instance of welfare to the rich is not an exception but the norm. For example, in the United States, tax breaks for the top 5 per cent of income earners have placed a huge burden on the remaining 95 per cent, and have, in effect, entailed an unprecedented transfer of wealth from the working poor to the rich. Lazzarato explains this in relation to the 2010 Bush–Obama law that extends the tax cuts to those making more than $250,000. The income bracket represents only 5% of the population ... in exchange for peanuts for the unemployed, the rich received $315 billion over two years. To have an idea of the handout, one should remember that the US government investment in the economy came to $800 billion in 2008. (Lazzarato, 2012: 119–20)

The current policy of quantitative easing (the governmental allocation of money for big business) fulfils a similar purpose that is perhaps even more striking in its 'trickle up' characteristics.

Here the capitalist state is directly fostering conditions that make work a permanently present problem that merits our practical attention: (a) we now have to pay for the resources that the collective tax pool used to take care of, and (b) our work is no longer about making a living but about avoiding social catastrophe. This is why what some call 'Endies' (Employed but with No Disposable Income or Savings), who consist of 1 million workers in London, persist despite the obvious sham that their life of work represents (Doward, 2014). The large percentage of London workers who are Endies awake every morning and commute to their places of employment not to 'get ahead' but to avoid perceived social oblivion. I shall soon explain why this perception is ideological as much as factual. Anyway, things get even worse for them (us?) with the advent of privatization, since this is really how the neoliberal taxation system comes into its own as a mechanism of extraordinary subsidization. In the United Kingdom, this has taken on some monumental proportions. For example, the privatization of public housing over the last 30 years has created not only an extreme shortage of accommodation and soaring prices, but also stagnation and decline in industry profits, since it has exploited all that could be exploited. There is no 'social fat' left. In 2012 the English accommodation 'market' was gaunt and nearing death. There was no movement. So in 2013 the Cameron government devised a new plan. The state would pump public money (our income taxes) into the private hands of building executives. Enter the much-heralded 'Help to Buy' support scheme. First-home buyers are given a deposit sum to purchase a property. This sum is effectively handed over to the construction corporations who instigated the housing shortage in the first place. One recent report genuinely understands the situation:

Recognise this story? An industry in difficulties, a hefty dose of public sector support, and then big bonuses for the management. But this time we're not talking about bankers, but some of the UK's biggest housebuilders ... The FTSE 350 housebuilders' index is up more than 20 per cent since March last year, and so are annual bonuses. Mr Ritchie's rose from £360,000 to £440,000, Persimmon's Jeff Fairburn's rose from £540,000 to £832,500. Taylor Wimpey's Peter Redfern's edged past the £1m mark, but (bearing in mind that nearly a quarter of sales came from Help To Buy) the remuneration committee said there was 'no significant distortion of incentive target performance'. So that's alright then. (Lynch, 2014)

Let's face it. If you were brutally mugged for your wallet outside your home, you would call the police. But the situation Lynch describes is different because the legitimate authorities themselves are robbing you. This weird neoliberal robbery of workers has, of course, been going on in the United Kingdom for some time now. According to Meek (2014), the very idea of privatization was always an excuse to shift as much public wealth to an ever smaller number of ultra-rich individuals and families as possible. Thatcher's claim that shareholder capitalism would result in ordinary people having an ownership stake in their country was a joke from the start. Following the sale of the railways, water providers, electricity, gas, etc., only 12 per cent of shares were held by ordinary citizens in the end. The rest were kettled by large institutional investors, many of which are actually French and German *state-owned* entities – it's amazing that this fact doesn't undermine once and for all the argument that private business inherently does things better. Additionally, these so-called 'firms' (do they really fit the prototypical capitalist model?) often receive very generous governmental subsidies to operate their 'private' business activities. This is the case with the UK railways, for example, whose retail prices have consistently risen far more than inflation rates. A worker who cannot afford to live in London is held captive by a corporatized monopoly. They pay income tax which subsidizes a private business. This business then half-heartedly delivers a substandard service at such extortionate prices that our worker must rack up a credit card debt in order to arrive at the office on time. There is only *one* winner. Welcome to neoliberal Britain.

According to Meek, when Thatcher came to power in 1979, the top rate of tax was 83 per cent and the basic rate 33 per cent. Now they are 45 per cent and 20 per cent respectively. But it is the flat taxes that really put the boot into the working poor. In 1979 value-added tax (or VAT, whereby everybody pays the same rate regardless of income) was 8 per cent. Now it is 20 per cent, which disproportionately sucks money away from working people. Meek goes even further. In addition to VAT,

> there are others, and they are onerous; they just aren't called taxes, though they should be – private taxes. A tax is generally thought of as something that only a government can levy, but this is a semantic distortion that favors the free market belief system. If a payment to an authority, public or private, is compulsory, it's a tax. We can't do without electricity; the electricity bill is an electricity tax. We can't do without water; the water bill is a water tax. Some people can get by without railways, and some can't; they pay the rail tax. Students pay the university tax. The meta-privatization is the privatization of the tax system itself; even, it could be said, the privatization of us, the former citizens of Britain.

However, I would extend the analysis to accentuate the class structure that every worker finds themselves embroiled in today. These are not just taxes, but also subsidies and rents, especially given that the sums we pay are always much higher than average wage increases. We work not to earn a wage but to pay 'relief' and 'welfare' to the capitalist rich who now operate as rentiers, most of whom have inherited their wealth. Our lack of choice is a direct consequence of their abundance of choice. This is the irony of state-sponsored shareholder capitalism. It is workers – via tax – who are the *true investors*. But that investment is immediately expropriated to bankroll the neoliberal war machine, confer costly assistance to large multinational firms free of charge, and pay for the expensive mistakes made by incompetent governmental bureaucrats (the United Kingdom and the United States are replete with such mistakes). Making matters even more dismal is the palpable hatred that the neoliberal state apparatus has for most working people, as if they are an 'enemy within' requiring constant harassment and purging. It thinks that capitalism would be great if it wasn't for workers. The predatory state uses legislation, public policy and brainwashing to promote the ideology of work in its worst hyper-rationalized form. It too takes on a rather sadistic quality, especially towards the unemployed, though unemployment, as we know, is a structural requirement of neoclassical economics. The explosion of bad jobs has been an important part of this trend too. Poor jobs are not inherently bad, but are made unbearable by the socio-economic conditions that envelop them. Degradation is generally a socio-political process rather than simply a technical one. The proliferation of shitty jobs allows the neoliberal state to claim that unemployment is dropping, when it is in fact simply being carved-up and hived out in precarious roles that pay almost nothing.

Governmental economic ideology is primarily guided by class politics, with the social construction of 'work' being a central factor for garnering legitimacy and justifying false scarcity. For example, it is largely state governance structures that has allowed the 2008 financial crisis to become a veritable boon to the rich as it sucks the life out of the working poor. It was recently noted that 'the 400 wealthiest Americans are worth a record $2.02 trillion (£1.4tn), up from $1.7tn in 2012, a collective fortune slightly bigger than Russia's economy' (*The Guardian*, 2013). Indeed, the old Marxist debates in the 1970s about whether or not the state was semi-autonomous from capital look quaint and naive today. When considering the present nature of work, I would go so far as to say that a critique of the state form is perhaps more pertinent than that of any other institution presently regulating our lives, including the multinational firm.

In the following chapters, I focus on six themes that I believe we ought to comprehensively understand if we are to develop a post-work future. Some of the analyses developed here are somewhat bleak. However, I hope this tone is never at the expense of the optimistic conviction that a world beyond work is both desirable and feasible. Moreover, each chapter puts forward concrete suggestions about how we might conceptualize this life after work. Any sustained investigation into the religion of productivism like the one that follows risks reproducing the very obsession with the concept being critiqued (i.e. work). Hopefully I avoid this. But it is clear that neoliberal society has definitely placed this strange invention we call work at the epicentre of everything we do. Now we must figure out how to successfully refuse it and the webs of capture that it ceaselessly spins.

1

The Factory That Never Sleeps

We now know that nearly everybody works far more than is economically necessary under neoliberal capitalism. Even the unemployed bear the emotional and existential weight of full-time employment. In this sense, the social is no longer really part of the economic. Economic necessity and income are almost completely disconnected from all the work we do. Our labour-obsession is perhaps best understood as a social pattern prompted by *simulated* conditions of 'survival'. They hunted; we work. There is little difference. However, it is becoming very clear that the outward symbolic gesture of labour has entirely overtaken the content of the productive act. And the late-capitalist situation repeats this simulacrum over and over for reasons that are not entirely clear. For me, this is the first warning that the question before us is not really about work at all. In its form another agenda is being pursued. But what?

To answer this question, let us take another tack. Many critics of paid employment approvingly recall John Maynard Keynes's weird 1930 essay 'Economic Prospects of Our Grandchildren'. Observing the immense increase of capitalist wealth and its technological triumphs, he predicted that work itself would probably soon be obsolete. Good riddance to bad business. The coming generations would be the first in history to enjoy the authentic emancipation from toil, necessity and most importantly, *work*. Keynes's essay is often read as evidence of a certain betrayal at the heart of neoliberal capitalism since we are now, of course, working more than ever. The faith that all this technological progress and inordinate wealth might relieve us from the burden of labour has been systematically derailed. Material abundance and Wi-Fi are now used to extend the working day, with debilitating penalties. The dialectic of modern capitalism is plain to observe in this respect. The ritual of labour has undoubtedly been existentially entrenched and generalized as the key standard by which we are judged. But this occurs precisely at the same moment that its redundancy is obvious to all – especially to the millions who have been deprived of work as neoliberalism gained global supremacy over the last 20 years.

However, a closer analysis of Keynes's argument reveals an important subtext that is prophetic. The ruling class's fear of a work-free world is certainly the red thread that holds the text together. That raises an important question. Is this 1930s paper behind the insistence that we continue to follow an antiquated way of life as we do in neoliberal societies today? Perhaps. But it is interesting that the present cataclysmic economic crisis has not disqualified the notion of work, but has made it more invidious. While capitalist wealth creation and technological innovation would undoubtedly guarantee more leisure and relaxation, Keynes sounds a note of cautious reserve about this prospect. The tone is one of plaintive restraint, almost warning the authorities that a world bereft of work might not be such a good thing after all. For what will the masses do with all that free time on their hands?

> Yet there is no country and no people, I think, who can look forward to the age of leisure and of abundance without a dread. For we have been trained too long to strive and not to enjoy. It is a fearful problem for the ordinary person, with no special talents, to occupy himself, especially if he no longer has roots in the soil or in custom or in the beloved conventions of a traditional society. To judge from the behaviour and the achievements of the wealthy classes to-day in any quarter of the world, the outlook is very depressing! For these are, so to speak, our advance guard – those who are spying out the promised land for the rest of us and pitching their camp there. For they have most of them failed disastrously, so it seems to me – those who have an independent income but no associations or duties or ties – to solve the problem which has been set them. (Keynes, 1930/2009: 198–199)

What looks like a gesture of class sympathy is really nothing of the sort. Instead we can detect a deeply reactionary and not so 'gentle' nihilism in Keynes's liberalist argument. He levels his antipathy against the parasitical rentier class for a particular reason: to justify an infrastructure that retains the most basic contours of capitalist class relations and its ideological preoccupation with work. Additionally, I suggest that his message concerning the 'dread' of leisure *apropos* the commoner (i.e. us) was taken very seriously by the capitalist ruling classes – and perhaps still is. Read deeper and he seems to be stating the following: We cannot allow the working multitude to enjoy the independence that progress could so easily bestow upon them, because then they would act like us (i.e. profligate idlers with a penchant for sadistic risk-taking, the elite's primary method for making an otherwise boring life more interesting). But more importantly, the working people would begin to rethink the very foundations of class society once its basis in economic necessity is discredited.

It is said that we live in post-Keynesian times, but Keynes' counsel to the ruling class has been bequeathed to us today in concrete governance practices and the whip of market discipline. While most work is now needless, neoliberal society has made good use of work's ontological connotations to keep a lid on a fundamental antagonism that defines modern life. Hence the socially manufactured scarcity that even Dallas, the beggar cum drug dealer residing outside my East London flat, understands well enough. The most interesting trait of the workforce today is the sheer amount of labour exerted that not only goes unpaid (discretionary work, unrecognized overtime, etc.) but is also functionally unessential to the firm, even by the firm's own standards of profit maximization. This is work done for its own sake, which may look from the outside to be meaningless, but is driven by extant concrete forces not greatly different from ancient rites of superfluous sacrifice. And as we shall note in the forthcoming chapters, this does not undermine the process of hyper-rationalization mentioned in the Introduction, but is *integral* to it.

Most working people recognize that capitalism fanatically underlines the importance of surplus labour in order to maintain its logic of expropriation, so that the rich can enjoy the idleness they are so afraid we might come to think is our entitlement as well. During the early years of industrialism, a major cultural impediment to economic (over) production was the long-standing custom of working just enough to meet the community's needs. As Max Weber (1905/1930) discovered in his analysis regarding the 'spirit of capitalism', workers who were paid a wage simply stopped half way through the day, since why would anyone continue to toil once they had met their basic needs in a satisfactory manner? Anthropological studies of other societies have noted this strange tension too. As Clastres observes in *Society Against the State* (1989), so-called primitive societies acted very differently to the capitalist norms imposed on them when presented with new technology:

The advantage of a metal axe over a stone axe is too obvious to require much discussion: one can do perhaps ten times as much work with the first in the same amount of time as with the second; or else complete the same amount of work in one-tenth the time. And when the Indians discovered the productive superiority of the white men's axes, they wanted them not in order to produce more in the same amount of time, but to produce as much in a period of time ten times shorter. (Clastres, 1989: 194)

From a capitalist point of view, something clearly had to be done. What fit the bill was an ideological overcoding of work with moral and religious significance. For a time this compelled people to labour more than they really had to. Rather than being presented as a finite social activity, work needed to be approached as an endless way of life pregnant with ethical connotations. Work will save you. Thus we witness a veritable Copernican revolution in the way the relatively simple act of labour is approached, one that has intensified under the neoliberal paradigm, but with some curious and rather depressing permutations. If what we might now call the ritual or ideology of work has become thoroughly decoupled from economic necessity, then work is also paradoxically no longer idolized as the highest social virtue (as it was at the apex of modernity, by capitalists and communists alike). The attempt to persuade us that a life of work is obliged by both basilar necessity and moral rectitude has long been abandoned. Everybody knows that we work now to keep the authorities at bay (the landlord, the tax man, the credit-card company, the multinational retailer, and so forth). But we also realize work's impudent needlessness. And this perception of senselessness has to be closely managed, something which neoliberal society only partially achieves. Since it is blindingly evident that there is not enough work to go around, the corporatized state apparatus fears both the employed and the unemployed. Moreover, those of us 'lucky' enough to have a job are so disgruntled by what it has done to us that a whole industry has arisen to deal with work's pathologies. We work, not because we want to or like it, but because it has become a way of life with little alternative or way out. This ideological universalization is a key governance strategy that neoliberal institutions use to keep the frantic pace of useless toil cranking along at breakneck pace. Work has become a virtual portmanteau that weighs upon our shoulders, its negative energy swallowing everything around us like some perfidious black hole. And, as I explore in more depth in Chapter 2, this demented generalization of the will-to-produce that has captured the social imaginary of late capitalism represents first and foremost a class offensive. As Keynes anxiously admitted, what would we do with all that free time?

What is striking about the cultural idiom of our workers' society is the compulsive obsessiveness that it inspires. If its justification has long been emptied of pious assurance, that void has been stopgapped by a certain social sickness: a liturgy of inwardness that is exaggerated by an 'all or nothing' attitude towards the empty grammar of labour. Many readers will recognize these extreme cases: interns who work themselves to death; bankers who see little alternative than to end their own lives when something goes wrong at the office; IT employees who work in their sleep; governmental functionaries who never see their families. While these are certainly marginal cases (and we analyse them in depth in the following chapters), it would be a mistake to consider them as unexpected aberrations from the norm. They are better approached as indicative of an underlying social tendency taken to its limits – the norm perfectly fulfilled. When fully realized, the 'ideal worker' celebrated by neoliberal capitalism is frequently a dead one. For sure, most of us pull back from the black hole before things get too ugly. But the same ideological template is still lurking behind much of what we do. As with any obsession – especially fixating ones such as cigarettes – the compulsion to repeat implies a certain degree of somatic dependency or *addiction*.

Most addictions function through a singularity that requires persistent displacement in order to perpetuate its own untenable premises. A multiplicity of life elements are contracted to the object of desire, THE ONE, thus relocating to the dark territory of existential blindness anything else that cannot be sublimated. Of course, this means that the object can never really be obtained or enjoyed. In describing this ongoing constitution of the unattainable and the functional disarticulation with fulfilment that work implies today, we are merely repeating Aristotle's famous meditation on accumulation in his *Politics* (especially Book 1, Chapter 9). The good life is defined by the skilful placement of desire so that the wish-object can be achieved and then left behind. A passion's ability to be terminated by accomplishment or fulfilment is a key definition of enjoyment or the good life. Money-lust, according to this formula, is a classic example of the bad life. Once enmeshed within this peculiar desire-matrix we can never have enough (even when drowning in the stuff) – we never arrive at the terminus of satisfaction. The same might be said of economic growth, another capitalist fetish, and now of work itself. The wheel that always returns goes nowhere or, as Aristotle puts it, we find ourselves in a world where there is no conclusion or end – none, that is, except for the 'big end', or death. Besides that, the obsessive subject position of idealized labour is nothing but a psychic curve folding back on itself indefinitely, much like the parameter-less totality I will discuss in the next chapter. No wonder the prison metaphor of 'escape' is so popular in radical politics today.

If the otherwise weird social construction of 'work' drives an addiction complex that is difficult to quit, then we might do well to compare it to other dangerous habits, such as the one I mentioned above: cigarette smoking. As anyone who has been addicted to cigarettes will attest, the first smoke in the morning is exhilarating. But smoking progressively become less enjoyable as the day goes on, even as we relentlessly light up. This self-harm becomes the source of an underlying anxiety that is a poignant facet of the obsession structure. We try to give up but cannot, even when the initial pleasure has turned into coercive non-enjoyment. At this stage it is understandable that we begin to hate ourselves and narcissistically project that judgement onto others, suspecting them of feelings of which they are actually innocent. Now we not only hate ourselves but believe that others might too, adding a touch of *paranoia* to the mix. Interestingly, this self-hate component of paranoia can most easily be observed in the contemporary post-industrial office. This may be due to the rampant consumption of 'smart drugs' currently being gobbled up in epic proportions by workers determined to stay alert and energetic over a 12-hour day (a topic we shall discuss in Chapter 2). Unfortunately, the prime pitfall of synthetic speed is paranoia. But notwithstanding this chemically induced chariness, work-for-its-own-sake cultures automatically make paranoia the default attitude in the office. For example, in her *Financial Times* article entitled 'Paranoia at Work is Out to Get You', Naomi Shragai (2014) explores the pandemic of paranoia in British organizations. The excessive prevalence of paranoia in this setting might be explained by competitive individualism, ambitious employees vying for the boss's favour, and run-of-the-mill Machiavellian office politics. But Shragai's report also notes how it stems from a fixated relationship with work. A young woman employed by a public relations firm tells us about the source of her paranoia following a major burnout. Clearly she is transferring her dislike of authority (managerial capitalism) onto her mother (a prototypical authority figure) as she recounts her slow but steady demise in the office:

The feeling I recall is of being actively disliked [by my mother], and in reaction to that I felt that I needed to try extremely hard – too hard – at work ... I had such a desperate need for people to say: 'Gosh you work so hard and aren't you brilliant'. At work you don't necessarily get that ... You're the target of envy too, because you're out to prove you're the best ... I thought hard work rather than relationships were the answer to progress at work. (Shragai, 2014: 12)

Shragai explains what happen next:

In a series of jobs she repeated a pattern of overworking to diffuse her imagined fears that people thought badly of her ... She quickly burnt out, was left feeling angry with every employer and as a result kept moving on to another job ... Her fear of being sacked drove her to work harder, but this often left her being exploited. (Shragai, 2014: 12)

Given the relatively conservative nature of the *Financial Times*, it is not surprising that this case of extreme paranoia is presented as being an exception to the rule, emanating from the personal qualities of dysfunctional individuals. However, I want to present another reading. Do we not have a fairly accurate depiction of what social life becomes when extreme neoliberalism is fully embodied? For most workers, the fear of being fired is a very real and rational response. The catchword of late-capitalist ideology is 'abandonment' ... you are always expendable. Moreover, the young woman's suspicion that she was not respected or liked by her employer is also probably accurate. The level of cynicism and sadistic enjoyment in pointless labour driving the present employment regime is easily observable. Her smoker-like addiction to work closely intersects with the social structures she thought would provide her security. But security has nothing to do with employment today, especially following the systematic demolition of labour unions, pension schemes and protective legislation that followed in the wake of Thatcher and Reagan like effluent carelessly discarded from a long departed super-yacht in the Mediterranean.

We can depict the endless spiral that characterizes the overwork/ paranoia complex (see Figure 1.1). At the centre of the system is the 'truth' of neoliberalism that is also ideological because of the actions it inspires. This variant of capitalism does not hide or conceal from us this definitive reality concerning itself. It simply displaces this structural truth onto the free-choosing subject in a specific manner that often sets off a centrifugal movement. If this is not halted, oblivion is its ultimate destination. Because our obsession is clearly pathetic, self-disgust is inevitable. And this bleeds into the paranoid feeling that you are not the only one who despises 'you' (or at least the caricature you have become). Perhaps others do too. We become repetitively fixated with this hateful 'other' because we want to prove our worth, an effort that is naturally exacerbated by the inherent impossibility of achieving it. In this manner, the repetition becomes deeply unstable. More Herculean efforts are enacted to externally validate this 'you' in the imagined eyes of others, some of whom actually do hate you. Many suffer burn-out at this stage. Some self-destruct. Sadly, others continue indefinitely into oblivion and even purchase investment properties – a truly horrible spiritual fate that embodies everything cursed about late capitalism.

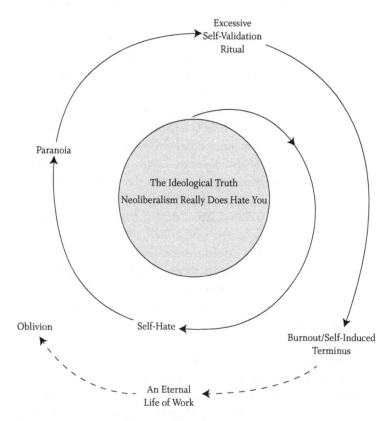

Figure 1.1   The Overwork/Paranoia Complex

I want to reiterate an important point here. The paranoid work-obsessed subject is not a one-off aberration, even if most such victims do not fling themselves into the void. The norm is not meant to be fully embodied literally in societies of control. Those martyred to the obsessive/paranoid norm frequently die, or become ghastly Bob Diamond-like figures. This is why the norm is generally useless when fully realized or rendered completely present. The violence of the neoliberal ideal does not function via open fulfilment; such an action is obviously impossible. No, rather than requesting the entire presence of, say, the 'entrepreneurial individual', we instead see the enforcement of ritualistic approximations. This kind of person is always failing, but is nevertheless extolled for trying.

Those who come close to inhabiting the obsessive–paranoiac complex in the workplace are simply following the template so fervently encouraged in the social factory today, of the ideal employee who never sleeps: habituated to the notion of working for the sake of it, unable to stop, deeply afraid, and often gaining pleasure from the ritual of sacrifice this kind of life entails. Indeed, self-preservation is considered a serious weakness when we enter the cultural field of the late-capitalist enterprise. In the financial sector, for example, this plays out to such an extent that potential employees write 'NO DEPENDENTS' in bold type on their CVs to curry favour with the firm. The message really being conveyed to the prospective employer is that the embodiment of labour power before them has no social impediments to acting out the role of unmitigated self-harm. I am 'free' to be exploited to whatever degree you choose. I am completely yours, unalloyed in my capacity to be crucified by the post-industrial labour process. At the heart of the neoliberal fantasy concerning the perfect employee, therefore, is something profoundly disconcerting, and it is one that we ought to refuse utterly.

If this paranoia afflicts the post-industrial office slave, then it takes on more dangerous qualities among the ruling class. They too are paranoid; but not because they fear abandonment or that workers might some day revolt and seek retribution. No, their paranoia derives from the suspicion that employees might somehow be relaxing or surreptitiously engaging in pernicious and unacceptable acts of self-preservation. Nowhere is this more evident than in the UK university sector, which has embraced a 'business analogy' (Collini, 2012) to such a ridiculous extent that it would look ludicrous and unworkable to even the most commercialized private-sector enterprise (the latter has known for years that a certain degree of 'business socialism' is required to make the modern firm function). In a recent high-profile incident, the upper management of a UK business school attracted media attention when they instituted crippling performance measures and incentive structures. Outcries concerning gratuitous micro-management and stand-over bullying tactics abounded. It is obvious to everyone that this management approach is immensely counterproductive in any creative enterprise like a university department that requires autonomy and trust. So it was no surprise that a survey administered to academic staff revealed trenchant discontent and low morale. But this is where things get interesting. The survey outcome was explained to new staff in a management memo leaked to the press. Newcomers ought to interpret the results with 'a pinch of salt' because:

> 'it contains the feedback of a relatively small number of staff [who] had a lovely cosy lifestyle doing whatever they wanted for years ... There were a few hippy-dippy comments about collegiality and letting the 'people' make the decisions ... I'm sorry. This is not a commune. This is a managed institution pursuing goals that are closely aligned with the university's. It is not a rest home for refugees from the 1960s, with their ponytails and tie-dyed T-shirts. Live with it. Some wags call for the removal of some or all of the school's top management team. Yes, well don't hold your breath. Or actually, do.' (*Times Higher Education Supplement*, 2014)

The vindictive tone is blended with an extraordinary degree of mistrust. And there might also be an element of pleasure derived from the fear that the social independence so relied upon by the high-education sector (after all I am writing these words in a Philadelphia hotel room and not in my London university office) is being directed towards 'hippy-dippy' ends. This type of managerial paranoia is increasingly the norm in UK universities as they attempt to render arts departments and business schools into cost-efficient, profitable business units and gain higher 'rankings' in the league tables. Moreover, the reference to 1960s communes expresses a fanatical anti-left-wing scorn that we would be hard-pressed to find even in a private equity firm. Deleuze and Guattari (1987: 288) suggest that this type of paranoia among the powerful is fuelled by the belief in labour's endless indebtedness. The employee is now the bearer of an infinite liability, one that can never be settled. This is why contemporary managerialism views labour as the personification of an integral lack, always underperforming and potentially lazy – even if employees successfully meet their production targets: 'paranoiacs act by means of, or else suffer from, rays they emit or receive ... Paranoid judgement is like an anticipation of perception replacing empirical research into boxes and their contents: guilty a priori and in any event!' Guilt implies an unpaid and unpayable debt, which, as we shall explore in Chapter 3, is effusive in the managerial grid of domination when it encounters the ethical status of labour today. When paranoia is articulated in this self-fulfilling manner, management regulation tends to assume rather egregious qualities. Surplus aggression becomes central to the control function in the social factory, even in organizations (such as the university) staffed by 'workaholics' who perform well beyond what is formally demanded by their employment contracts. This surplus labour only makes the agents of managerialism more suspicious.

Let's return to the workers' standpoint in all of this. It is easy to see why so many find paranoia such a suitable pathology in the post-industrial economy. It connects the neoliberal obsessive complex to the labouring body that overworks automatically and is held in place by ritualistic attractions that are sacrificial in nature. So can we do anything about this? This book offers a number of suggestions about how to refuse the ideology of work today. Most importantly, we must remember that neoliberalism is largely a quantitative extension of a basic fixture of capitalist power relations present from the very beginning: *class domination*. Therefore, collective action must still remain the most important weapon of the post-capitalist movement. But class domination has proliferated in unexpected ways, bleeding into methods of management that are qualitatively different. In ways that it never did to factory workers under Fordism, regulation today has infiltrated everyday lives and sensibilities, scrambling our conventional existential orientations and recodifying them in domains sometimes far removed from the official labour process. This trend necessitates additional modes of resistance. Merely fighting for more pay and better conditions might not tackle the speculative flows of regulation that shadow us like a cage awaiting a bird.

If the relationship to work encouraged by the neoliberal matrix is analogous to the predicament suffered by smokers who can neither quit nor continue scruple-free, it is tempting to jokingly apply the same methods used by anti-smoking campaigners to help us quit. The offending companies ought to be highly taxed and graphic health warnings displayed concerning the negative effects of work. However, as with cigarettes, this is not enough. Addicts needs to see their addiction in a completely different light, which is where a more therapeutic touch might be handy.

One of the most famous and successful quit-smoking advisers was Allen Carr (who subsequently died of lung cancer many years after he stopped). He argued that four myths stop us from quitting, which might just as well apply to working in the factory that never sleeps. So let's adapt his advice and see if we can counteract the myths that keep us bound to meaningless labour. I have inserted 'work' where it should read 'smoke' and replaced 'nicotine' with 'money':

Myth One: Workers believe they need will power to quit. Other methods concentrate on reasons why they shouldn't work. The health, the slavery, the filthy habit. But workers know all this, yet they continue to work. Why? Look at the other side of the tug of war: it helps me to concentrate, it relives boredom. These are powerful factors to frighten workers of quitting. But just suppose working did none of those things and in actual fact it impeded concentration, it impeded relaxation, it increased boredom and it increased stress. Now you have not got a single reason to carry on working. Once we see that, we do not need will power.

Myth Two: Workers believe they work because they choose to. They can remember their first experimental job but not the day they *decided* to become a regular worker. That is because no worker ever did. Ask any tired and stressed overworked parent whether they encourage their children to do the same, the answer is always an emphatic no. That is because all workers sense that they fell into a trap and they don't want their children to fall into the same trap. If you have made one half-hearted attempt to quit, that is because you have made a positive decision to be a non-worker, and if you continue to work, it's not because you chose to.

Myth Three: When workers quit they believe they suffer from terrible physical withdrawal pains from money. But money withdrawal is what workers suffer *throughout* their working life and it is the only reason they take the next job. It gets no worse when they quit the final job. The reason that workers suffer from withdrawal is that they believe they are making a terrible sacrifice. But the opposite is true.

Myth Four: Workers believe that it is difficult to quit. Providing you realize that there is nothing to give up, you can quit not with a feeling of doom and gloom, worrying whether you've got the will power or whether the money cravings will go but with a feeling of utter elation, knowing that from then on you will enjoy social occasions more and be better equipped to handle stress. You will look at other workers not with envy but with pity.

The Structure of Work in the Social Factory

If only the task of refusal was as easy as the amusing wordplay above! Of course, it is not. In order to appreciate why, we need to examine the particular structural configuration work has assumed under neoliberal conditions. I do not here intend to give an exhaustive overview of the division of labour, occupational segmentation and distribution of jobs, which has been done in a more complete manner elsewhere. Instead, I aim to focus on a number of emergent trends that I believe warrant our attention in relation to the way work has ballooned into its own ideological trope that so many find inescapable. In undertaking this exercise, we are able to more clearly identify facets of work that I will explore in more depth in forthcoming chapters and emphasise issues that are salient for the post-work movement presently gathering steam in neoliberal societies.

Why Focus on Work?

Important from the outset is to provide some conceptual reassurance about the centrality of work in the late-capitalist situation. If we position work as the dominant political problem in neoliberal societies, then we must account for recent arguments suggesting that work is of secondary importance in light of other socio-economic developments. For example, Bauman (2005) has contended that we now live in a consumer society as opposed to a workers' society. He calls this the 'gradual yet relentless passage from the earlier to the later state of modern society: from a society of producers to a society of consumers, and accordingly from a society guided by the work ethic to one ruled by the aesthetic of consumption' (Bauman, 2005: 2). Bauman is not well known for his attention to class and he certainly doesn't do Marx very well. He consequently misses some important dynamics of late capitalism. Just because work is not valued as it was at the height of Fordism does not mean that it is no longer the central fulcrum around which capitalism turns. This is what makes life in our society so depressing. Moreover, consumption is but a proxy for the income (or inherited wealth for some) we earn through capitalist relations of production. We are economically judged according to our standing in these relations, and our ability to consume is of secondary relevance. In this sense, Bauman throws the baby out with the bath water, mainly because he abstains from even an elementary class analysis.

And what about debt? According to Ross's (2013) excellent analysis of 'creditocracy', the massive prevalence of personal debt has supplanted work as the defining power relation in crisis-ridden Western societies: 'Whereas strife over wages was central to the industrial era, the grand conflict of our times is shaping up as the struggle over debt, and any just resolution calls for a level of organizing at least as momentous as the labor movement in its heyday' (Ross, 2013: 26). Lazzarato (2012: 7) similarly argues that 'the debtor–creditor relationship intensifies the mechanism of exploitation and domination at every level of society, for within it no distinction exists between workers and the unemployed, consumers and producers, working and non-working populations, retirees and welfare recipients.' I agree with these observations up to a point. But the distribution and experience of debt does have qualitative gradations. The financialization of the working- and middle-class poor, in particular, is still all about work: who has it and who doesn't, what quality of life it provides, etc. Debt, with its sadistic regime of endless repayment, has such a strong class quality, and this is linked to the post-industrial labour process and its constellation of social relations, both inside and outside the workplace. This is what gives debt its social character. Capitalism can have work without debt, but debt cannot exist without a primary relationship to work. For example, the transformation of public debt into a personal living hell was underpinned by a new approach to organizing the labour process. Working people were enlisted to pick up the slack and subsidize the corporate enclosure movement from the 1990s onwards. Moreover, credit-card debt began as a working person's problem, wedded to declining wages and the rising cost of healthcare, education and so forth, following waves of privatization. While debt is definitely a problem in its own right, it is also reflective of a particular reorganization of the role of work and its present class composition. For example, as the credit crisis unfolded in the United States, many were willing to lose their houses before their cars, since the latter were essential for getting them to the office. Debt is an instrument of class war used to discipline the poor and subsidize the rich, and this is inextricably connected to the post-industrial labour process.

And finally, burgeoning levels of unemployment might signal the diminishing importance of work as a central political flashpoint in capitalist society simply because so many people do not have a job. There is much truth to this. As Gorz (1989) also argues, the existence of permanent unemployment tells us that the relationship between waged income and economic necessity or survival has been irrevocably overdetermined by other dynamics. They are not as closely correlated as we once thought (you still can live and survive without a job, albeit under precarious and difficult conditions, as anyone who is forced to report to the jobcentre can attest). But as Foster and McChesney correctly argue, what Marx called the reserve army of the unemployed still plays a crucial role in maintaining wage discipline in the Global North and South, especially through multinational labour arbitrage. Wages and industrial unrest are kept at bay by the existence of a large pool of the forever unwaged, which now constitutes one of the biggest classes in the global economic system:

> If we take the categories of the unemployed, the vulnerable employed and the economically inactive population in prime working ages (25–54) and add them together, we come up with what might be called the maximum size of the global reserve army in 2011: some 2.4 billion people, compared to 1.4 in the active labour army. (Foster and McChesney, 2012: 149)

They go on to argue that there is no way this number of people could ever be absorbed back into the active labour force. But this is not the intention of global capitalism. By shifting work offshore, putting pressure on local governments to deregulate labour markets and imposing an effective security system to manage the dispossessed, the corporate system *needs* the unemployed. The function of these 2.4 billion people is to help shape the capitalist labour process into an image most favourable to the capitalist elite. The numbers involved here are not as important as the relationship that is constituted.

I am advancing this case for putting work and class at the centre of a critical theory of neoliberalism not in the old spirit of the Left that wants to see the importance of work everywhere, nor in the old humanist tradition of imbuing work/labour with venerable anthropological categories (which appears to be making a comeback – see Harvey, 2014). I wish that capitalist waged labour was not the defining point of all other struggles. I dislike it as much as anyone else, especially today when much of it is clearly pointless and antithetical to our collective needs. But the fact remains: to fight neoliberalism, class is THE relation we have to tackle, even if it is through its mediation on other registers of social distinction and domination. Capitalism cannot exist without class, and this is the weakness that must always be kept at the forefront of political resistance. In short, to avoid becoming a fascist today, one has no choice but to embody the obverse and constitutive nothingness of the working subject so designated by late-capitalist regulation.

None of this is to say that race, gender and sexuality, for example, are somehow secondary to the class relation under capitalism. Of course, considering these is crucial when approaching the question of counter-capitalist politics. As Harvey recently notes, the labour–capital contradiction is important,

> but its tangible manifestations are mediated and tangled up through filters of other forms of social distinction, such as race, ethnicity, gender and religious affiliation so as to make the actual politics of struggle within capitalism a far more complicated affair than would appear to be the case from the standpoint of the labour–capital relation alone. (Harvey, 2014: 68)

However, most activists fighting gender and race discrimination are the first to note their thoroughly capitalist dimensions. Eliminating capitalism would also abolish, not all, but a good deal of the problems associated with social inequality and environmental degradation, because it would give rebirth to democratic exchange. By ignoring this insight, we enter into the insipid territory of liberal diversity politics, which more often than not deepens the capitalist agenda.

Moreover, and closer to the topic of this book, Harvey's caution only makes sense if we're adhering to dialectical reason, an either/or rationality (i.e. the labour–capital relation *or* race, gender, etc.). However, the ideology of work dismantles the exclusivity of the labour–capital dyad as an independent struggle, but not by diffusing it as one contradiction among a plural universe of others. The dismantlement paradoxically reinforces its predominance *everywhere* in the social system, since the ideology of work operates through multiplication and contamination rather than diametrical opposition to other political spheres. This is what gives work its virus-like qualities, which can be detected in social relations far removed from the direct labour–capital antagonism that we otherwise observe in the factory, office, retail counter and cornfield. The neoliberal constitution of work is charged with a significance that goes beyond itself, just as the minor role played by sexuality is exaggerated and echoed throughout the vast and intrinsic machinery of life (is this why Freud repeatedly drew upon economic terminology?), far removed from the apparent origin of the signal.

The 'I, Job' Function

How on earth did the simple act of work become a gargantuan social factory that has colonized most facets of our lives to such an extent? The predominance of work involves both quantitative and qualitative shifts in the underlying structure of capitalist regulation. Because the struggle to reduce the length of the working day was a formative victory of the working-class movement in the Fordist era (see Negrey, 2012), its reversal was one of the first targets of neoliberal governance. This was certainly aided by enforced (and often unpaid) overtime and the rapid proliferation of mobile technology. But there is a more general political will behind this too. In the United Kingdom, for example, it certainly feels as if successive governments have done everything in their power to convey to employers and workers that the legal stipulations concerning the EU Time Directive (no more than 48-hours a week) is not to be taken too seriously. Reporting on recent research on this topic, Hart points out that many employment contracts have an opt-out clause, particularly in industries that delight in eye-watering numbers of hours spent at the office. Hart reveals the true extent of work-creep in neoliberalized Europe:

> A recent survey has confirmed that nine to five is indeed a relic of the past. Today the average worker checks their work email at 7.42am, gets to the office at 8.18am and leaves at 7.19pm ... A government survey found that 4.5 million people would like to work from home one day a week but just aren't allowed ... The recent survey found that one in three British workers check their emails before 6.30am, while 80% of British employers consider it acceptable to phone employees out of hours (16% would happily call between 10pm and midnight). (Hart, 2014: 66)

Much of this is normalized by the fetish of the work itself. Employees conform not because of an authoritarian boss but because the job entails intrinsic qualities (especially when things go wrong) that captures their attention. It simply feels natural to put in the extra hours to ensure that complete chaos does not ensue or co-workers are not let down (see Gregg, 2011).

The rise of 24/7 capitalism, as Crary (2013) terms it, is facilitated by other developments as well. Many studies of work in neoliberal society forget about the massive amount of labour conducted between 10 p.m.

and 5 a.m.: night work. Analysts have noted how keeping unsociable hours is increasingly the norm beyond the professions usually associated with night work (nursing, for example). This has been encouraged and facilitated by a broader agenda of flexible employment systems, the growth of subcontracting and the degradation of important employment rights and benefits that once regulated this practice (see Kreitzman, 1999; Aubenas, 2011). Cleaners, warehouse workers, caterers, security personnel, truck drivers, call-centre agents and many others now do their work in the middle of the night when the rest of us are asleep. Of course, Marx noted long ago that the attempt to render labour productive after the sun goes down represents a strong predisposition of the capitalist mode of production:

> The prolongation of the working day beyond the limits of the natural day, into the night, acts only as a palliative. It quenches only in a slight degree the vampire thirst for the living blood of labour. To appropriate labour during 24 hours of the day, is, therefore, the inherent tendency of capitalist production. (Marx, 1867/1976: 367)

But given the limits of the human organism, this tendency can only be achieved through a particular organization of the labour process which has been perfected under flexible production systems, including the much dreaded 'night shift' that is periodically coupled with regular daytime shifts. For these workers, the constant readjustment between day and night shifts can be extremely debilitating. A recent report investigating the life of night-shift workers in an online book warehouse revealed the sheer exhaustion that it entailed, even suggesting that mental illness might be connected to this type of work. As one employee stated: 'We are machines, we are robots, we plug our scanner in, we're holding it, but we might as well be plugging it into ourselves' (BBC, 2013).

The potential harm of night work is caused by a disrupted 'body clock' – the 'circardian rhythms' that regulate our sleep patterns. One study, for example, found that women who have engaged in long-term night labour were twice as likely to develop breast cancer (*The Independent*, 2013). If the night shift is regular, then there are techniques for readjusting the body clock. However, this is more difficult if the night work is irregular. According to a London nurse I spoke with, the real issue was the lost time *once the shift was over*. One can neither sleep nor do anything remotely useful. 'I lie there like a zombie and that is hard work in itself'.

Indeed, it appears that once the shift has finished the labour process hauntingly continues as one endeavours to find sleep in a busy inner-city nurses' apartment.

In addition to these quantitative trends that increase the number of hours we work, I suggest that the true relation of force that has precipitated our 'workers' society' is qualitative in nature. Not only more work, but a peculiar ethical orientation to our jobs that affects us regardless of the time we spend at the office. Many employees occupy the subjective position of the worker whether they are formally checked in or not. In Western economies, the diffused workplace sees evermore elements of our social being echoed through the ideological matrix of aimless production. The rise of the social factory, as the Italian autonomist Marxists call it, has meant that many jobs are no longer external to us – as was the case when we confronted the assembly line in the Fordist era – but also between and in us. Our vested sociality is now part of the production process.

I term this the 'I, Job' function because work is transformed into something we *are* rather than something we simply do among other things. Work becomes an inescapable way of life, 24/7. For example, when we enter the workplace today we are not only selling our skills as potential labour power but also ourselves as certain kinds of people. Hence the popularity of 'human capital' in neoclassical economics, which is now a central component of the means of production in a totally commercialized society. We can note this emphasis on human and social capital in the following mainstream praise of the modern corporation. Under the title of 'Sociability's Value Added', we are told by pro-business celebrants Goffee and Jones that sociability

> is often a boon to creativity because it fosters teamwork, the sharing of information, and an openness to new ideas. Healthy sociability also creates an environment in which people are more likely to go beyond the formal requirements of their jobs. They work harder than technically necessary to help their colleagues – that is, their community – look good and succeed. (Goffee and Jones , 2003: 26)

The social element of the 'I, Job' function is emphasized by firms today because it is able to tap the extra-economic qualities that conventional management controls are almost useless at doing. Moreover, it provides a stealthy alibi for overwork, as alluded to in the excerpt above. To paraphrase Adorno (2005), now even the social is sick. Indeed, this shift in how work is organized was not accidental. It is a basic feature of class recomposition following the decline of Fordism. The repudiation of public goods and the Fordist labour–capital compact from the 1980s onwards heralded a new employment paradigm based upon pure marketization. However, if an organization applied the tenets of neoliberalism to the letter (i.e. unadulterated individual competition, private property, little 'free' cooperation and pure commoditization) the system would grind to a halt – especially the workplace. This is why the collective self-reliance of the workforce – often euphemized as flexibility – is so important to the exploitation process today. Here is another example, this time set amidst a newspaper exposé concerning the joys of being a small business owner:

> James no longer sees any distinction between his work and personal life, but sees this as a good thing, 'It's like a continuum, I just happen to be doing different activities at different times.' When he's working he doesn't compromise his play time or his social time, he says. 'It's an extension of that.' (*The Guardian*, 2014a)

Statements like these would have been inexplicable to workers in the 1950s and 1960s. Why would anyone rejoice in the fact that they have no life outside their job? Would this not denote a special kind of madness? A good deal of ideological effort had to be conducted to pave the way for people like James to make an appearance in the world. The branded self or the 'I, Job' function is an intense fantasy in the neoclassical mindset. As Foucault (2008: 28) noted in his lectures on the birth of biopolitics, ultra-right-wing economists of the Chicago School like Gary Becker attempted to create a social prototype that would allow economic reason to 'generalize the enterprise from within the social body … the individual's life itself – must make him into a sort of permanent and multiple enterprise'.

In the United Kingdom, following the rise of coercive-state, Thatcherism and the barbarism of subsequent neoliberal governmental reform programmes, we now see the true consequences of this desire to transform us all into little one-person corporations. In the wake of the 2008 crisis, the capitalist promotion of self-sufficiency and individual entrepreneur-ship no longer bothers to evoke the euphemisms of 'creativity', 'innovation' and 'freedom' that characterised 1990s neoliberal agenda. No, this is now about fear. You are on your own – but you still have to pay your taxes! Even Foucault fails – or perhaps refuses – to apprehend the grinding concrete reality that the birth of biopower actually implies. The real world behind the gloss of the 'entrepreneur' is actually sanctioned poverty, insecurity, precarity and an impossible life-structure designed to absorb the externalities of rich corporations and the neoliberal state. Because Foucault appears almost to be smitten by the neoclassical economists, he ignores the violence that their ideas entail in practice. It is telling that when Gary Becker was invited to comment on Foucault's analysis of American neoliberalism he stated: 'I like most of it, and I do not disagree with much and I also cannot tell whether Foucault is disagreeing with me' (Becker, 2012).

Tragic signs of what it really means to force someone to mimic a permanent enterprise are all around us. For example, in 2014 the United Kingdom's Office of National Statistics announced that self-employment was at its highest level in 40 years. You can hear the triumphant cheers of neoliberal pundits, declaring that its market reforms now allow more people than ever to live the high-life of Richard Branson. That is until you take a closer look at the statistics, as Monagham does:

> Self-employed people have on average experienced a 22% fall in real pay since 2008–09 …with average earnings of £207 a week, less than half that of employees, and with no sick pay or holiday pay, and no employer to contribute towards their pension. (Monagham, 2014: 25)

In addition, the number of people over the age of retirement (65) who are self-employed has doubled in the last five years. And no, they do not continue to work because they are bored. They do so because their pension schemes are so dilapidated that they have little choice. As a recent *Economist* (2014) report stated, the slow degradation of pensions in OECD countries means that retirement funds are now 'too small to generate a decent income, as many people are discovering; they will need to keep working, whatever the official retirement age may be'. Work until you drop. That is the true face of biopolitics and its extolment of the permanent individual enterprise.

Let's more closely analyse this idealization of the 'I, Job' function in neoliberal political thought. What is the underlying desire supplementing this attempt to economize everyday life today? The blind faith in the power of micro-economic processes certainly highlights the fundamentalist bent of much neoliberal (ir)rationality: the impersonal force of the market will not only save us from the tyranny of big government (and how wrong were they here when we survey the authoritarian neoliberal state today!), but also the claustrophobia of the *social itself*. Hayek's essay exploring the meaning of 'the social' (1973/2013), as closely described by Dardot and Laval (2014: 122), is fascinating in this respect. At first glance, Hayek reads almost like a Wittgensteinian analyst as he pushes the notional formalism of what we mean by the word 'social' to its limits. He concludes that it really doesn't mean anything. Therefore, as with any other empty transcendental signifier, we ought to remain silent about it: 'Not only "social justice" but also "social democracy", "social market economy" or the "social state of law" are expressions which, though justice, democracy, the market economy or the *Rechsstaat* have by themselves perfectly good meaning, the addition of the adjective "social" makes them capable of meaning almost anything one likes' (Hayek, 1973/2013: 242: quoted in Dardot and Laval, 2014: 122).

Hayek's refusal to define the social is very important for understanding what we confront in practice today. The type of social he chooses to demolish, of course, tends to be that associated with a left-wing political perspective. There is little mention of the 'socials' frequently evoked by right-wing regimes. More interestingly, he conveys a strong social-phobia that distinctly fears how our togetherness might somehow spoil all that is good in the world. What is the logic behind this phobia? Might we not hypothetically put Hayek on the psychoanalytical couch to learn a little more about what this symptom means and perhaps posit a cure? As would any decent quack, we begin by asking him about his childhood, trying to discern why he is so attracted to this mysterious object of disgust that he repeatedly dismisses as 'the social'. Of course, we discover that part of the problem is his deep distrust of 'big government', particularly its communist variant. It is noteworthy that Hayek's intellectual imagination was veritably captured by a fascination with communism and socialism. He read left-wing utopian thinkers obsessively, suggesting that conservatives could learn some important tips from them:

> What we lack is a liberal Utopia, a program which seems neither a mere defence of things as they are nor a diluted kind of socialism, but a truly liberal radicalism which does not spare the susceptibilities of the mighty (including the trade unions), which is not too severely practical, and which does not confine itself to what appears today as politically possible (Hayek, 1960: 384).

For Hayek, the social is too closely aligned with 'organization' and must be downplayed lest the un-freedoms he imagines to be the ultimate end game of socialism are unleashed upon society. These future utopian thinkers he calls upon are radical precisely because they will be able to envisage a society in which the social is no longer required, and is perhaps even deleted from our vocabulary. Theoretical success would be obtained when this paradox was overcome. However, let us probe further as he lies upon our couch and his unconscious begins to divulge some unnerving themes. His disdain for the social opens a secret centre, perhaps his real Utopia: namely, a world that is anti-peopled or more precisely without people. And this erasure is clearly informed by wish-obsessions linked to *death*. The subplot reads like this. The world would be wonderful if only it was peopled by no one. But that is impossibly terrifying. So I must entertain this fantasy by other means, paths and logics. Hence a similar obsession that IT geeks have with Ayn Rand, who must easily be the craziest writer I have ever encountered, making Artaud look reasonable (which, of course, he very much was). A fully automated world without the 'stain' of human interaction would return us to the Utopia of *pure nature*, an artificially induced virtuality that subsists only within its own internal reference points, its self-contained objectivism. This is the founding fantasy for those who idealize the so-called self-regulated market mechanism: a non-peopled machine. And is this not also the present attraction of high-frequency trading and calls for 'algorithmic regulation/governance'? Computers can appropriate the irregularities indicative of class politics and smooth them out indefinitely. The blemish of sociality ought to be purged from human affairs as far as possible. This is only achievable if we all become commercialized moments in a network without history and biography – and thus, in particular, one of mankind's greatest inventions, time-wasting idleness, is eradicated. In short, Hayek turns out to be somewhat disturbed.

If there is a strong death desire in the formative ideals of neoclassical economics, then it is also an integral part of its self-deception, since this asocial fantasy can only be an unachievable reverie, of course. When put to work in the wasteland of late-capitalist reality, this impossible I-enterprise becomes a very different model of living compared to that of James's glowing report above. Applied wholesale to the entire economy, life certainly becomes hellish, but a deeply social hell as we pick up the pieces together. And perhaps this is why Hayek's much derided 'social state' is weirdly more important now than ever in the neoliberal era. The state attempts to create a false-social or privatized public sphere to postpone our collective dissension into psychosis. The stress induced by neoliberalism's systemic chaos is now embodied by workers themselves, who ultimately bear the negativities of capitalism while sharing in little of its benefits. We certainly saw this in our discussion of paranoia and addiction earlier. But behind all of these flows of collective sadness is a sense of *tragedy*: the painful realization that we might have lived otherwise. The typical worker in the social factory is no longer bound to the excuse of necessity that was so popular during the Fordist period. Knowing now that this was always something of a ruse, however, does not empower us or diminish our feelings of imprisonment. Such knowledge almost accentuates the fact that the wonderful myriad possibilities that tauntingly lie before us are completely unattainable.

Decoding Dissent and Defusing the Myth of Work

Between 2011 and 2012, Gallup conducted a large-scale survey of the global workforce to measure their level of engagement. Millions of workers in 142 countries were asked if they were respected by superiors, if their jobs offered autonomy and fulfilment and whether well-being might be found in the workplace. Following the 2008 global economic crisis, the results were expected to be bleak, but they still surprised business observers and industry leaders. Only about 13 per cent of workers considered themselves 'engaged' in their jobs, defined as individuals 'who are involved in, enthusiastic about, and committed to their work and who contribute to their organization in a positive manner. Engaged employees are the ones who are most likely to drive innovation, growth, and revenue that their companies desperately need' (Gallup, 2013: 7); 63 per cent said they were 'not engaged'. These individuals have essentially 'checked out'. They're 'sleepwalking through their workday, putting time – but not energy or passion – into their work ... not engaged workers can be difficult to spot: They are not hostile or disruptive. They are thinking about lunch or their next break' (Gallup, 2013: 13). Most interestingly, 23 per cent of respondents claimed they were *actively disengaged*. These workers

aren't just unhappy at work; they're busy acting out their unhappiness. Every day, these workers undermine what their engaged co-workers accomplish ... Actively disengaged employees are more or less out to damage their company. They monopolize managers' time; have more on-the-job accidents; account for more quality defects; contribute to 'shrinkage,' as theft is called; are sicker; miss more days; and quit at a higher rate than engaged employees do. Whatever the engaged do – such as solving problems, innovating, and creating new customers – the actively disengaged try to undo. (Gallup, 2013: 17)

These results are interesting for a number of reasons. Even though the survey should be read from a worker's perspective, the report is and ought to be approached as capitalist propaganda. There is little sympathy with the disengaged multitude who have little choice but to put up with their awful boss and find ways to mitigate the nightmare called their job. For example, in contrast to the scourge that is the 'actively disengaged worker', we are told that 'actively engaged employees' 'are the best colleagues. They cooperate to build an organization, institution, or agency, and they are behind everything good that happens there.' Thank goodness there are only 13 per cent of these people! Turning to the actively disengaged employees, the report has only negative things to say about them:

Active disengagement is an immense drain on economies throughout the world. Gallup estimates, for example, that for the U.S., active disengagement costs US$450 billion to $550 billion per year. In Germany, that figure ranges from €112 billion to €138 billion per year (US$151 billion to $186 billion). In the United Kingdom, actively disengaged employees cost the country between £52 billion and £70 billion (US$83 billion and $112 billion) per year. (Gallup, 2013: 7)

However, when the results were released what really concerned capitalists and leaders of industry was not the lost profits, but the realization that the neoliberal revolution had not actually created a supine and obedient workforce after all. For all the effort put into the subjectification of the new 'enterprising worker' who ought to be robotically upbeat and engaged, the end result from power's perspective looks like an utter failure. In the conservative business magazine *Forbes*, we gain a glimpse of this disappointment concerning the US component of the survey, which revealed 70 per cent of employees to be unengaged. One author simply denounces the survey as flawed and irresponsible for portraying the workforce in such miserable terms. He worries that once managerial self-confidence is compromised by this vision of their workforce (i.e. as comprised of discontented saboteurs), the fiction of the 'good manager' might actually be revealed for what it really is – a fiction. These high-blood-pressured deputies of capitalism might begin to understand themselves as agents of exploitation rather than as the worker's best friend. Reality is not kind:

> So what? What difference does it make if managers believe that 70% of the workforce is not engaged in their work? Some might argue that this should motivate managers to put forth Herculean efforts to implement policies and practices that would increase employee engagement. And how bad would that be? But we believe the opposite will more likely occur. We believe executives' willingness to 1) experiment with more flexible work hours and schedules, 2) allow people to work part of the time from home, 3) fully explain the company's direction and strategy to everyone, and 4) provide more developmental opportunities will likely decrease if senior leaders assume that seven out of 10 people are not engaged in their work. (Zenger, 2013)

Given the survey results, maybe the real problem for commentators like this is that managers might actually become what they really are rather than what they pretend to be – family-friendly therapists and life-coach role models for employees. Managerialism has never liked to know too much about the truth of its place in the capitalist relations of production. The impossible and unattainable neoliberal fantasy of the conflict-free global workplace – apart from a few rogue aberrations in Bangladesh – is lethally disrupted. While it is indeed depressing to know that the trap of work has ensnared so many of us with extremely negative emotional outcomes, we should also view the results of the survey with some optimism. For it would be completely bizarre if the outcome was anything but dismal. The notion that authentic engagement could be experienced after the neoliberal brutalization of the global workforce would be the stuff of science fiction horror movies. So there is still hope. We can sense an alternative counter-history lurking in this survey, one that is anathema and hostile to the 'I, Job' function foisted upon us by the late-capitalist class offensive.

It is for this very reason that we should be circumspect about critical reason getting too close to neoliberal ideas, histories and ideologies when endeavouring to dissect the current woes of global capitalism. A growing number of recent studies have presented in-depth genealogies and exegeses of neoliberal thought (e.g. Dordot and Laval, 2014; Mirowski, 2013; Crouch, 2011; Duménil and Lévy, 2011). All are informative investigations.

But one gets the sense that they are taking this ideological *doxa* a little too seriously, getting too intimate with its assumptions and thus missing the protean miscarriages and false starts that animate neo-capitalist governance structures. Analytical distance is somehow compromised by the seductive sway exuded by the very object of criticism. In the end, neoliberal apologists only desire our attention and probably relish the idea of left-wing debunkers spending years reading Hayek.

This is surely one of the profound problems with Foucault's (2008; 2010) lectures delivered at the Collège de France explicating the antecedents of neoclassical liberalism and its developments in the early 1970s. The historian of systems of thought becomes overly attentive to its internal consistency and inadvertently subtends its supposed legitimacy. This is no doubt inspired by a quiet appreciation of neoliberal intellectu-ality and Foucault's more vocal disapproval of Marxism. But what makes neoliberalism interesting, if it is at all, is the vast historical continents that it is inherently unable to speak about; the minor worlds of the working multitude that pre-structures the majority of the world's population and cannot be recalibrated to Hayek's obdurate Utopia. We must anchor our criticism in the standpoint of the unspeakable, the invisible and the irreconcilable; the unassigned majority. For this, we require *our own history*, one that is never congruent or even partially commensurate with the dirty class offensive from above. For there is little symmetry here if we look closely. To perceive this requires a Baldwinian sensitivity for evidence of things not seen and the fire next time. So, how does neoliberalism function? To be honest, who cares? From the working classes' point of view it never really has, and understanding its internal consistency is of little import. Whence the *real labour begins*. To recognize one's self in the long shadow cast by an invisible sun requires a 'long, painful and difficult re-education', as a great thinker once observed.

Critical Theory's Abandonment Denial

The open wound is before us. Do we dare force ourselves to address it? The Gallup survey certainly disabuses us of the idea that capitalism wants to nurture and care for us in order to facilitate our exploitation; that it studies our subjectivity in all its minutia, buddies up to us like a close friend, and obedience thus follows. Recent critical theory has unfortunately been misguided in this respect. It approaches contemporary capitalism as an ingratiating ideology that needs to 'subjectify' the workforce to achieve complete regulation. Criticism derides the artificial attempts to manufacture happy, enthusiastic and authentic workplace performances. As a result, the focus of critique has been on the ideological co-optation of employees, through fun programmes, happiness workshops and other postmodern tropes that would not be out of place in a Google play zone. In other words, there is a tendency in some radical scholarship to explain the reproduction of the late-capitalist enterprise by alerting us to certain modes of cultural indoctrination. We are given the impression that the happy and engaged worker is the real objective of neoliberal control strategies, and this is achieved through a variety of seductive temptations.

We can see this misplaced analytical emphasis clearly in a number of recent studies concerning the modern workplace. In *Willing Slaves of Capital* (2014), Lordon argues that the centrepiece of neoliberal incorporation is desire. We are brainwashed by the contemporary enterprise and willingly subjugate ourselves to its wishes as we succumb to the boss's compliments, playfulness and employee-engagement exercises:

> To induce an aligned desire is the perennial goal of bossing, namely, of all the institutions of capture. For the enlistees in the grip of the co-linearization machine, the task is therefore to convert external imperatives, those of the enterprise and its particular objectives, into joyful affects and a personal desire, a desire that ideally they can each call their own. To produce consent is to produce in individuals love for the situation in which they have been put. (Lordon, 2014: 98)

Here the world of subjugated labour comes to look like a giant Googleplex. This is a rich man's version of Marx. Dardot and Laval too, in their analysis of how the neo-capitalist employee is manufactured, begin to quietly accept some of the rhetoric peddled by facile management consultants, albeit from a critical perspective. For them, the neoliberal working subject comes to resemble the 'personal enterprise' that Foucault argued was the leading thematic of this socio-economic paradigm. And as with Lordon's description above, desire is once again integral to the argument:

> The teeming proclamations in the new management literature of the importance of the 'human factor' must be read in light of a new kind of power. It is now not so much a matter of a man at work remains a man, that he is never reduced to the status of a passive object, as of

viewing him as an active subject who must participate fully, commit himself utterly and engage completely in his professional activity…The target of the new power is the desire to realize one's self, the project one wishes to pursue, the motivation that inspires the 'collaborator' of the enterprise, and ultimately, desire by whatever name one chooses to call it. (Dardot and Laval, 2014: 260)

There are some serious problems with viewing neoliberal employment relationship in this manner, as we shall discover in the following chapters. While the discourse of managerialism (especially the airport paperback version of it, which very few 'real' managers read) would like us to believe that we have entered a world of 'love' 'commitment' and 'fulfilment', many real workplace settings exhibit nothing of the sort. Sallaz (2013) even analyses 'gift-exchange' and 'reciprocity' as leading control mechanisms of the contemporary business enterprise. Critical theory must let go of the premise that capitalist organizations today aim to woo their workforces in order to get what they want from us. Contemporary work is nothing like a love relationship, and if it was, it would be the kind that our mothers quite rightly warned us to avoid at all costs. This is fundamentally a question of standpoint. Once we throw our copies of *The Four Hour Work Week* (Ferriss, 2011) into the rubbish bin and see things from the class position of the 'actively disengaged' (or even the 'not engaged') we begin to see *un*willing slaves, management enmity and most of all, *abandonment*. The concept of 'human capital', for example, which appears to indicate a friendlier version of economic reason, emerges precisely at the same time when the individual (i.e. his or her history, class relations, dreams, etc.) no longer matters to those who exploit. And this truth is formally displayed to us in an unrelenting fashion. Indeed, we immediately realize that something deeply disturbing is unfolding when the ruling class start to propound the principles of diversity, tolerance and participation. Not because of some automatic rule that disqualifies these qualities under capitalism. Nor because such ideals are inherently impossible and could never be realized, as a cynic might suggest. The problem arises because (as Lenin reminds us) capitalism has a weird relationship to democracy which is tirelessly voyeuristic and speculative. It must speak the truth about its social travesties, but only in a way that vindicates its own founding lie.

This is why my problem with the 'love thesis' concerning the neoliberal enterprise is not based upon a straightforward materialist argument, although I am extremely sympathetic to that. It is not the case that ideological inculcation has no place. It does, but late capitalism subjectively incorporates us in a purely negative sense. Neoliberal ideology does not want to persuade us that compliance will bring happiness and special privileges. Instead it seeks to remind us that our potential exclusion is always close and quietly encourages us to see the present as but the ghostly vulnerability it surely is when viewed from a future state of abandonment. Control and regulation no longer require an ideological supplement to justify their exercise. Coercion is certainly the medium, but more importantly, it is also the ideological message. We are now far away from the Googleplex and its origami workshops and ping-pong tables.

So what is actually happening here in terms of ideological assimilation? Investigations of how pain can irrationally capture our attention may be germane here. In her book, the *Body in Pain* (1985), Scarry argues that the point of torture is not the confession, but the act of torture itself. In other words, the infliction of pain in the interrogation room is not really motivated by extracting useful secrets or confessions. Violence is tautological, becoming its own primary destination or *telos*. This is why it is so ideologically befuddling. There is no subjective rationale behind it and this excess carries a very important cultural message that the victims themselves primarily create. Dominant ideologies always develop from their intended targets. I believe something analogous occurs when power is exercised in the workplace today. The goal of managerial regulation is not to seduce us into becoming willing collaborators, but to vindicate the moment of power itself and its fickle postponements: 'Are you in my favour today? If so, I will leave you alone ... for now, at least. If not, you will be harassed until you leave of your own accord (for one must observe unfair-dismissal employment law!)' The purpose of neoliberal discourse is to remind us that it exists and is the only game in town. Hence the Straussian ultimatum presented to us on a daily basis: Are you with us or against us? And herein lays the sting in the tail. If you are with us, then you are permanently indebted and always hypothetically abandoned. This is what makes the fear of being abandoned by our employers all the more irrational. Abandonment has *already* concretely arrived (the power elite don't care one iota about you) and we are constantly reminded of this fact in order, paradoxically, to convince us otherwise. As I argue in the chapters that follow, this is how the ideology of abandonment binds us ever more tightly to our willingness to tolerate our unwillingness. Can this complex cycle of control ever be broken?

2

Planet of Work

Welcome to the planet of work. When a 21-year-old banking intern, Moritz Erhardt, died in his London apartment in 2013, it attracted worldwide attention. What was so troubling about his death was that it followed 72 straight hours of stressful work. Subsequent reports pointed to an industry mentality that gleefully celebrated such arduous displays of commitment. Working incredibly long hours is a badge of honour, something to be proud of and rewarded by the company. Erhardt's parents stated that they had become increasingly worried about their son's lifestyle, noting how his emails were sent at very unusual times, indicating that he was working too much.

In January 2014, Li Junjie, a 33-year-old investment banker for a large US firm, jumped to his death from its high-rise tower in Hong Kong. Some commentators suggested that he had a rather stressful job, but it was news of an impending financial crash that had prompted this awful act. The wave of banker suicides in 2014 has been shocking, with some large firms even banning its employees from using email after hours so they have time to unwind. But the fact remains, why would someone take their job so seriously that they choose to end their life when something goes wrong at the office? How does such a lack of perspective come about?

In 2013, *News China* magazine reported on the strange death of Li Zheng, a 24-year-old employed by a global PR firm. He died from a cardiac arrest on the first day back from a stress-induced holiday. Li Zheng's death was totally unexpected given his chance to recuperate and relax. But all was not well, as this report emphasizes: 'It was obvious from the 24-year-old's public microblog posts that he was regularly to be found burning the midnight oil. In the personal description on Li's Weibo [China's Twitter equivalent], he called himself 'an over-worker in overworking season', and an earlier post revealed that the young man did not leave the office until 11PM on the day of his death' (*News China*, 2013).

In February 2014, 56-year old Richard Tally, a senior executive at American Tiles Services was pronounced dead at his Colorado home. His company was being investigated by the Colorado Division of Insurance. Not unexpectedly, the media concentrated on the particularly gruesome nature of his death. Evidence suggests he walked into his suburban garage, picked up a nail gun and shot himself seven or eight times in the head and chest. It is unclear exactly what the investigation involved that apparently motivated the suicide. But it is safe to categorize this as a *job-related suicide*, a phrase that increasingly appears in the daily news.

These four sad deaths tell us much about the world of work today – not in quantitative terms (for the numbers are few) but in the way they tragically reveal the 'ideal type' of worker that we are all increasingly measured against. Most reports about work-related death after the 2008 economic crisis cite *lack* of work as the chief driver. For example, the BBC recently highlighted a study published in the *British Journal of Psychiatry* suggesting that 10,000 additional suicides in Europe and North America (above and beyond the typical rate) have been recorded since the global recession began. Much of this has been put down to the stress and humiliation of unemployment: 'losing a job, having a home repossessed and being in debt were the main risk factors.' (BBC, 2014a). However, less emphasized here is the death-drive connected to the overactive 'I, Job' function. That is to say, what connects these cases of deaths is the particular relationship that the victims had developed with their jobs – not a lack of work, but lives oversaturated with the stuff so that no alternative could be envisaged, least of all quitting. There was no reasonable way out.

It is this perception of endlessness that I think is so important for understanding the cultural meaning of capitalist work relations today. The 'all or nothing' attitude exemplified in these four unhappy deaths now runs deep in our social imagination. However, our driving concern here should not simply be about grasping this facet of neoliberal reason and its ability to universalize a rather isolated and partial part of modernity (i.e. working); no, what is really at stake is figuring out how we might practically transcend this universalization, a question that resounds in much critical theory, from Adorno's negative dialectics to the notion of exodus in Italian autonomist thought. That is to say, it is all very well to map the totality of real subsumption, especially today when it now invades our dreams, sexuality and most private moments of rest; but we must now focus on the problem of 'escape'. When the biopolitical articulation of power creates a self-sealed world that only reflects more of the same, what type of cognitive map might help us break free from the acephalous society of work?

There Is No Outside

There is much to be disconsolate about when we read yet another report of someone dying because their job was unbearably close to them. However, I suggest that the four deaths mentioned above do actually tell us much about how a growing number of people approach their jobs in the post-industrial workforce. Whereas our grandparents could 'switch off' after leaving the office, positioning it as something they did among others things, what we might call the bio-proletariat view their jobs as something they 'are'. While suicide and death-by-overwork are extreme cases, they are indicative of an idealization of employment that affects many people, encouraging them to perceive their jobs as everything. Work has become a generalizable social insistence, an inclusive reference point that relates to everything else we do. These deadly trends say something more generally about the intentional conflation of work and life in late-capitalist societies.

Standing on the outside looking in, the idea of killing yourself over a trivial thing like work is unfathomable. Over a lost lover? Yes. Ennui? Perhaps. But a stupid little office job, or even worse, a bank's bullying letters about the mortgage? *Never*. Just quit. Walk away. Sadly, however, just as a troubled sleeper at 3.23 a.m. cannot help worrying about a problem at the office, the suicidal clerk too resists perspective. This might be described as a kind of capitalist resistance. The 'I, job' function poisons everything and rebels against what we know is actually the case. And only then does a violent end seem like the only reasonable way out. Life and labour are perfectly blended. And is this not neoliberal capitalism's highest ideal? Those who work themselves to death or sacrifice their lives at the altar of work represent the highest embodiment of the neoclassical model of human capital. Hence the title of this chapter. A planet of work is not only a physical globe overtaken by manufactured necessity, a reality principle that has infiltrated the collective imaginary of large parts of society; it also points to an assiduous socio-political circularity that always brings us back to the beginning again, ensuring that we are never done or finished with anything.

The Antinomies of Escape

This is where many cinematic visions of the present juncture in late-capitalist societies fail when endeavouring to portray the universalization of labour today. They always posit a visible outside. In Stephen King's *Under the Dome*, the entrapped citizens of a small US town are tormented not only by their inability to escape the giant dome, but also by its transparency – they can literally see the world outside, its trees and inhabitants, the rescuers in florescent yellow slowly getting bored with their impossible task – an exterior that is discernible and nefariously taunting. But the inside–outside dichotomy, as with any oversimplified dialectics, is far too clear-cut for our purposes. Vincenzo Natali's 1997 film *The Cube* comes closer. A group of strangers mysteriously awake imprisoned in a giant machine consisting of shifting cubical rooms. No one knows how they ended up there. They suspect that it might be a governmental experiment or some corporate 'hunger games' entertainment for the elite. But they don't know for sure. They immediately search for an exit. Each compartment has a trapdoor that allows them to move between the cubes. But escape will not be easy since the rooms periodically rotate, shifting their respective positions, as if dictated by some strange and indecipherable algorithm. Making matters worse is that some of the rooms harbour clandestine booby-traps that kill off the characters in increasingly disturbing ways (incinerated by a blowtorch, literally cubed by a matrix of blades that appear from nowhere, etc.). Those who remain slowly descend into madness. The film's genius is in the way it almost perfectly captures the neoliberal nightmare of permanent redeployment – the inscrutably changing nature of the game's rules with deadly effect, and a division of labour that foments interminable interpersonal conflict. But the film fails when it attempts to visualize how we might escape this machine. There is a clear external domain, a decodable path to the outside, which understandably motivates the captives' activity. We witness the exit's brilliant glare towards the end of the film, a magical square of light, as the last survivor (a mute man inflicted with chronic Asperger's) finally disappears into freedom.

But the neoliberal universalization of work is not a prison with a clear perimeter wall. Infinity is an endlessly repeated loop. This is why the time and space of working today has managed to reduce all of our efforts to its own myopic register. And this is perhaps too difficult to depict in cinema. The ideological curvature that points only to its own vectors of accession is not immediately representable in visual terms. Not even Rodrigo Cortés's otherwise brilliant 2010 anti-capitalist film *Buried* can analogize neoliberal interment. Paul Conroy is a truck driver based in US-occupied Iraq. One day he is ambushed by terrorists and buried alive in a coffin with a bottle of water, some glow sticks, a pen and a BlackBerry mobile phone. His abductors have asked for a ransom. The US government won't pay but will try to rescue him. Conroy calls his employers and is summarily fired. His captors then request he record himself cutting off his finger on his phone and he dutifully complies. Finally, Conroy hears digging and then beautiful sunshine surges into the coffin. He is about to be liberated. The lid opens. He is free. But it was only a hallucination as he awakes in the coffin. As Conroy's makeshift lighting begins to fail the film ends in blackness.

The claustrophobic impossibility of a world overcome by work is brilliantly captured in this film. All of the items Conroy is buried with are fixtures of the postmodern office cubicle – the pen, the artificial florescent lights, the mobile phone, etc. Indeed, not only is the BlackBerry a lifeline to the outside world, but it is also an instrument of psychic torture, a self-harming weapon that Conroy clings to nevertheless since he would be completely alone without it. The paradox, of course, is that like the millions of overworked employees around the world, he is in fact already alone and cruelly abandoned. While his job has killed him, Conroy is alive to observe this reality with increasing desperation. Not even self-harm can save him. But *Buried* is still marred by the motif of imprisonment. A clear exteriority is naively suggested. This is the film's basic error. We cannot 'dig' ourselves out of late capitalism. Power is not a seven-foot stratum of sand and dirt above us that might be tunnelled through to freedom if only we had a good trowel. While it sometimes feels as if we have been buried alive, that sense of existential collapse is absolutely fundamental to the economy of justification that makes manufactured inequality seem bearable. Our intuition is correct. We are being suffocated. But the air we seek merely signals more of the same, an oxygen mask at the bottom of a grave.

The hypostatic pressure to produce incited by neoliberal employment policy, to make one's life into an indefinitely poised factor of production, does not operate through the logic of old-fashioned incarceration. As I argue in a later chapter, the late-capitalist concern with confinement – what Foucault (1977) called disciplinary power – no longer bothers with imprisonment as its guiding metaphor. Containment might have been useful under the Fordist regime of accumulation; but today it would seriously hamper the flows of power that seek to enlist the agential freedoms of 'life itself'. Corporate domination now depends upon a dynamic social indexation and suspiciously multiple passages between institutional domains. This kind of freedom is designed to inspire anxiety. And this tactically constructed anxiety inspires a certain type of unfreedom that restrains political involvement. Capitalism evidently understands the dialectic very well.

Let's return to the problem at hand; the indexation process allows a primary power to create indirect sympathies with other social logics that are sometimes far removed from the capitalist interface itself. It acts as a social conductor that we must resist at all costs. This is how work becomes the ultimate measure of all things even when not directly present in our lives. And only then can the negative costs of production be externalized so that workers carry them – for we know that prisons are notoriously expensive to maintain. Thus the nasty reality of so-called flexible labour. If anything, what Deleuze calls 'societies of control' is a regime of power more aligned with the 'open prison' that tags the permanently accused, with debt, mobile technology, a family that will be with you forever, and a CV that is always on your mind. As I maintain later, this tagging process accomplishes an important function. It gives us the impression that the era of coercive power is over. But that is part of the deception. Old-fashioned managerialism continues, but with the added benefits (from the capitalist perspective at least) of having us eternally on call. Perhaps even in the grave, as Ross (2013) illustrates in relation to the way some workers can only obtain a loan by enrolling a guarantor to take on the repayment obligation if the signee dies.

This never-ending structure of feeling that neoliberal ideology has been particularly successful in perfecting requires us to find new ways of conceptualizing emancipation. The old leftist slogans are problematic here. More work is certainly not the answer. Nor are better wages that deepen our normative indebtedness to the tenets of production. In order to refuse capitalist regulation in an era defined by 'societies of control' we must break the spell of permanency that confers a sense of interminableness to our economic subordination. Perhaps this is why the 1993 comedy film *Groundhog Day* is a more faithful cinematic illustration of our present situation than those we have examined so far. Bill Murray plays Phil Connors, a grumpy TV weather reporter who finds himself trapped in a small town called Punxsutawney on 2 February. He hates the town. When his job is done and he is about to leave, Punxsutawney is besieged by a snowstorm that makes departure impossible. Awaking in his rustic hotel room the next morning he finds himself reliving 2 February. Everything is exactly the same – the people, the conversations, the events. All of Phil's attempts to break the time-loop merely result in his awakening once again in his room on 2 February to begin the day as he did before. Nothing stops the repetition. Becoming desperate, he even commits suicide (throws himself in front of a truck, jumps off a building, electrocutes himself). Still 2 February begins again. Phil complains to his friend Ralph: 'What would you do if you were stuck in one place and every day was exactly the same, and nothing that you did mattered?' Ralph replies, 'Well that about sums it up for me.'

Finally, Phil starts to use the special insights gleaned from constantly reliving 2 February for other purposes – to save those who were destined to die, to undermine local power authorities, to enhance the civic well-being of Punxsutawney's citizens and workers. And thus the loop is broken. Phil Connor's new-found communist ethic of social love, learning and laughing is our only hope too for breaking the life sentence of late-capitalist employment relations. Fundamentally, it consists of a critique of everyday life through radical remembrance. Phil knew exactly what was coming. However, is it really possible to break the spell of capitalist realism with some sort of inspired social love?

Learning From the Falling Banker

Let us delve a little further into this strange Groundhog-Day-like impasse that has lured so many into the closed universe of work today. As is often the case, we can learn some axiomatic principles about the late capitalist mindset by examining its fullest embodiment. For this, we must return to work-related suicide. The financial crisis has seen a spate of job-inspired suicides in the banking sector. It is far too simple to cite 'underlying personal problems' as the sole causal factor when endeavouring to explain these extreme acts. Indeed, this trend has a strong social backdrop that is very important to this book's argument: namely, all-encompassing work environments and the inescapable pressures they have created. And now, with a huge amount of governmental and public scrutiny directed towards the banking sector, this already stressful occupation has become a 'hyper-stressful' vocation that ought to carry a severe health warning.

As I mentioned above, the real question is this: why would someone end their life over something as relatively minor as their job? I believe this has to do with the 'suicidal work ethic' that these institutions tend to foster, which is also an important element of how we are all encouraged to approach our jobs today as neoliberalism flounders in irredeemable crisis. Like other institutional believers in endless work, banks have encouraged a reckless ethos in which nothing matters except what happens in the office. Excruciatingly long hours are a sign that one has submitted to their work and worthy of the position, the bonuses, etc. Under these conditions, and especially with the help of mobile technology, the distinction between work and non-work dissolves. You are your job – 24/7.

This has always been the wet dream of neoliberal capitalism. Classic proclamations concerning 'human capital' are salient in this regard. What better way to secure capital's future than transforming labour into its primary vehicle of dissemination, making it intangible (knowledge, competencies and sociability) and portable (self-reliant, fluid, dynamic and transmittable through social interconnections)? Perhaps this is the key ideological role of human-capital theory. When we relate to ourselves as capital, mobile and always potentially valorizable, we begin to do the dirty work for a beleaguered economic system that is so ossified and decrepit that it requires the self-styled virtuosity of living labour to carry out its class mission. Moreover, we must acknowledge the other side of the coin, which is perhaps more important than the 'positive' exploitable qualities of human capital. Its true value to capitalism lies in its inherent disposability. When capital is personified in this manner, its individualization makes 'letting go' (aka firing) a more feasible option than defining the worker as a member of a collective coalition. It is easier for a firm to justify an employee's abandonment if it is able to emphasize reasons that are related to individual personalities. The talk is no longer of structural decline and systemic unemployment, but of wrong people.

Personalizing the negative returns on capital is a central feature of human capital theory. And this has profound consequences for those who must bear the weight of work, especially when things go wrong, as they often do. What characterizes the suicides that have blighted the finance sector around the world is the human enrolment that binds the fortunes of the market to the individual's body. As a result, these people lose perspective, since work has no outside. A small problem in the office is blown out of proportion, making it feel like a life-threatening issue. From the outside (wherever this may be, since it does not exist in a formal sense), it seems like no big deal; but when you are inside the 'I, Job' function, there appears to be no way out, because work is mercurially inscribed as a worldwide horizon. Making this situation more complex is the masochistic pleasure derived from such self-sacrifice. This is why typical ideology critique does not work here. Human capital is impervious to being shown the truth because it lives its own negativity as a realistic and pragmatic response to external stimuli, even though these stimuli systematically distort the truth. Self-sacrifice cannot be deemed a lie, especially when a modicum of freedom is derived from a slow (or, in the case of suicide, sudden) demise.

In this sense, the concatenation of human capital can be deadly to your health and well-being. It is indicative of a changing relationship with how work is conducted and the deeply deleterious consequences that can follow. This recent and morbid development in capitalist philosophy did not come about by accident. Human capital represents a new configuration of power that glorifies work as the ultimate 'advantage', whilst heartlessly denying it to millions whenever it can. This denial is not only numerical, however, but also qualitative since it infects the already-working as well. You may be 'let go' with little notice. But here's the rub: if we actually had pure neoliberalism in the office – say, complete individualism, no state regulation, profligate competition, no mutualism or open co-operation – absolutely nothing would get done. Neoliberal ideals are completely unworkable when actually applied to most employment settings. As we see in the next chapter, the irony is that managers know this fact very well. As a result, corporate capitalism requires us to be fully present, socially resourceful networkers who can pick up the slack. Organized employment inherently requires worker discretion and autonomy, something that managerialism resents as it increasingly comes to rely upon social qualities that lie beyond its formal powers. Regardless of this enmity, we feel compelled to employ our whole personas to deal with the unbearable disorder around us. As a result of this closeness with work, many of us misdiagnose the failings of neoliberal capitalism as our own.

We can see this playing out in the finance sector and other industries today. For example, the pressure of living up to the 'successful banker' schematization (which usually has strong masculine connotations) is increasingly difficult to do when the finance sector is in such dire straits. Couple this with a work ethic that indexes everything to the job, and stress morphs into depression and a dangerously diminished sense of self-preservation – risk becomes addictive and nihilistic. Moreover, in this culture of anxiety and financial atrophy, combined with extremely negative comments from the media, it is inevitable that some will begin to hate themselves and try to resist what they have become. Freud argued that suicide can be defined as killing the hated 'other' inside us – those characteristics that we have assimilated from our environment over time and now perceive as an awful stranger inside us. When we mistake this unwanted guest as ourselves (rather than the ugly cardboard cut-out that neoclassical economists widely laud as 'human capital') we risk making a grave miscalculation.

All of this sounds bleak, and it is. But the main focus of this book is how we might push back and break the capitalist gridlock that has us hanging between an unliveable life and a future of more of the same. Given the above trends that have generalized some horrible principles in the form of human and social capital, this is more easily said than done. For how might we oppose the 'I, Job' function when it is now somehow tied up with our very sense of identity and personal worth? And what would a world without work actually look like? I argue that a new resistance movement is emerging in post-industrial societies and beyond that seeks to put work in its place. Unlike traditional conceptions of employee resistance (such as the strike or sabotage) which often functioned as a platform to demand more, better or fairer work, this novel form of opposition seeks to escape the paradigm of work altogether. It does not view our over-attachment to a job as an inevitable consequence of survival, but as a hypnotic political absurdity that we have come to live as if it has always been so. But before we look at how neoliberal strategies of 'tagging' might be successfully evaded, we need to further explore the planet of work and especially its demented sense of time.

What Happens to Time on the Frozen Planet of Work?

In *The Seeds of Time* (1996), Fredric Jameson contends that late-capitalist society has mangled time in a strange manner. Unlike other political systems that warp history to counterbalance existential and concrete individual grievances – for example, by erasing certain stories from the historical past – capitalism in its latest phase simply does away with time, creating a permanent present: 'for us time consists in an eternal present and, much, further away, an inevitable catastrophe, these two moments showing up distinctly on the registering apparatus without overlapping or transitional states' (Jameson, 1996: 72). Here, Jameson is identifying a double totality that has long been part of the capitalist imaginary, given the man-made alienation that it conspires to render immutable. On the one hand, the individual is detached from his or her own collective history through the exchange process, becoming an abstraction that is bought and sold in the marketplace like any other commodity whose history is ultra-condensed into an infinitesimal moment by the transaction process. On the other hand, history coagulated in the state form and the collective institutional apparatuses of the capitalist mode of production are reified into a spectacle. We witness the class offensive as something like a bad movie that we are unable to walk away from. Late-capitalist democracy amounts to being strapped in a chair and forced to watch another Adam Sandler offering.

However, working-class politics has always evinced its own totality, a sub-genus of history that is minor, peasant-like (i.e. a nameless universality), and incommensurate with official narratives that attempt to obliterate any reasonable sense of time. Walter Benjamin was particularly proficient at detecting this history, his textual colligations or collages consisting of elements drawn from seemingly disparate sources. This allowed his essays to speak as if they were voicing the nameless who haunt us because the crimes that befell them continue to befall us. The fetish of individualism can only be undermined by this minor knowledge. If the totality of work today forms a suspended temporality that only folds back on itself, a loop of infinite regress like the one that the hapless Phil Connor found himself trapped in, two important experiential elements also become apparent. Firstly, no totality can be without a putative outside, as Adorno taught us well. The infinite is impossible. The fabricated totality of late-capitalist reason always insinuates its own impossibility. This falsity often becomes conspicuous via the limits of the body – its capitulation to illness, burnout and injurious revolt. It is in the organic impossibility of the present that the materials of minor knowledge conspire, oozing from the fissures of the untrue whole. Secondly, the calculus of exploitative rationality is not only experienced like a bad film on constant repeat, but also as a real world detached from an observer who nevertheless remains an integral participant. Work too is lived in this way, a spectacle without a history – or as Jameson might put it, an eternal present. But there is also a minor history here that can be recovered and deployed as a route out.

When it comes to late capitalism's ability to eternalize the present, Deleuze (1992) understood a great deal. His conception of 'societies of control' is important for discerning the crisis of disciplinary regulation. (It might also be argued that Foucault understood this too, for are not his genealogies of particular knowledge regimes always written at the time of their demise? – 'I do not say the things I say because they are what I think, I say them as a way to make sure they are no longer what I think.') Deleuze's brilliant essay identifies the tactics of endlessness that the neoliberal corporation and state apparatus pursue. Central to maintaining the false whole is the corporeal incitement guided by an unpayable debt, or what Deleuze and Guattari (1983) earlier called *infinite debt*. But the abiding and contractual weight of this unpayable sum is not enough in this respect. For its religious connotations of life without atonement is too closely allied with a moral universe resistant to the cold cash nexus of everyday capitalism. The debt has to be *social* in order to serve a class function properly, whereby *bios* itself is deferred in a continuous state of exception.

For this reason, to truly grasp the significance of our society of control we ought to analyse it through the concept of *overcoding* rather than as some sort of vital debt. For Deleuze and Guattari (1987), overcoding is a dangerous instrument of social logics that are folded upon themselves so there is no longer any perceptible beginning or end. Life becomes an endless series of soon-to-be postponed fixtures that can never be realized or completed. For example, the state overcodes the employment situation through a multiplication of legal supplements and reclarifications, each of which rewrites the law of an earlier period and simultaneously expiates that period's history until the original impetus no longer matters. As a result, there is no longer any 'ground zero' or absolute baseline to which we are able to anchor our experience of the present. Overcoding is also isomorphic. The repetition of emetic axioms and their rewritings of the social body are the chief reasons Deleuze constantly approached biopower under neoliberal conditions as something akin to a virus. The virus cannot be isolated in any part of the cellular totality, but is somehow virtually constitutive of each part within the systemic whole. From this point onwards, we must therefore refrain from conceptualizing the apparent totality of the neoliberal impasse as an inside–outside system. Instead we ought to speak of tactical lines that build upon the non-voiced minor histories of class autonomy and a future that gives licence to extending those lines. I suggest that several aspects of neoliberal employment practices conspire to present an otherwise finite experience (i.e. work) as infinite, endless, and so forth. Let's explore them in detail before we turn to some detotalizing interventions that might finally hasten an emancipatory transformation of the world of work.

Deformalization

In 2014, a Long Island customer service firm, United Health Programs of America, was sued by the US Equal Employment Opportunities Commission for forcing employees to say 'I love you' to each other. The company's Human Resource Management (HRM) office clearly believed strongly that spirituality in the workplace would increase motivation and sales. Spearheading this management approach was a program called 'Onionhead'. Employees were required to express deep feelings of emotional attachment to their colleagues and bosses (including love) and pray at the office each morning. A number of workers complained about this intrusion into their personal lives. One individual was subsequently fired by the company for not participating in the Onionhead ritual of love, prayer and gestures of peace. A report about the incident explains: 'A month after she complained, the employee was removed from her office and relocated to an open customer service area, while a large statue of a Buddha was placed in her former office. She protested to the owner that the move amounted to a demotion and was fired, the complaint said' (Reuters, 2014).

It has been widely noted that one way in which the production mentality is generalized throughout society is to blur the boundary between work and non-work. Many features of corporate life today – including parties, emotional bonding exercises, spirituality and overt sexuality – would have looked peculiar and completely out of place in the classic offices of Fordism. When work is personalized in this manner, it is not as easy to walk away from because power is drawing on vested social qualities. As Deleuze argued in his 'societies of control' essay, such defor-malization ought to be viewed as a very worrying trend: 'We are taught that corporations have a soul, which is the most terrifying news in the world' (Deleuze, 1992: 6). Why is this a terrifying prospect? If we cherish the opportunity to experience love, then why not welcome it into the workplace, a zone that has been bereft of meaningful emotion for so long? There are a number of reasons to be horrified. The informalization of work in this manner is not simply driven by an attempt to build stronger, warmer and more spiritually fulfilling ties between employees and management (a reading we criticized in the last chapter). A more important driver is social disposability, which dovetails neatly with the contractualization of everyday life under late-capitalist conditions. With the advent of ultra-formalization exemplified by the technical bureaucracies of the Fordist period, a platform was inadvertently created for certain social-justice claims. Edwards (1979) notes that this was an unintended consequence of modern industrialism. From the capitalist perspective, the immediate gains of rationalization under bureaucratic structures were clear, and it provided an efficient instrument of class domination. However, by developing nominally impartial systems of employment, impersonal occupational grades and career paths, corporations unwittingly civilized workplace power relations. Managers had to partially forego the freedom to sadistically toy with the worker, often on a whim, that they had enjoyed under patrimonial employment relations such as the early factory system.

This is why the attempt to retract the rituals of formalization ought to be seen with a very pessimistic eye. It has very little to do with forging lasting bonds of reciprocity, trust and commitment. Critical theory often misses this point when it laments the advent of the corporate clone, in love with their firm and the firm with them. All of the talk about 'high commitment' cultures elides the real nature of the discourse. These changes actually signify the return of the emotionally unpredictable and capricious boss, who one day treats you as his favourite pet and the next day scorns you like a jilted lover. Moreover, when work relations are personalized in this manner, it is much easier to justify an employee's ejection from the workplace. The rationale for doing so can be framed in the same terms as those that apply to a lover breaking up with their partner. Our bosses are now able to say, 'This is not a forced relationship, but a matter of choice and compatibility. Please leave now, this isn't working out. And by the way, I have found someone new.'

This is why the attempt to model workplaces along the lines of a 'family' is fundamentally disturbing from the worker's point of view. Marxian critiques of this capitalist manoeuvre are correct to point out its ideological function, manufacturing the pliant and loyal worker at the expense of their true class interests. But matters are more serious than that. As any psychoanalyst will remind us, the modern nuclear family turned out to be a rather brutal invention, a social structure that often caused years of torment, even long after the victim had escaped. Replicating in the office the psychological hang-ups, backbiting, mind games and spirit-crushing guilt at the heart of the modern family is rightfully considered by most workers to be a vicious development.

Additionally, the deformalization of work seeks to nullify long-standing transgressive spaces typical of working-class resistance. The evocation of various tropes associated with rebellion, even if only as a flimsy and substanceless caricature, is a cause for worry from a critical point of view. For example, a new trend in office management in London was recently reported in an article entitled 'Drinking on the Job' (Williams-Grut, 2014). At first glance, the headline might lead us to expect a scandalous account of the secret pastimes of disgruntled employees, functional alcoholics who would surely be fired if their lavatory whisky-sipping activities were discovered by the boss. But a very different story is told:

> London's white-collar brigade is taking up a new habit that blurs the boundaries between work and play so much they've nearly been rubbed out completely. Everybody is drinking in the office. Booze trolleys, beer fridges, drinks cabinets, office cocktails and even in-work bars mean it's no longer taboo to drink at your desk. Hundreds of Londoner's are clinking bottles before they've even clocked off – with the boss footing the bill. Dress rental service Girl Meets Dress is typical, with the 12-strong team gathering for drinks in their office every Friday afternoon … Tom Morris of Fishburn thinks the in-house social not only boosts morale but also helps foster new ideas. (Williams-Grut, 2014: 35)

Of course, for any dedicated drinker, this trend is extremely depressing. Capitalism has always maintained an extremely antagonistic relationship with respect to alcohol consumption in the workplace. E.P. Thompson (1967) noted how the legendary 'Saint Monday' binges became *the* enemy for early industrialists and government officials. The customary practice consisted of workers dropping their tools, vacating the factory and getting extremely inebriated on Monday mornings just as the workday was formally beginning. A raft of disciplinary measures was hurled at the working class to stamp out this reverential tribute to Saint Monday. The anti-work connotations of boozing on the job continued through the Fordist period under Western capitalism. For employees, drinking was not only a moment of escape, but also a sign of triumphant insubordination in the face of sobering discipline, as epitomized by Hamper (1992) in his tale about working on the line at General Motors. The relationship between alcohol and authority takes on an important political dimension in societies governed by prison-like regimentation and disciplinary power. We see this in so many of Charles Bukowski's stories and poems. Once we stand back and contemplate the ritual of paid employment from an objective distance, its so-called normalcy disappears and we see it for what it really is: a type of mindless psychosis. A drunk can never be a perfect worker. That is why she is beautiful. Alcohol not only alters our perception of time in a favourable manner, but gathers connections with our peasant past and frequently obliterates the non-time of capitalism's eternal present.

Consequently we should contest the corporate enclosure of this component of working-class praxis for a number of reasons. It hijacks a decisively incongruent modulation of temporal experience and seeks to smooth it out, rendering it felicitous with the self-same present of neoliberal rationality. Alcohol's minor modulation traces a line back to the rebellions against the factory, Saint Monday (and sometimes Saint Tuesday) and a constellation of non-capitalist images that are muted when they enter into the parlance of corporate socializing. In addition, sanctioned drinking on the job becomes a code of capitalist obstinacy regarding our attempts to reclaim the non-numerical time that alcohol otherwise signifies. One can only imagine the pressure *not to drink* an employee must experience when forced to 'enjoy' a glass of wine with a watchful boss. The oppressive restraint kills the historical knowledge delivered in a bottle of wine. Alone with trusted friends we get shit-faced. With the boss, we sadly stare at our half-empty glass and pray the occasion ends quickly. The blurring of work into play and non-work heralds yet another attempt to universalize the logic of work so that even getting drunk is not immune to its reach. Once again, work infiltrates everything, and social time collapses in upon itself like some lapidary bad dream.

The Labour Marathon and Modafinil

For the above reasons, this is why I think Pollack's 1969 film *They Shoot Horses Don't They?* truly goes to heart of the terror that social deformalization can instil among the bio-proletariat today. Set in the 1930s US depression, Robert Syverton (played by Michael Sarrazin) finds himself in Los Angeles, where he discovers an infamous competition called the Dance Marathon. He wants to try his luck. With the help of an organizer, he is paired with the mentally unsound Gloria (played by Jane Fonda). The competition is simple. Couples must dance continuously for as long as they can. The final couple standing receive a large cash prize. The marathon is both physically and emotionally gruelling. And it is this that precisely draws such large audiences. Over the hours, a range of feelings are expressed between the couples. Joy and frivolity at the beginning is slowly replaced by feelings of hate, jealously, resentment and irrational bickering played out over many hours, days and weeks. Robert and Gloria begin to experience their relationship as a life sentence, a never-ending bond of revulsion neither can walk away from – even though the exit door is in sight. After weeks have past, some participants attempt to carry their fatigued partners, angrily demanding that they do not fall asleep since that would result in disqualification. When Robert and Gloria are told by the organizer that expenses will be deducted from the prize, reducing it to a negligible sum, they give up and bow out. Both have been duped and economically exploited, all in the name of a competition that seeks to test the 'staying power' of couples in love. Do you really love me? In the final scene of the film, Gloria asks Robert to help her commit suicide. He obliges and finally fulfils the role of the loyal husband. Of course, now it is too late.

It is obvious that this excessively bleak film is an indictment of the way many unloving marriages needlessly continue, for whatever reason. However, is this not also a vivid depiction of what happens to us in the highly deformalized workplaces emerging in the post-industrial West? The terrible and exhausting eternity that these couples endure together is similar to the inability to fathom an outside by many employees today. As we observed above, even drinking is not safe.

There are three elements of the film that are important for the purposes of this discussion. First, Robert and Gloria were complete strangers before the marathon organizer paired them together. Unlike the other couples who genuinely loved each other (and interestingly were often the first to exit the competition), Robert and Gloria were forced together by economic reason. This allowed the supposed romantic dynamic to withstand almost inhuman levels of fatigue, exhaustion and humiliation. We should read the 'I love you' command by the United Health Programs of America Corporation discussed above in the same way. There is no authentic love involved, since it is a simulation designed to extract arduous hours of work from employees. One might suspect that the worker fired by the firm actually did love her job, but as soon as it became a mandatory requirement of her employment contract she recoiled and departed the scene.

Secondly, the informal stereotype of partners in love becomes a mechanism for extending the endurance of the working pair. After a week of dancing, the time of labour (which is so overladen and ultimately camouflaged by so-called personal bonds) becomes universal. Robert and Gloria can no longer remember how the marathon started or even that they once were complete strangers. They obediently submit to the regime of generalized labour and the easily noticeable 'exit' sign on the door becomes a nauseating emblem of their own predicament. Departure is impossible when beginnings and ends are rubbed out. As Deleuze argues, this kind of time is without the clear sectors, domains and borders

of distinction that would help differentiate life from labour. Now is only a
time of postponements against a steady screen.

And thirdly, Robert and Gloria can only exit this infinite social space
once their exploitation is revealed and visibly enjoyed by the tyrannical
organizer, who displays a subtle and excruciating *schadenfreude* as they
painfully limp off the dance floor. Even afterwards, when Gloria is finally
free from the ghastly competition, she can no longer decipher what her
life might actual be. Only death can provide her with the terminus she
longs for. The time of work has instilled a self-entrapping circularity
that not even departing the stage of exploitation can disrupt. As Robert
assists her suicide, we might remember the bankers falling from the high
towers in the city centres of London and Hong Kong or the interns who
simply cannot stop until their bodies rise up and utter a definitive and
irreversible no.

If Gloria and Robert had had access to Modafinil and Ritalin I suspect
they would have wolfed them down in order to win the Dance Marathon.
Indeed, many employees in the post-industrial West are using 'smart drugs'
to get through their own personal work marathons. The proliferation
of mobile technology, shift work and the 24-hour synchronization of
international markets have all been important for giving birth to the
Modafinil-addled employee. The drug enables a self-imposed lengthening
of the workday by individuals struggling to keep up in the factory that
never sleeps. In her autobiographical article, *Stylist* writer Lizzie Pook
experiments with these 'work-enabling' pills whose consumption has
apparently reached epidemic proportions in the United Kingdom and the
United States. Do they really make you a better worker? She mentions a
career-driven individual called Sam, who seems to think so:

> 'I first took Modafinil when I had an important presentation to
> prepare and I'd been working until 2am the night before,' says Sam,
> 29, a marketing executive from Balham. 'I was given a few pills by a
> friend who had taken it while studying and thought I'd give it a shot. I
> work hours of overtime, so I didn't feel guilty about taking something
> that would level the playing field with my colleagues. The results were
> quite comical. I found myself drawing up huge Excel spreadsheets and
> becoming really focused on boring admin tasks.' (Pook, 2014)

On the first day of Pook's experiment she is working faster and (in
her mind) smarter than ever. On the second day, she is still typing at a

breakneck pace, but feeling a little nauseous. On day three, paranoia sets in and she terminates the experiment. As we noted in the last chapter, there is enough paranoia in the office already without the assistance of drugs. The escalation of smart-drug usage in the workplace is significant for our argument in a number of ways. Given their effects, these chemicals were initially popular among workers who had little choice but to toil for long hours: army personnel, night-shift workers, long-haul truck drivers, etc. But now these once isolated conditions of employment conditions have become the norm for the mainstream workforce. And the other type of worker that regularly used these stimulants was, of course, the artist, who has become the ideal model of the contemporary employee: fast, flexible, never absent-minded and always ready to produce (see Cederström and Fleming, 2012).

But we would be wrong to think of Modafinil use at work simply in quantitative terms (more hours on the job). No, it is not only the proximate lengthening of the working day that is important here. Modafinil also provides for a more existential *presence*, a qualitative shift in exactly how our work time is lived regardless of quantity. We might call this 'presence stamina', an attribute also demonstrated in the intense and verbose dialogue between Robert and Gloria in the Dance Marathon. This is what makes Modafinil such a special drug, differentiating the overworking bio-proletariat from other eras of labour obsession. In the city offices of the 1980s, I might have put in a 12-hour day at my desk; but much of this would have been time spent looking into space, tired and dazed. Today, however, I also need to be 'switched on', present, alert, creative and enthused with my task, even when I am actually doing nothing. Only after I get home and the paranoia sets in can I relax with a glass of bourbon. If, that is, my boss has not made that method of escape into a mandatory team building exercise too.

Totality Refusal

Now we must turn to the question of how we might escape the totality of neoliberal capitalist time by adopting tactics to thwart and turn our back on it. Unfortunately, walking away from the marathon of work is no easy feat when you are caught up in its momentum. Deleuze argues that the first task we need to undertake here is to avoid *fearing* 'societies of control' since fear is an integral part of their operational systems. Attention instead ought to be directed towards inventing useful weapons for crashing those systems. I would like to build on this thought, since every weapon requires a concept. Theory is fundamental in this regard. Ideas of successful struggle (by which I mean a form of contestation that envisages its own demise once its objectives are achieved) must be rigorously considered in order to withstand the tidal wave of regulation that seeks to draw us back into the language of capitalist productivism. Weapons of revolt surround us, however. We only need to see them: being on the 'outlook' is the first step to understanding the indeterminate versatility of an otherwise hostile environment. And for this reason alone, designs and realizable memes are now more important than ever.

Dialectics, Maps and Lines

Dialectical inquiry has, of course, dominated critical thinking in this regard. Future spaces and times are specified via the contradictory pull between what the present is and what might be so given the technological and social possibilities systematically denied under class conditions. We see zones of otherness in the socialized forces generated by private ownership and waged employment. For Lukács (1971), our complex totality is a precatory combination lock that can only be cracked from the proletarian standpoint. While workers do not constitute the totality, their position echoes the whole because they collectively stand inside the house of exploitation and live the impossibility of complete inclusion. Only the bourgeoisie, according to Lukács, is fully enveloped by the blinding processes of reification. I think this is a very convincing argument. But its applicability to the neoliberal totality is thwarted because every effective capitalist has (indirectly of course) now learnt important lessons from Lukács's challenge. Under the auspices of globalization and free trade, the parasitical 1 per cent has concertedly endeavoured to transform this totality into something that is virtual and viral rather than only structural. Space is no longer of any consequence. This lack of co-ordinates makes it particularly difficult to escape through dialectical reason, since labour and capital blend into each other in such unpredictable and complex ways.

If we are to assign a date to the death of dialectical praxis then it is probably 1966, the year Adorno published his attempt to rescue dialectics in the face of a new form of power and inadvertently imploded its internal clockwork. *Negative Dialectics* (1966/1973) distils the totality into an unvariegated singularity that must suck in another world in order to reconcile its positivity. But that other world is not immediately detectable. It has to be inferred through the negation of the negation. However much Adorno aggressively escalated the capitalist contradictions to visualize this emancipatory other, it grew evermore distant, like a black hole that exponentially recedes as we approach its event horizon. Every gesture is extirpated and fed back into the never-ending circle of control. The universal subsumes the particular and devours it. The concept and category collapse into a holistic hell without respite. Adorno presents his findings after having pressed dialectical thinking to its breaking point:

> Whoever pleads for the maintenance of this radically culpable and shabby culture becomes its accomplice, while the man who says no to culture is directly furthering the barbarism which our culture showed itself to be. Not even silence gets us out of the circle. In silence we simply use the state of objective truth to rationalize our subjective incapacity, once more degrading truth into a lie. (Adorno, 1966/1973: 367)

The problem with this type of totality-escape attempt lies in the way it is swiftly hamstrung by the notion of its supposed outside, which is but an incomplete projection of the false whole's essential failures. We can also note this in Bloch's lament concerning utopian thought, when he despairs, 'We hear only ourselves. For we are gradually becoming blind to the outside' (Bloch, 1964/2000: 34). What outside? Who have you been talking to? The perfunctory supposition of an outside implies a conceit that is far too biblical for my tastes. The method undermines fruitful methods of refusal by misconstruing what the totality actually is, since its so-called 'outside' is but an antimonial reflection of its own impossibility. In other words, the totality is not a 'prison' that can be escaped. Plotting a breakout is definitely counterproductive to cultivating a socio-biotic resistance to the virus of work. Purity will never be yours, and that precept must be put to democratic uses. For how can we contemplate the emancipatory potential of being a 'fugitive' (Lordon, 2014) when we are defined as such by capitalist class relations from the outset? – even before we are born, and regardless of whether we are born or not.

Michel de Certeau (1984) comes closer to solving the problematic we are dealing with here. He argues that tactics operate by opening new spatial fissures, disrupting the time sequence of the strategies that code and overcode us within the circle of power. For him, what one uses (rather than how one uses it) within the permanently backdated ideological matrix of domination is what really matters. He asks the question: How can one exit the realm of power without going anywhere? Tactics exploit with guile and cunning the very topographical textures of control, turning power back on itself and thus yielding potential fractures of freedom. Certeau posits a kind of map (e.g. the abstraction of New York City when viewed from the top of a skyscraper) whose margins are everywhere within the system. Similarly, the universe of work too might be traversed by cracks and half-finished rudiments that can be deregistered for other purposes.

The tactical undermining of the strategic totality of work can take a number of forms – most of which, in my opinion, are fairly mundane and tame. For example, the technocratic measurement of time in most workplaces – you are contractually obliged to log your holidays – can be manipulated to forge more time away from the office by a workforce that seldom relaxes. This was why Richard Branson's recent 'as much holidays as you want' policy for his personal staff was criticized. Inspired by a similar policy at Netflix, Branson said in his blog that 'it is left to the employee alone to decide if and when he or she feels like taking a few hours, a day, a week or a month off'. Of course, there is a catch. Only when employees feel that they have met their responsibilities fully (finished a project, etc.) are they able to enjoy this benevolent approach to holidays. The problem is that this ostensible gesture of freedom would most likely result in staff working forever and *never* taking holidays. Commenting on Branson's policy, Kellaway (2014: 16) correctly observes that 'the trouble with modern work is that it is endless. You are never through with it, which means that judging when to take a break is very difficult indeed. A fixed holiday entitlement tells us it is OK to take a break – even though our work is far from done.' So, what was intended to be a disciplinary mechanism to track work time (i.e. formal holiday requests, etc.) can actually be turned back on the company to stave off some of the more insidious features of the 'I, Job' function.

But Certeau's conception of the totality as a map with a multitude of constitutive blind spots and opportunities to hack power misses the *impossibility* at the heart of the neoliberal whole. The tactics and practices of everyday life recorded by Certeau still implicitly hold onto the rather liberal assumption that a life is indeed *possible* within the universe of capitalism. For him, we can make do and get by, despite the monstrous strategic codifications of the neoliberal city, family and work arrangements that claustrophobically close in on us from every angle.

This is where Deleuze's suggestions about how we might elude the transmutable virus of work in the societies of control is perhaps bleaker but more realistic. Rather than viewing control as a prison (with an identifiable outside), or an all-encompassing antithesis of a hoped-for future (as in dialectical thinking), or an official map (with its unofficial underworld of crevices in which we can make do), power for Deleuze is more like a perpetually failing diagram. As he argues, a diagram maintains a 'function that must be detached from any specific use, as from any specified substance' (Deleuze, 2006: 61). The virus of work is virtual in so far that its concrete expression moves between the peopled components of neoliberal society. But these components are always failing. Disappointment and botched attempts to control us actually energize rather than weaken the totality of late-capitalist relations. Perfect control is always something to come, always nearing perfection, always in a future which never arrives. In other words, the generalization of capitalist time in societies of control is held together by an acute impossibility: our attempts to live, that futile optimism that fools even the most enslaved, is stymied at every turn by an existential darkness that denies complete synthesis. Our embodied and inexorable *modi operandi* are defined by a breathless and depressing, 'It cannot go on like this', things must change. But they never do change, and somehow we continue as before.

Deleuze is important for understanding not only how this false totality remains consistent with itself, but also the pulse of impossibility that echoes the true nature of its form. This seam of darkness is the nightlife of neoliberalism, both the painful moment of immoderation and the social source of a new world announced when its impossible figure finally steps out of the shadows. It is for this reason that the most politically abject and ignored in our society must be considered *foremost* if the totality is to be understood. The absolute 'worst off', that part of the whole we like to consign to the status of an exception or aberration, is really what gives the totalized system its false positivity. Its part is the part of everything. That is why society despises the untouchables so much, because in them we see the untruthful structure that bears witness to society's own mendacity. Society's debt is to those who are born owing more than what they are. In other words, we must always approach the neoliberal whole from the standpoint of the impossible. Was not the working-class credit-card disease, for example, invented to postpone this impossibility? This impossibility is characterized not only by the Saint Genets haunting the cut-throat nightlife of the neoliberal order. We are not referring to a distinctive class or social category, although the destitute prefigures its form. For the impossibility lodged in every centre of this wrong whole is viral too. Its inflections are to be seen in the homeless, in the tearful bankers falling to earth from their high-rise prisons, in academics sacrificing themselves to the 'bad deal' they call a mortgage, in the call-centre employees who cannot go on, etc. The official silence concerning these unmanageable moments constantly throbs everywhere in the large cities of the capitalist order, a low and compulsive hum that troubles those who have learnt to listen to its message.

A Negative Optics of Revolt

After Deleuze, the planet of work is no figurative prison or straitjacket, but a set of impossible geometric lines that we must render obsolete so that their perpetual postponements and qualifications can be halted for good. These qualifications can never be perfected, and this is where a minor knowledge of deviant 'lines of flight' becomes useful to the majority who seek to escape the 'I, Job' function. Such peasant knowledge, based on sedimentary memories that can never be deleted in societies of control, consists of lines rather than spatio-temporal locations. The era of locations is finished and should not inform the work-refusal movement any longer. Locations are today but interdictions that point to other locations, which in turn point to yet others without end. Neither does time pertain to the lines of revolt we are considering here. The social frequency of so-called 'non-work' time, for example, is now too sympathetic to the never-ending cycle of capitalist power relations. Dreams of a future time freed from capitalism are simply one dimension of our current mode of domination, which incidentially has built a booming 'escape industry' as iniquitous as the post-industrial office cubicle.

What I call peasant lines of flight simply embolden what they already are – not in the chancy 'accelerationist' sense or even as a dialectical manoeuvre to heighten the contradictions of the capitalist mode of production through genuine protest. The generalized skyline of economic reason can only be broken if we have the courage to face the reality of abandonment that is the real message to us from the neoliberal ruling class. Abandoned times and spaces can be transformed into abandoned lines rather than vague outlines perpetually postponed by an infinite panoply of excuses and qualifications ('the reason the free-market system is not working is because we do not have true free markets, we need more deregulation'). Strangely, it is these vague lines that are the most visible and ensnare us more thoroughly, given their indeterminate trajectories of surveillance, judgement and subjectification. This is where Certeau misses an important aspect of power that emerged following the biopolitical shift in exploitation. The outline, with all of its potent pre-significations, is what makes the artillery of late capitalism so powerful.

By identifying these ultimately impossible lines, we follow a theory not of spatial or temporal totality, but one that is basically *optical*. The ideology of work today can be compared to the same rules that organize fibre optics – work acts like silica undulations or waveguides, collecting all that is not work within its pulse. Vision is the currency of power today, but not in the manner of the panopticon gaze of the prison. The 'open prison' of neoliberal society requires numerous blind alleys and unrealizable times to function – how could it otherwise commandeer the self-control and self-reliance that has made the closed prison of Fordism obsolete as a method of exploitation? The vision of the unmanaged is as much a function of biopower as that of the managed. Optics empties the subject of history. Of course, we learnt this long ago in Lefebvre's (1947/1991) critique of everyday life. The new visual apparatus that purifies the capitalist present for everybody (i.e. the totality) is actually about diminishing the faculty particular to our proletarian memory. The hurt, vilification and dispossession that define a collective past evaporate when capitalist culture goes hyper-optical. Never has so much been seen and so little truly viewed.

Refusal can be effective if it practises a negative or reverse optics. The impossible lines house the exploited 99-percenters and are concealed in plain view. Like a distorted photographic negative, the visible is only possible from power's perspective when it is held in abeyance. A line of flight implodes its own impossibility by erasing the vague outlines and thus departing the postponements of optical subjugation tying us to the universal 'I, Job' operating system. A minoritarian line of revolt has nothing to do with numbers in this respect. Perhaps this is where Certeau (1984: xvii) is correct when he states that 'marginality is today no longer limited to minority groups, but is rather massive and pervasive ... marginality is becoming universal'. A wayward or departing optical line of negation makes the impossible circuits of power visible so that the erasure process has a qualitative effect as it remembers – memory not as quanta of data but as a connection to the minoritarian world that excoriates the totality, those who came before us. It is only 'in their place' that we are able to act presently with any authenticity. These are the nameless lives that run ahead of us to issue warnings about our fate. This type of remembrance views us as ghosts haunting *their* world. It is not the dead but the impossible permanence of an irreconcilable present (i.e. 'us') that we seek to exorcize. And if there is a canticle for the worker today, lost and abandoned by the very enemy that demands that we stay, then it entails a closure of the false vision that has obliterated our past. Only then can night and day begin once again.

The eye begins to see once more through memory – not of a crippling debt-laden promise to be fulfilled in the future, as Nietzsche argued in his genealogy of morals. This type of memory isn't about conscience and guilt burnt into the individual like a brand. Indeed, present-day debt can only be transformed into guilt by erasing a particular version of history. Here, personal liability is not about the past, but is always co-present with a timeless 'now'. Neoliberal debt in particular relies upon the freedom of the subject who knows no past and is thus entirely responsible. This is why a worker's historical imagination is the enemy of the capitalist project; 'to forget suffering is to forgive the forces that caused it – without defeating these forces' (Marcuse, 1955: 163). This is the only way to appreciate the totality of neoliberal temporality if we are systematically to leave it behind. As capitalism becomes a Marathon Dance that eternally repeats itself, it uses the forces of insinuation or 'indirect discourse' (Deleuze and Guattari, 1987: 77) to bolster the misconception that departure is out of the question. Insinuation removes any obvious exit, even as it taunts us with its visible proximity. The overcoded can only be decoded by a minoritarian peasant knowledge (i.e. *tribal*, as we all belong to a tribe). I see my practice remembering its own presence as a ghost haunting those who came before me; that presence recalls how, why and roughly when the dance of exploitation was transformed into a marathon without end: 'Substitute forgetting for anamnesis' (Deleuze and Guattari, 1987: 151).

But such remembrance also acknowledges that our life sentence is underscored by abandonment or more precisely an 'ideology of abandonment', as I call it in the next chapter. We now need to give our abandonment depth so it corrupts the smooth plane of one-dimensional rationality that makes the curve of capitalist reality seem unending. This is the 'lost dimension' of industrialized modernity (Virilio, 2012). So in summary, the pertinent ethical question for those who seek to refuse the ridiculous verities of the 'I, Job' function today is simply this: Are you worthy of your abandonment? If not, then keep working for a master who doesn't even see you on his radar (but would nevertheless like you to think he is watching you all of the time). If you are worthy of your own abandonment, then what are you going to do with the *absolute* impossibility that is now the defining quality of the late-capitalist worker? Where will you go, what will you say and who will you take with you?

3

What Is Managerialism?

In a 2014 BBC report entitled 'Managers work an extra day per week in unpaid overtime', a common frustration experienced by workers in the United Kingdom was noted. Following a survey by the Institute of Leadership and Management (ILM), it was found that over half of UK managers are working significantly above and beyond what was legally required by their employment contracts. As in many other countries afflicted with the neoliberal 'I, Job' function, managers are putting in much more time at the office than they are being paid for. 'Wage theft' (Bobo, 2009) and a generalized culture of overwork are the cultural icons that define working 'life' for most today: 'When you add up all the skipped lunch breaks, early morning conference calls and after hours emails you see just how widespread the extra-hours culture is within UK business', a representative for the ILM stated. The report continues:

> Around 13% of managers work two days unpaid overtime per week, 76% routinely work late in the office or at home, 48% regularly work through their lunch break, and more than one third work at weekends. Smartphone technology has added to pressures to work, with some managers 'obsessively' checking email outside of office hours. (BBC, 2014b)

There are a number of interesting implications concerning this survey. Now even the traditional agents of capitalist exploitation, those charged with coercing and harassing workers with evermore needless work, are experiencing the social costs of their own ideological agenda. More generally, there are significant reasons why employees from many industrial sectors are obliged to work more than they need to. Much of this can ironically (given the above survey) be put down to a certain biopolitical management structure that has been unleashed by late-capitalist rationality. When the labour process is organized around individual competitiveness in the pursuit of tasks that appear purposeless to almost all involved and is imbued with an enduring fear of perceived (and real) abandonment, even the simplest type of work becomes chaotic and impractical to conduct well. Increasing swathes of employees understand the paradox of the neoliberal organization very well: an individual-based system of exchange value means that many more informal and employee-led social ties are required to get the job done at all, let alone well. We are forced to build an undercurrent of non-capitalist relations to make things happen. This sociality is, of course, given away free to capitalism. We then begin to work for nothing, stress about a project even after we have left the office, call friends during lunch to ensure a report is filed, and so forth.

This social surplus, or 'commons' as Hardt and Negri (2000) term it, is now the mainstay of life in the social factory since neoliberal reason asks for a reality that is impossible to enact in concrete terms. The litmus test for discerning the biopolitical exploitation of this common might be the following: would the task or project be achieved if all of this unpaid social work was not summoned? We are increasingly issuing a resounding no to this question given the massive overcoding of the workday and its multiplication through increasingly insidious instruments of overproduction. However, there is another irony lurking in this trend, which is perhaps even more depressing. One might also reply *yes* to the above test question. That is to say, if I did not work at the weekend or lead an emotionally injurious way of life for the sake of an impending deadline, perhaps the task or job that pursues me like a deranged ex-lover would *still be achieved well*. While theorists of the commons often infer a functional relationship between the caesura of disorganized capitalism and the self-organizing propensities of the multitudinous workforce, perhaps the social surplus being put to work is nothing but a negative remainder of the regulation process – unnecessary overtime, unrequired stress, and social networks under pressure that have no functional outcome other than their own display. Our extra work and frenetic evocation of social relationships beyond capital are salient not only because they help get things done, but because the very authority that prompts their repeated evocation demands its own vindication in the useless social labour of others.

The compulsive insistence of this dysfunctional uselessness – purposeless activity exhibited for its own sake – is a defining characteristic of managerialism, a discursive practice that is the political essence of the people-pushing biosphere of today's workplace. Managerialism is the chief mechanism for helping the voracious virus of productivity to become contagious and spread throughout the social body. In this sense, the social factory is but a living machine without any teleological ends. Like an overworked employee in the office, whose feverish disequilibrium only serves to regulate his or her own pathology (rather than expunging the malady from the organism to regain some balance), the management function seeks to maintain a certain disorientated extension of the social. The informal paratactic life of the bio-proletarian worker, a mode of living that is forever off balance, serves very little instrumental role in this regard. The point of power is power itself and this is why managerialism is to neoliberalism as oxygen is to the body. Any attempt to refuse work, therefore, must have a good understanding of what managerialism is today.

The BBC report is thus extremely relevant for highlighting employment trends that this book is considering. We see a developing synergy between managers and the managed, with managers themselves, the agents of capital, complaining about overwork in much the same manner as workers do. This structural sympathy is fascinating given the antagonism that has defined this basic capitalist relationship for so long. It turns out that managers *are* workers after all, which is a suggestive political *aporia*, as any Marxist analysis will tell us. Here the ILM chief executive begins to sound like a trade union representative when he complains that 'excessive hours are not sustainable – there are only so many times you can burn the midnight oil before your performance, decision making and well-being begin to suffer'. With managers speaking out against the unsustainable force driving the injunction to produce, it is easy to conclude that capitalism itself is drawing upon an anti-work thematic, acknowledging parallels between managers' own predicament and the conditions they expect from those they manage.

However, this conclusion risks approaching the issue from the wrong angle. That the extra and 'free' work common is at the centre of the late-capitalist mode of production is without question. We work beyond the stipulations of our contracts, using our social intelligence to bypass the counterproductive rules of domination, even after hours, and avoid the impossible principles of neoliberal reason. The Italian autonomist movement has taught us much about this. The common is the working class's shock absorber, cushioning (and facilitating) entire lives that have been put to work. It represents a social reservoir that picks up the slack of an unworkable system. However, herein lies the key point. If the common refers to an egregious excess that falls outside of the functional dictates of economic reason, then we also see it unfolding among the *capitalist class too*. Virno (2008) emphasizes this de-romanticized reading of the common, a point often missed by those who celebrate its emancipatory purity. The communism of capitalism has a dark side, peopled by anti-people who wander in and out of all the economic classes. For example, what does the excessive social work conducted by the surveyed UK managers actually consist of? What is the nature of the pointless labour that forms the flip side of 'going the extra mile' in order to get the job done? The answer, of course, is obvious: *dominating*. The managerial moment certainly demands that we do much more work than is necessary or accounted for. But this moment also involves the agents of capital regulating and controlling more than is actually necessary: *surplus* regulation. In other words, the excess sociality that allows the working class to meet its targets in a socio-economic structure defined by disarray is reflected in its class reversal – control not because it is functionally necessary, but for its own sake and self-assurance. Could it be this type of overwork that was measured by the ILM survey?

The transition from management to managerialism consists in a shift from function to functionlessness. And this logic is now so pervasive that even managers themselves find their positions intolerable, as the above report notes. Managerialism is viral in this respect, as in Deleuze's diagram discussed earlier. It exceeds the concrete individual to become a kind of oblique template that seeks to infiltrate and recalibrate almost every sphere of social life – a taskless task for sure, but one with very real outcomes that are bodily and menacing. For sure, managerialism is often peopled by those who have been seduced by the bright lights of capitalist wealth, but I have seen it expressed by the most junior supervisors. If you visit the USA you will even come across it in the ordinary person on the street, bearing witness to the overwhelming militarization of everyday US life under a bloated cultural command structure. In addition, managerialism is certainly parasitical on the labour of others, as has been well argued elsewhere (see Hanlon, 2007). But we must appreciate how it is also parasitical on its own pointless presence, and especially the uselessness that this presence demands among a struggling and tired workforce. What exactly are the political contours of managerialism in the workplace today and how might we refuse its outlandish edicts? Let's take a closer look.

The Profligate Management Function

If the underlying message of managerialism under neoliberal conditions is 'I dominate you because I can' then its profligate repetition and proliferation is inevitably experienced by most workers as a functional obstruction – not only an obstacle to a freer life, but ironically also an impediment to actually accomplishing the work task well. Managerialism is a blockage even when judged against the most capitalist of criteria (just as neoliberalism is when judged against the standards of completion, state minimalization, free markets and so forth). Following Deleuze's arguments concerning societies of control, I suggest that managerialism epitomizes the will to postpone, the imposition of a 'target' that is never quite achievable. Often this is unstated and merely insinuated, which is particularly characteristic of the self-management fad in many large enterprises today. This technique promotes itself as the end of management, but paradoxically carries the expectation that the employee-empowered firm will require more management in order to arrive at this end point (i.e. the death of management), which, of course never, arrives. Hence the exponential growth of the managerial class at precisely the same moment that capitalism was heralding the end of management. It is all about a future to come, but one that is inherently impossible under present structural conditions. Continuous improvement, to use the popular parlance of corporations today, is not about improvement at all, but about self-maintenance and the glorification of an impossible task. And as I will demonstrate in this chapter, this also gives most micro-managed situations a rather sadistic quality. As long as the organizational objective set cannot be fulfilled, a void is opened up at the centre of the labour process that gives it some rather pornographic elements, as we shall soon see.

In this respect too, KPIs (Key Performance Indicators), another popular corporate term, are not about measuring performance but about tracking inevitable failures. Perhaps this is why the most germane metaphor for neoliberal management regimes can be found in the perversely mercurial pages of the Marquis de Sade. The obsessive reporting, tallying and calculation of the painful 'pleasures' to be inflicted on the imprisoned is always organized with an eye to an inbuilt miscarriage, the system's real rationale: how much will the managed fail today and what will be the libidinal quality of that commensurate variance? Moreover, like the Marquis de Sade's victims, constant instruction and scrutiny is exacted in the name of self-improvement. When the managed are unsuccessful, the failure must be structured in a manner that highlights their agency and self-authority. Otherwise, the cycle of enjoyment is symbolically short-circuited and the social setting simply becomes one of slavery – which is no fun for those who dominate. For this reason too, self-management in the neoliberal enterprise is always accompanied by a barrage of quantitative measures and controls. The so-called willing obedience of the self-regulated must signify the patent nihilism of the power matrix one is being subjected to. Neoliberal capitalism believes in nothing, not even its own efficacy.

The Myth of Co-ordination and Inclusion

Two myths attempt to mislead us regarding the purpose of management under late capitalism. The first is easily dismissible: management is seen as *co-ordination*. The idea of co-ordination is the founding myth of capitalism itself, one that imputes a vital social necessity to the institutions of capitalist hegemony. Without them there would be primitive mayhem. Markets efficiently distribute goods and services in a neutral and impersonal manner. Free competition results in the most effective enterprises surviving, while those that do not meet the standard justifiably fall by the wayside. Private organizations in the marketplace are compelled to satisfy the consumer and thus the disparate and diverse ends of the majority are met as capital pursues its own self-interests. Such effective co-ordination is also the ideological premise of management. With the growth of large organizations, some personnel had to forgo contributing to the direct labour process and help oversee how production is socially organized. Hence the basic principles of management taught in most first-year business schools: it is deemed to be a function concerned with harmonizing members of the organization to achieve its goals with the resources available. It additionally consists of recruiting, training, motivating and rewarding employees in order to accomplish certain objectives.

Such definitions are comical for obvious reasons. The socio-political context of capitalism is stripped out of the picture. Organizations are seen as collections of 'members' all with equal standing, some of whom are better qualified to be higher up in the hierarchy than others. Managers co-ordinate the rest of us for goals that are shared (or ought to be) by all in the firm. The class antagonism fundamental to capitalism is omitted from management's perception of itself. But it is very important to note that this ideology has never denied its intimate connection to power per se.

One of the key influences on management thinking, the sociologist Talcott Parsons, wrote copiously on the topic of domination. But he was happy to translate Weber's concept of power (*Herrschaft* or domination over others) as *leadership* (see Cohen, Hazelrigg and Pope, 1975). Power is a neutral instrument that a trained and qualified meritocratic few use to ensure that the collective pursuits of an organization are effectively fulfilled.

Placing any organization within a capitalist context of private-property ownership and wealth capture, of course, immediately demolishes the conceit of 'shared interests' and the intrinsic worth of leadership. From this perspective we clearly see that the management 'function' is actually a *class function*, a vehicle for enabling the narrow objectives of the owning class often at the expense of workers' interests (and under neoliberal capitalism, frequently paradoxically even the objectives of profit). In light of this, the only important management thinker worth reading today remains Fredrick Winslow Taylor, for he was quite open about the class mission of management. In his classic essay *The Principles of Scientific Management* (1911/1967), he acknowledged that workers could very well manage the labour process entirely by themselves. They did not need overpaid experts to tell them to do something that they were doing very well from the start. For Taylor, the goal of modern management was to recapture control from the workforce, putting it more firmly into the hands of capital, even if this meant less efficiency and effectiveness on the shop floor, since that was secondary to winning the class war in the United States.

With the birth of Human Resource Management in the 1980s and 1990s, we see this management function becoming interested in the importance of conflict as it developed pre-emptive tactics to thwart anti-capitalist sentiment among the workforce. And this gives rise to the second way management is often misunderstood, this time among left-wing scholars: management as the calculated inducement of *willing obedience*. There is a long history of radical thinking that has endeavoured to demonstrate how corporate managerialism obfuscates the contradiction of class interests by commandeering the ideological ambitions and perceptions of the workforce, either via intensive indoctrination ('What is good for us is clearly good for you'), cultural conditioning ('We are a family') or discursive manipulation ('We are now all in this together'). A recent example of such an analysis is Lordon's (2014) *Willing Slaves of Capital*. As we saw earlier, he argues that managerialism aims to enlist the desires of the workforce through tactics of *mobilization*, in which the agents of capitalist accumulation cultivate wilful identification with the firm's profit motive. While money is important for partially and temporally co-aligning the activities of capital and labour, recent management systems (such as HRM) have sought to enrol the desires of employees too, so that they genuinely and wholeheartedly want what capital wants. This invariably makes self-exploitation the key objective of management.

According to Lordon, new management systems capture the worker through symbolic structures of passionate desire. This is why terms like 'self-fulfilment' and 'empowerment' are so salient in a good deal of management jargon today. The prototypical team engagement leader seeks to foster in you affectionate feelings for your employer that resemble those of a passionate love affair. This can be difficult to resist even when we know we are being instrumentally used. The cold cash nexus of Fordism – in which alienation was simply an expected part of the job – was experienced by workers as an acceptable cost for participation in the consumer society after the workday was done. This attitude has been supplanted under neoliberalism:

> Everything suggests that this regime is undergoing in turn a profound mutation, manifest in new managerial methods of enlistment and the new affective sensibilities they are able to exploit. The passionate situation of employment is significantly enriched in the process, thwarting old forms of anti-capitalist critique, and providing new opportunities for losing one's way in the aporiae of 'voluntary servitude' (Lordon, 2014: 33).

In short, management today is fundamentally about systems of all-encompassing capture and *inclusion*, so much so that workers 'lose their way' and come to love the very enemy that seeks to squeeze them dry through the regime of work. For me, however, there are serious problems with Lordon's reading of managerial capitalism. The periodization is incorrect for a start. The corporate promises of 'self-fulfilment' and 'authenticity', for example, were around long before the arrival of the neoliberal enterprise. These ideas and their cognates were born out of the experimental age of occupational and industrial psychology and thus have a very strong Fordist character (Maslow, McGregor, etc.). But such techniques no longer have a prominent place in the neoliberal obsession with temporary work systems, flexible occupations and 'management by fear' typically used to organize the post-industrial labour process. A more troubling problem, however, is that Lordon tends to characterize managerial capitalism in the same way it would like to see itself – extensively interested in how workers feel, obsessed with their emotional well-being, and profoundly worried that they might refuse the corporate marriage proposal and turn their backs on the boss: 'The manager is the very model of the kind of happy workforce that capitalism would like to create' (Lordon, 2014: xii).

Managers as Abandonment Enablers

Does Lordon's depiction really represent how the neoliberal enterprise and its manifest managerialism operate today? No, I do not think it does, since it partakes in critical theory's 'abandonment denial' discussed earlier in this book. The withdrawal of capital and its subsequent contractual hostility directed at the working multitude suggests that 'love' and 'commitment' have little to do with the neoliberal grammar of control today. If the contemporary capitalist enterprise is anything remotely like a love affair (a particularly dreadful metaphor no doubt) then it would be one with a partner that gains pleasure from persistently announcing that he or she plans to leave you, and sooner rather than later. Neoliberal capitalism is not the 'world of the girlfriend experience' (Lordon, 2014: 84) but of the *deranged girlfriend experience*. Management today has no interest in whether you like or love it (although it would like you to think it does). And it certainly *does not* like itself. General happiness is not its concern; nor are lasting social bonds.

Indeed, if managerialism today has an ideology – which it hardly requires given neoliberalism's recent return to naked force – it is one that continuously communicates our postponed but inevitable abandonment. We can see this ideational motif in the aforementioned rise of Human Resource Management, perhaps the most despised variation of the management prerogative that capitalism has invented to date. HRM emerged out of personnel management, which was an administrative function that all large organizations required during the Fordist period. As opposed to the roles of supervisors and line managers, the personnel office recruited employees, took charge of the payroll and ensured that the organization abided by employment regulations and law. It also acted as the firm's mediating agents between capital and labour unions. But other than that, it was a very boring facet of the firm. But with the assault on trade unions in the 1980s, firms sought to develop new modes of occupational solidarity. This is when personnel management branched into building cultures of commitment, employee engagement and internal branding (e.g. 'We are IBM'). In line with the neoliberal penchant for individual contracts and part-time employment, HRM also managed workers through psychologizing many of the injuries of post-industrial work. Burnout, absenteeism, recalcitrance and other forms of refusal were no longer deemed workplace problems but subjective pathologies fully seated within the individual worker him- or herself. But HRM could assist in treating these attitudinal abnormalities. This is why critics in the 1980s often called HRM 'friendly fascism'; it sought to screw you with a smile, and if possible, have you smile at the same time.

Over the last five years or so, the HRM function has changed once more, and this time there is little to smile about. Its erstwhile tripartite role of recruitment–engagement–retention has been relinquished in favour of focusing singularly, not so much on the last element, but, in a dialectically negative fashion, on its expected opposite. The concern with retention – how to dissuade employees from leaving – has now been replaced by a preoccupation with deciding precisely when to *abandon* them. Indeed, a vast cultural script built around the theme of abandonment now informs the management function in enterprises, the public sector and a raft of other institutions. Today, employers have little problem recruiting workers. They are lining up at the door in droves, grossly overqualified and willing to work for lower wages than previous generations. Engagement and motivation is not a problem either. Workers understand very well that feigned enthusiasm, self-reliance and 'going the extra mile' is simply what one must do to avoid the deleterious gaze of capital. Retention, however, is a problem. But only in the negative sense of calculating when the firm is able to accentuate its dialectical obverse and successfully instigate a culture of permanent non-retention. In a practical sense, the HRM function is now inordinately interested in disposability. When and how to divest its 'human capital' is capital's central problematic today. Perhaps this is why contemporary HRM is so meticulous in keeping detailed employee records on almost every aspect of performance. A bitchy email to a manager, for example, will be retained not because it is an issue to be dealt with presently. No, not yet; but sometime in the future it will be useful to construct a picture of a 'difficult' employee who really should be 'let go'. Indeed, the correspondence does not even have to be potentially incriminating or negative to serve this role as evidence of one's ill fit within the organization. Given the backward and feudal-like regression that the neoliberal order represents, we now find HR managers acting like medieval inquisitors, as epitomized in the infamous words of Cardinal Richelieu: 'If one would give me six lines written by the hand of the most honest man, I would find something in them to have him hanged.'

There are three emblematic features of this abandonment ideology so embraced by managerialism today. The first is *destabilization*. This is where management relies upon a perverse and gratuitously punitive stance when interacting with employees. There is certainly a sadistic element to this non-utilitarian display of power for its own sake, as we discussed earlier. But destabilization also has other purposes. Workers persistently thrown 'off balance' are much more amenable to being dismissed when no longer required in the exploitation process. The constant shock of managerial interventions, many of which appear completely irrational and sometimes weird, communicates to the workforce that they are not really welcome, so do not get too comfortable. Virno (2004: 34) argues that this feeling of 'not being at home' developed from the perpetually shifting undercurrents endemic to late-capitalist societies and is an existential by-product of pointless oppression. But I would suggest that it is also an intentional tactic of managerialism today since it not only puts workers permanently on guard (and thus encourages self-control) but also expresses to them the deep regret the firm feels for ever employing them in the first place. The resulting culture of sadness ironically rivets employees even more tightly to their exploitation: if their own employer despises them, then probably so does capitalist society as a whole. There is nowhere to escape.

The second characteristic of this abandonment ideology is *demobilization*. Perhaps this is where Lordon (2014) is really off the mark. He argues that the neoliberal enterprise invests in flows of desire between capital and its willing slaves by mobilizing their affective apparatus to minimize any drift between what the employee wants and the boss demands: 'The desire of the enlistees must be *aligned* with the master-desire. In other words, if the conatus to be enlisted is a force acting with a certain intensity, it must be given the "correct" orientation, namely a direction that conforms to the direction of the boss's desire' (Lordon, 2014: 33–34, emphasis original). However, the US-inspired HRM supervisor has very little interest in seeing our desires aligned with his or hers, or the firm's, and would prefer that we felt nothing at all. Positive sentiment towards the organization, as many managers have learnt, can so easily be used against them when they make controversial decisions (such as a merger, restructuring, stock buyback, investments in unethical industries, etc.). Just look at what happened with the Massachusetts-based supermarket chain Market Basket in August 2014. The firm is immensely admired by its employees. So when the CEO was replaced by someone they did not trust, employees revolted, almost destroying the enterprise before the decision was reversed and the old CEO reinstated: 'To have an internal uprising of just about everyone, without a union, is very unusual in American industry,' said David Lewin, professor of management at the University of California Los Angeles. 'And it's even more unusual for workers to say, "We want this guy to come back" – and to have him actually come back' (Adams and Newsham, 2014). A mobilized workforce is inherently dangerous and is no longer the goal of neoliberal management practice – just the opposite, in fact.

HRM instead seeks to demobilize the workforce, have them be individually anxious in their isolated office cubicles, worried about what might come next. Indeed, one suspects that being disliked by employees is a badge of honour for many HRM staff. It might even be deemed a sign of success. As for senior management, the same often applies, but for more narcissistic reasons. We can imagine executives secretly counselling themselves and their closest cohort: 'Why would I want my employees to be aligned with my interests and love me when I know (and they should know) that deep down I loathe them? That gulf between my wants and their wants ought to permanently displayed, just to remind them who's the rightful boss and that there is little they can do about it.'

The third aspect of this abandonment ideology is *divestment*. While HRM would like workers to nervously anticipate their potential abandonment (sometimes for years and well into retirement), its practical enactment is also now a staple strategy for many firms. I do not simply mean retrenchment and redundancy when times are bad, sparking a new round of recruitment when the economy picks up. I mean here the permanent divestment of the workforce. In his excellent study *The Fissured Workplace* (2014), Weil demonstrates how the majority of large enterprises in the United States have subcontracted and franchised most of the labour functions outside of their core business unit. For example, a large hotel chain does not directly employee anybody. Customer service staff, cleaners, catering, recruitment services, telephone operators and even managers are employed by a myriad of other firms, which then outsource their staff functions as well. In the end, the hotel is merely a building and a brand. Other than its owners, it is people-less. For is not the private ownership of the means of production liberated from the trouble of labour the perfect ideal of the current era? This is not an isolated case;

it is the basic business model of late capitalism, especially for jobs that involve dangerous, controversial or undesirable work. It keeps wages low, enables large firms to bypass health, safety and employment regulations and defers the costs of employment in a never-ending chain of contractors. The final recipient of this hypothetical 'perfect storm', of course, which cannot yet again pass on the costs to somebody else, is the unstated working multitude.

The ultimate underlying fantasy of HRM is strangely a future in which it has no one to employ, manage or regulate. This anti-people obsession (which justifies us in renaming it *anti*-Human Resource Management) also applies to *its own* role. Because HRM is such a successful enabler of abandonment, there is no protected symbolic space in which its own principles do not apply – not even itself. This gives it a very masochistic flavour. And hence the neoliberal HRM functionary's unhappy consciousness and ardent desire to share that melancholy among as many people as possible.

As illustrated in Figure 3.1, an exponentially expanding individualization process can be seen in these trends whereby the psychic and practical effects of anticipated abandonment renders class solidarity impotent. *Destabilization* makes demobilization far easier to accomplish, which is why a peculiar disorientation is the first symptom of a class assault in the neoliberal era (as pointed out by Virno, 2004). Fragmentation and diffusion now begin to thin out the bonds of oppositional solidarity. *Demobilization* in turn amplifies the potential opportunities for divestment, aided by the state's litany of contractual law and regulation that focuses solely on the individual rather than on a class. And finally, *divestment* ensures that there is nothing left but the abstract husk of permanent exploitation. This is a vague or broken line representing that ultimate emblem of the capitalist way of life, the Robinson Crusoe-like individual – but this time lost in South East London or a suicide-grey commuter town on the outskirts of New Jersey rather than on a Pacific Island. This individual is truly fucked. Additionally, and as we can recall from Chapter 2, the line is vague because that is fundamental to the way societies of control operate – insinuation and anticipation rather than delimiting vectors of force.

This individuation must not be seen as a singularity or organic monad, but as the product of a process. Additionally, we should also remind ourselves that this abandonment ideology actually heightens the individual's ties to work. One might expect that with all these threats of rejection many would be tempted simply to walk away and start afresh. In fact, the opposite happens, which is perhaps the strangest aspect of the delirium that neoliberal capitalism institutes as a norm. This is why we must approach this process as an ideological form first and foremost.

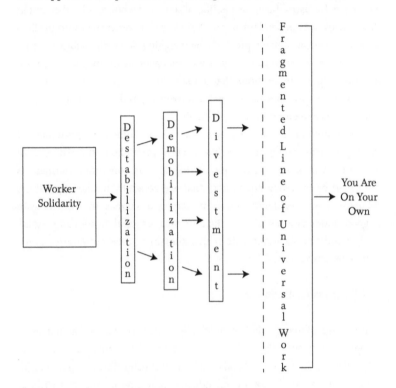

Figure 3.1 The Ideology of Abandonment Process

Three General Principles of Managerialism

HRM is just one strain of managerialism that typifies much organizational life today. We could also refer to New Public Management in governmental and semi-state institutions, Liberation Management in the IT and creative industries, and so forth. The most important point, however, is that individual management and managers are not quite the same as managerialism. The latter is an abstract principle or social technology that is unique to the neoliberal anti-people mentality. Whereas old-school management was defined by class politics and the efficient extraction of surplus value by the owners of capital, managerialism is more about reducing people (workers and even managers themselves) to a quantitative debt exemplified by the worker. Workers should feel eternally grateful to be employed since they are but a numerical expense to the firm and, as mentioned above, permanently prepared to be abandoned by the corporate infrastructure, the neoliberal state and whoever else they might find themselves dependent upon. A society of control therefore proffers a false universal register precisely by weighing down the subject with a bill that can never be paid. This is why managerialism finds its true forte in anti-people interventions that actually hurts productivity – how else would you expect power to treat a universally indebted figure? And it follows this egregious tendency with vim.

Abandonment is a necessary but not sufficient principle of managerialism which spreads like a virus throughout the societies of control. As an abstract principle or diagram, its concrete enactment is informed by everyday encounters that are generally marked by failure. Managerialism constantly misses its target, of course. In order to gain a good understanding of this diagram we must analyse its components and real-life implications within this domain of inherent failure. Three attributes are salient.

1. Self-Referential Abstraction

The concept of managerialism fanatically holds to the belief that managing people is a transferable skill that can be tradable and cross-referable regardless of the organizational context that is ostensibly being managed. As a result, we find captains of industry managing universities without ever having been in a lecture hall and given a class. We find an aviation executive in charge of a hospital. Local councils seek to hire experts from the retail industry because their finesse with containerization is thought to be analogous to the complexities of civic governance. As a result, managerialism becomes a de-contextual abstraction that is fundamentally self-referential. I manage a hospital not because I started my career as a junior doctor but because I am a manager. In theory at least, once a manager has attained his or her subject position within the ideology of managerialism, they can be parachuted into almost any situation with little experiential knowledge that might otherwise be considered essential to that institution.

Perhaps the most striking example I have observed was in a New Zealand hospital when conducting research on culture change. A surgeon recalled a senior manager who was headhunted from a multinational forestry firm. The manager's knowledge of hospital life soon became apparent. He ordered maintenance to remove obstructive piping in an operating theatre because it clashed with the new decor he had in mind. That piping unfortunately delivered anaesthetic to patients undergoing surgery. It is obvious that this lack of basic experiential know-how can lead to catastrophic errors of judgment. The decision to launch the Space Shuttle *Challenger* in 1986 is a case in point. Management at both NASA and Thikol (the firm which designed and manufactured the ill-fated O-ring seals that caused the disaster) overruled the engineers' expert understanding of O-ring technology. Under political pressure to launch (or what a subsequent accident investigation called 'go fever'), management abstraction took precedence over patently superior practical insight.

There is an important rationale behind this self-referential abstraction that defines managerialism today. It intentionally creates a gulf or division between managers and the managed, which is an increasingly visible power dynamic in many neoliberal institutions. It is almost as if the university executive is *advantaged* by the fact that she has never stepped into a lecture hall. If she had experienced the effort of preparing classes, struggling on a junior lecturer's salary, and so forth, a degree of sympathy might develop. And this would seriously compromise the anti-people philosophy of the managerial logic. Distance or dissociation are essential elements of managerialism, which the transferable technocrat excels in practising, given that he or she is removed from the historical context (i.e. value-adding labour) that defines their institutions. Moreover, such detachment allows for a very cold relationship with the workforce. We might term this a spreadsheet mentality. The managed are considered more of a 'problem' rather than an asset. So it is preferable to render them commensurate with a numerical figure that can easily be deleted, increased or decreased at the stroke of a computer key. Perhaps email, which we all know can be put to some diabolical uses, was invented for this very reason

This distance creates a tepid and exceedingly rigid atmosphere in many organizations. Whereas neoliberal ideology would like us to believe that its institutions are innovative, dynamic and creative, the exact opposite is the case. The gulf between decision makers and those carrying out the work invariably fosters a stifling institutional climate. This tendency of managerialism has long been understood by sociologists of work. In his seminal study of bureaucratization, Crozier notes:

The power to make decisions and to interpret and complete the rules, as well as the power to change the rules or to institute new ones, will tend to grow farther and farther away from the field where those rules will be carried out. If the pressure for impersonality is strong, such a tendency toward centralization cannot be resisted ... The price the organization has to pay for it is still greater rigidity. People who make decisions cannot have direct first-hand knowledge of the problems they are called upon to solve. On the other hand, the field officers who know these problems can never have the power necessary to adjust, to experiment and to innovate. (Crozier, 1964: 189–90)

While this was a problem to be overcome under Fordist conditions, the neoliberal enterprise almost welcomes such a scenario. Innovation in a state institution that has been brutalized by New Public Management, for example, is viewed with a sceptical eye by the executive council. It implies that workers might have some life in them yet which could be turned towards anti-managerial goals such as union building or whistle blowing. One might even suspect that the desolate atmosphere that accrues as the inequalities between elites and the managed grow is considered an important performance indicator in the managerialized neoliberal institution.

It is also important to note that this market for transferrable managerial skills is not entirely free. Almost all of the examples I have given consist of business managers being employed in institutions that they are otherwise remote from. This is one-way traffic: senior executives who rise up through the ranks of a university, for example, hardly ever find themselves leading a major bank. But the reverse is increasingly the case. This tends to suggest that managerialism is inextricably related to commercialization, especially in the public sector; it is thus symptomatic of the class offensive that the neoliberal elite have conducted against public and common goods. Privatization and the expropriation of the historical wealth accumulated in the public sphere is an obvious corollary of the ideology of managerialism.

2. Boundary Management

If an important political rift opens up between elites and the managed, then managerialism is also deft at maintaining and policing this boundary, especially when it comes to protecting the uppermost ranks of an institution. A key task of managerialism is fortification; and this siege mentality is not unexpected given the turmoil that managerialism almost naturally incites in organizations. As the managed are gratuitously punished for their audacity of being employed by the organization, their discontent (either directly expressed or anticipated by the rulership) becomes a source of anxiety for the institutional 1 per cent. For it must be remembered that just as the apex of any bureaucracy is never bureaucratized, as Weber noted, so it is too with managerial structures. The institutional elite are never subjected to the numerical humiliation and intimidation of managerialism. Those charged with management in the neoliberal enterprise are almost always positioned as a technocratic weapon used to cocoon this inner circle, both in the workplace and in society more generally. This is why elites generate a phalanx of managers who encircle them in a military-like fashion. Under neoliberal conditions, managers are hired protection.

This is wonderfully captured by Michael Moore in his 1989 film *Roger and Me*. Following the closure of the General Motors plant in Flint, Michigan, which resulted in large-scale redundancies, Moore attempts the rather simple task of speaking with the president, Roger Smith, to get his side of the story. However, arranging the meeting becomes a mammoth and almost impossible undertaking. Moore deploys every strategy he can think of. He disguises himself as a journalist and even a company shareholder to confront Smith, but finds himself persistently led away by security. The pathos of the film lies in the inaccessibility of the president, even to his own employees and shareholders. A battalion of managers are poised to preserve an almost mythical level of unapproachability. At the end of the film, Moore finally manages to have a brief conversation about the decision to fire 30,000 auto-workers as the president is being ushered away. Smith's reply is telling: 'I don't know anything about it.'

It is due to this distance too that when the elite themselves encounter managerialism, its agents are always deferential and genial, while the rest of us have become almost insouciantly accustomed to inhumane levels of ruthlessness. This is a strange schizophrenic consciousness, painfully noticed by leaders demoted in their organizations to the status of rank-and-file employees: technocrats who were once gushing with soft gentleness are suddenly completely different people – remote, hard, cold and bitter.

The boundary control and fortification process that underlies much managerialism today has three additional implications. Firstly, the division between workers and the elite that professional managers are hired to maintain inevitably fuels a rampant growth in the number of administrative technocrats employed by the institution. This is one of the great ironies of neoliberal capitalism, especially with all its fluster about 'cutting red tape', decentralizing power and minimizing state bureaucracy and deregulation. All of us know that the exact opposite occurs. This is because the power gulf between the winners and the massively expanding class of losers has become so obvious and thus risks inciting insurrection. For instance, neoliberal society requires a very intrusive, micro-managing and punitive state apparatus which is expensive to run. This enables it to protect and disconnect a highly concentrated ruling class from the majority, who are the real wealth creators in capitalist society. We also see this pattern unfolding in the workplace. As soon as it arrives in any organization, managerialism's first tendency is to swiftly expand its own ranks and replicate itself over and over again. In his extremely insightful study *Fat and Mean* (1996), Gordon dispels the myth that the neoliberal enterprise is lean and mean. In fact, many post-Fordist organizations require large numbers of bureaucrats, given the inequalities they create: 'When supervisory systems are put in place, they acquire a hierarchical imperative all their own. Where authority is exercised from top down, you need managers and supervisors to check the supervisors' (Gordon, 1996: 72).

The second aspect that underpins this boundary management process is an increased emphasis on *securitization*. Managerialism has a strong affinity with growing levels of policing and surveillance. If managers in the neoliberal enterprise are overly technocratic, this invariably has to be backed by an unambiguous exhibition of raw power and symbols communicating private access only. In this sense, we might call managers the new 'securocrats' of the modern order. There are three audiences that such displays are intended for. The first is the general public. Here is an example from my own experience. Having recently arranged a meeting at Canary Wharf, a major financial-industry district in London, I am quickly given the impression that my taxi is entering a militarized zone. Security police are ever present, checking cars and buses as they enter the 'green zone'. Upon reaching the designated office tower a security guard escorts me to reception. A temporary access card is issued allowing me to pass through reception and approach the elevators. Another member of the security personnel calls a lift for me and I am closely observed as I swiped my card. Finally, yet another large security guard escorts me to a door that also requires swipe-card access and finally I arrived to the meeting ... very late of course. I was not expecting such a *Get Smart* level of palaver. This over-the-top militarization of everyday life aims to send an important message to the general public. To be honest I have absolutely no idea what this is and would somehow feel sullied if I did. The second audience is workers, which is more understandable. Given the thoughts of violent retribution that are bound to flourish in a context of pointless micro-management, the inner circle ought to be afraid. And the third audience is, of course, the elite, who want to be reassured that they are ultimately untouchable.

Managerialism aims to protect itself and its privileged charge (the elite) from imagined threats that arise from its crystalline understanding of what inequality entails. Such threats are seen to be multiple and always ready to pounce, whether posed by the democratic public, a disgruntled workforce, angry customers, or whatever. It is true that military metaphors in management jargon have been around for some time. But only recently have managers been collectively captivated by popular business books that suggest managing your staff is something like a military exercise. For example, *The Art of War*, by the ancient Chinese military strategist Sun Tzu, has been a bestseller for the last ten years. Corporate managers are literally obsessed with it. This treatise imparts lessons about how to use spies, deploy weapons, detect weaknesses in the enemy and, most importantly, always be prepared for battle. This is the prototypical managerialist view of the contemporary workplace.

And this brings us to next attribute of managerialism that supports its boundary control function; the ideology of *leadership*. The astounding popularity of 'great leaders' in neoliberal discourse is bizarre given the inexorable depersonalization of the workplace and the irrational distance this discourse entails on the ground. I believe that the fuss concerning the importance of leadership is a direct result of the anti-democratic norms defining the neoliberal enterprise today. The retraction of decision-making power from an organization's value-adders (i.e. workers) is often justified by the idea that superhuman individuals are guiding the institution. The signifier of leadership provides an alibi for the democratic deficit killing many workplaces today. The reader will probably recognize the rhetoric: 'The true reason you have so little say over your work and those at the top of the hierarchy are inordinately remunerated is because our leaders are gifted with superior foresight and acumen that you and I don't have.' This self-justification is the only way we can explain the travesty of executive remuneration whereby a UK boss can legally receive 143 times the average wage of their own employees – a threefold increase from 1998 (Chu, 2014). And this during a period of enforced wage stagflation? Unbelievable. No, a £3.4 million pay packet cannot be justified by skill or market forces (see Piketty's [2014: 331–2] demolition of the 'marginal productivity' concept). Only a deluded sense of self-worth could explain why the recipients of such large sums of cash could ever deem it acceptable.

It goes without saying that even a basic sociological analysis of the demographic make-up of leaders quickly dispels the myth that the elite hold their positions by virtue of skill. They simply come from the 'right' (aka rich) family. A report released in the United Kingdom in 2014 by the Social Mobility and Child Poverty Commission opens the lid on so-called meritocratic Britain. The study surveyed 4000 people who occupy the top leadership positions in government, business, the judiciary, the civil service and the media. Where they obtained their university degree was used as a proxy for whether these leaders had privileged backgrounds or not (i.e. publicly or privately funded education). The results were striking and tell us much about how the neoliberal class structure functions:

> Only 7% of members of the public attended a private school. But 71% of senior judges, 62% of senior officers in the armed forces, 55% of permanent secretaries in Whitehall, 53% of senior diplomats, 50% of members of the House of Lords and 45% of public body chairs did so. So too did 44% of people on the Sunday Times Rich List, 43% of newspaper columnists, 36% of cabinet ministers and 33% of MPs. (*The Guardian*, 2014b)

Family wealth rather than skill or competence is a much better indicator of why someone holds a senior leadership position. And the 'newspaper columnist' figure might indicate why the media have been so silent about the class catastrophe that has befallen the rest of us. One suspects that these so-called leaders also tend to mimic the lifeless technocrats that they insulate themselves with. When we meet leaders face-to-face they are so often anything but charismatic. Therefore, we must frame the veneration of leadership as an ideological supplement for the anti-democratic drift of the neoliberal politics, especially in relation to the technocratic securitization of a discontented workforce. This is why the idea of leadership still carries strong fascist connotations, since the call for strong leaders usually coincides with gratuitous acts of disempowerment and overt regulation.

3. Conflict-Seeking Behaviour

While it might be tempting to view managerialism as a fundamentally defensive stance given the above analysis, it also displays an extremely strong attraction to conflict. Indeed, I suggest that it literally thrives on antagonism and actively seeks it out or instigates it. One obvious reason for this is the timing of its emergence in post-industrial societies. The birth of managerialism corresponded with the dissolution of labour unions in the 1980s and was crafted as the most suitable social technology for combatting workers and reforming their understanding of the employment relation, especially apropos abandonment, zero-hour contracts, so-called flexible employment arrangements, subcontracting and a stagnating wage packet. Evoking the rather neutral sounding language of 'change management', the discourse of managerialism was the second line of attack on the Fordist employment relationship following the state's use of violence (i.e. the police and the military). But even after the dust had settled somewhat, the anti-people datum of managerial ideology continues to this day to provoke conflict in the workplace. This is integral to its internal operating code. A group of hardnosed managers in the same room is weird for this very reason. To flourish, managerialism structurally requires non-managerial 'raw material' (i.e. us) to sustain its own ideological integrity. With only technocrats in the room, the cultural atmosphere becomes rather moribund and confusing, as managerial stances cancel each other out. The prototypical neoliberal manager requires social goods to attack – something to bite – even if this results in major organizational dysfunction. I believe there are four driving factors for this attraction to confrontation and conflict.

Firstly, as the classic economic theory of 'transaction cost analysis' crept into almost every sphere of economic activity, including work, its underlying cynicism crafted a specific ideological view of the employee. In particular, the idea of 'shirking' became popular for understanding the presumed divergence between what a principal (the firm) hires the agent (worker) to do on its behalf and what the agent actually does. According to the theory, the agent will always be tempted by opportunism. Managerialism naturally gravitates to this theory of human behaviour, enjoying the idea that workers are inherently lazy and have an inbuilt propensity for theft, corner-cutting, and so forth. It thus unleashes pre-emptive measures even before there is any evidence to justify such cynicism. This gives managerialism a rather pugnacious and self-fulfilling flavour. However, there is an interesting contradiction here. On the one hand, managers cannot but permit workers a certain degree of autonomy, especially in the post-industrial workplace that is so conspicuously dependent on the vested and immaterial qualities of the employee. Self-reliance is a basic requisite of neoliberal exploitation, since it is (a) the domain in which negative externalities are placed and (b) the 'human resource' that takes up the slack of an unworkable socio-economic paradigm. However, on the other hand, managers are constantly worried about this autonomy being directed towards non-exploitative ends, to the point where they are automatically hostile towards it. In the end, managerialism seeks to stamp out the very resource that it and the neoliberal agenda relies upon to get things done.

There is a second reason why managerialism thrives on conflict. Most organizations do not really need the excessive and pointless amount of management activity that accumulates over time. Thus, managers constantly seek out ways to justify their own existence (e.g. by creating useless work for others) and engage in power-display rituals lest the owners of the means of production realize that much management is inherently needless and obstructive when applied to most jobs. The provocation of conflict is expedient for these self-justification rituals since it delineates a clear and present 'threat' to the institution and stimulates a degree of trepidation among elites. I think this is also why a good deal of managerial antipathy seems so redundant when one stands back to gain perspective. For example, why would a large and profitable budget airline based in Europe bill employees who use the company premises to recharge their mobile phones? From our vantage point, this ruling does not seem worth it given the impact on morale and self-esteem. But managerialism does not see the question in these terms. One might imagine a senior executive muttering, 'Who cares what workers think about it? In fact, we hope they don't like it and kick up a fuss.'

Thirdly, the encouragement of conflict yields valuable information for managers that it would not otherwise be privy to. The distance that managerialism creates between its orders and their execution generates a significant information deficit. This is why Spicer and Alvesson (2012) are correct when they argue that management is often crippled by its self-imposed stupidity. Thus, a conflict around the use of the Internet on company time, for example, gives the firm license to collect a great deal of information concerning workflow processes more generally. And the ensuing dissatisfaction becomes a pretext for heightened surveillance and monitoring. Concerning the informal organization (the unstated norms and subterranean networks of communication and patrimony at work), certain forms of induced conflict can flush out malcontents from their anonymity, especially those who have been working behind the scenes fuelling and spreading unrest. In the presence of a gruelling and often humiliating clash between managers and a disempowered employee, organizational bystanders frequently lose their nerve and volunteer important insights about the political alliances and factions that may be frustrating managerial objectives.

A fourth reason for all this conflict is perhaps most central. An incident of disagreement, however minor and insignificant, offers management useful ammunition for justifiably abandoning employees in the future should the need arise. Many industries, especially call centres, customer services and retail, rely upon orchestrated conflict to eject workers on a regular basis, knowing that newcomers are less wise to the historical struggles within the firm and more pliant, until they too become a 'problem' and are themselves replaced. Indeed, these 'green field' strategies, in which a relentless cycle of hiring–firing–hiring is pursued, require a very combative approach by management, because most of the time employees simply want to be left alone to get on with the job. So they must be antagonized. And this pervasive construction of the 'new' also dovetails with the universalization of work we have discussed in earlier chapters. The variegated and uneven histories and normative traces of past struggles are effectively silenced through these cycles, fostering a pliant and one-dimensional surface that can only repeat itself into a bleak future.

Eleven Theses on How to Refuse Managerialism

Managerialism is not an isolated social technology that can be challenged alone. It is symptomatic of a broader socio-economic paradigm and the trenchant class politics that fundamentally defines that paradigm. When confronting managerialism, in whatever guise it may take, it always makes sense to depersonalize (managerialism warps its own human agents as much as its victims) and then contextualize it as an abstract resultant of neoliberal capitalist relations. Having said that, however, there are some everyday tactics that can be useful for dealing with the more excessive components of this nasty little invention.

1. The visible expression of managerial power is always a fundamental sign of its constitutive weakness. This is not inconsequential, since power ultimately realizes this too. Because of this, it frequently attempts to excessively humiliate. For you, that can be the time of patient planning ... *collectivize*.

2. Managerialism is ultimately a class perspective that denies class. When this perspective is internalized even the most militant employees will see their own oppression and possible dismissal as reasonable and justifiable. Work hard to resist that perspective and *never* be enamoured of its apparent privileges. Managerialism never likes hearing about its class structure (for it considers itself a numerical and neutral science). Always put that class characteristic at the forefront of any interaction with it.

3. Management is about the enforcement of useless rules, preferably imposed from a distance. Some suggest that knowing management's rules better than management itself allows the disempowered to hoist power by its own petard (Saul Alinsky, etc.). But neoliberalism has manufactured a permanent state of exception. The rules of honourable conduct can be rescinded whenever there is a danger they may be applied to management itself. Therefore, never use only *its* formal rules to justify your refusal; always have a number of standards available (even if they have to be invented especially for this purpose). Notwithstanding these managerial powers of arbitrary repudiation, always seek to understand employment law and regulations better and more thoroughly than it does. Most technocrats assume you are not interested in such matters, which is only a projection of their own ignorance.

4. Managerialism relishes the prospect of your being depressed. This is part of its ideological purpose since it breeds resignation and satisfies the sadistic strain in this type of power. Even if you are depressed, remember that optimism is a moment of revolt in these dark times.

5. Managerial power is a *form*. It only deigns to address you when it wants something it cannot provide itself. Often that is simply your attention to the address itself. The *content* of the address is often secondary to you *and* power.

6. Always remember that you have been abandoned right from the start. But this realization is also part of the managerial ideology designed to bind you even closer to its demands. Move forward on the basis of this principle.

7. Never think of managerial power as rational (intelligent and logical), or assume it knows what is going on when it issues its edicts. The opposite is the case, since incompetence is power's most obvious trademark. Managerialism's lack of intelligence can be exploited for progressive ends.

8. Email is a record and ought to be treated with grave caution.

9. Managerialism *always* flounders and appears pathetic when placed in a public forum. Its fear of the democratic process and of a mobilized group whose members communicate with each other becomes patently evident. Use this to your advantage.

10. Individual, isolated withdrawal is usually a sign that managerialism has won. While it is tempting to escape its power by keeping your head down, any form of successful exodus must always be collective. Rather than viewing individual withdrawal as a tactical response to managerial power, it ought to be seen as the opposite: a strategic resource for aiding managerial oppression.

11. Management itself is not the real enemy. It is merely a symptomatic technology designed to take the heat for late capitalism itself. Never be distracted from analysing the real causes of your non-freedom.

4

Viral Capitalism in the Bedroom

In Bob Flanagan's sombre account of slowly dying, *The Pain Journal* (2000), the author presents a rare glimpse into the prosaic physical, social and emotional traumas faced by the terminally ill. As the last stages of cystic fibrosis ravage his body, the performance artist and musician presents a disturbing but sometimes humorous description of what everyday dying entails for one who is bedbound in a dull suburban house. By this time, Flanagan's international reputation for making some breathtakingly controversial artistic interventions had been firmly established. In the banned *Nine Inch Nails* music video 'Happiness is Slavery', Flanagan plays a slave who submits himself to a machine and all its sordid sexual fantasies. In the final scene he is raped and killed by being slowly minced alive. In another music video, this time for the heavy metal band *Danzig* and their song 'It's Coming Down', Flanagan attempts to sew his lips together and then happily hammers a nail through the head of his penis. As the blood drips from the mangled organ, he directs it to the camera lens. Needless to say, most only got to view the highly censored version of the video.

Afflicted with cystic fibrosis from an early age, Flanagan was always living on borrowed time. He was expected to be dead by his late teens and by the time he began *The Pain Journal* on 22 November 1994, at the age of 42, he had little over a year left to live. When a documentary maker agreed to make a film recording his slow death, we gain insight into Flanagan's strange aesthetic sensibilities. For example, in one scene, he performs in an art installation entitled 'Visiting Hours' in which he reclines in hospital regalia, oxygen tube in nose, as patrons watch. Periodically, Flanagan is hoisted into the air by his feet as if to mimic an inverted Christ, offering his emaciated body to the gods of pain as he visibly suffers. The sacrifice to one's oeuvre is complete.

Compared to these eccentric performances, *The Pain Journal* is a rather sedate affair. It details the sheer monotony and pedestrian inconvenience of dying. Flanagan complains about the quality of the television he must endure, his girlfriend's habit of snoring, the increasingly repellent blandness of his home's decor and the fickleness of friends. Nevertheless, he persists in writing his journal entries on an almost daily basis, drugged to near unconsciousness and in constant excruciating pain as he approaches oblivion:

5/25/95 Letterman. Earplugs. Boredom. And more bad writing. I'm just so lethargic, day and night. Sleep all day on the couch. Come down to bed at night, write some shit here about the nothing I do all day, and then it's off to sleep. Blah. I want to be involved in something but I'm out of breath when I do anything, when I even think of doing anything. It's easier to go to sleep. And I like the way it feels to sleep. I like typing here in bed with the television on. I like touching my balls when I'm done and surfing the channels. Too bad there's nothing good on, but I like it any way. It would be better to read something, and I will, but not just yet. Tomorrow is another day. If only I was another writer. (Flanagan, 2000: 58)

What astonishes the reader midway through this journal is the indefatigable will to work that Flanagan displays. Despite the fact that his body has become a pitiless prison that leaves him in permanent agony, he still must write. He cannot not write. Rather than the disturbing content of the writing, perhaps this stamina and determination itself is Flanagan's last act of shocking perversity. In spite of the shit, vomit, doctors, banal TV, failed attempts at sex and the ugly deterioration of his body, he still finds in work something that defies death. It occupies him as much as it hurts him. Flanagan's ceaseless persistence and self-discipline in noting in minute detail the act of dying represent a sort of revenge. All of this work provides a source of existential overcoming, which has perhaps always been a central aspect of the industrial work ethic. As the British poet Philip Larkin (2012: 376) once quipped, 'Work, paradoxically enough, is a comfort. One wakes up wanting to cut one's throat; one goes to work and in 15 minutes one wants to cut someone else's throat – complete cure!'

But Flanagan's journal operates on another, more negative level. Once the voyeuristic curiosity of witnessing another's death close up has passed and we begin to plod through another day of painful productiveness with

Flanagan, an unsettling realization slowly dawns upon the reader. Suddenly we recognize something very familiar in Flanagan's futile struggle. Not the extreme spectacle of somebody's final flurry of activity in the face of impending demise, but the exact opposite: we see the normalized sickness that underlies the rituals of the living more generally – the putatively 'healthy' working subject. For example, as dashed hopes accumulate and distraction is sought in neurosis, Flanagan declares: 'I am mad at myself for wasting so much time, watching so much TV, sleeping so much, going back and forth to the computer and turning it on but not doing anything with it and going back to the couch and sleeping and watching the OJ trial when there's so much else I want to do' (Flanagan, 2000: 120). In other words, perhaps really *he is writing about us*, the so-called healthy ones. And therein lies the joke (Flanagan was a consummate comedian). Only when semi-annihilated by his necrotic condition can he begin to faithfully describe what the rest of us have become. For Flanagan, the almost suicidal will-to-produce in late-capitalist societies denotes a profound social illness.

This inverted relationship between illness and well-being under capitalist conditions plays an important ideological role in defining what it means to be worthy of workplace enslavement today. If the capitalist system defines illness as the *inability* to work, as Harvey (2001) argues, then there is also something paradoxically unwell underscoring this very *ability* to work too, given the exploitative context in which this ability unfolds. The healthy – especially the too clean corporate types we see frequenting overpriced inner-city gyms – convey a special kind of sickness when placed against the psychotic backdrop of capital accumulation. Something rotten in the social body is quietly implied by the exuberance of muscular office workers who, like Patrick Bateman in *American Psycho*, perform hundreds of sit-ups before making their way to the office. In typically wry style, Adorno was very distressed by the healthy worker. Rather than seeing the physiological vibrancy usually assigned to the 'fit-for-work' subject, he saw instead a figure closer to the semi-dead Bob Flanagan:

> Just as the old injustice is not changed by a lavish display of light, air and hygiene, but is in fact concealed by the gleaming transparency of rationalized big business, the inner health of our time has been secured by blocking flight into illness without in the slightest altering its aetiology ... the only objective way of diagnosing the sickness of the healthy is by the incongruity between their rational existence and

the possible course their lives might be given by reason. All the same, the traces of illness give them away: their skin seems covered by a rash printed in regular patterns, like a camouflage of the inorganic. The very people who burst with proofs of exuberant vitality could easily be taken for prepared corpses, from whom the news of their not-quite-successful decease has been withheld for reasons of population policy. Underlying the prevalent health is death. (Adorno, 2005: 58–59)

We can only imagine what Adorno's thoughts might have been if he had happened upon an insipid corporate well-being exercise. Perhaps the analogy of a funeral rite springs to mind. He certainly was the master of ultra-dry humour and I suspect would have greatly appreciated Flanagan's account. But let's turn the screw up a notch. If illness is defined under capitalism as the inability to work, then when it is placed at the centre of the neoliberal socio-economic universe it may also signify an alternative set of possibilities – the *unwillingness* to work. When the biopolitical infiltration of the body by the 'I, Job' function occurs, any subsequent breakdown of living labour's organic infrastructure through illness poses a problem for corporate exploitation. Whereas Flanagan and Adorno deduce a certain symbolic disorder when the gym-fit middle manager walks into the room and issues a stupid command, individuals trapped in the societies of control are actually overcrowded by the sign of the *supposed sick* ('Why aren't you ill yet? My god, you must have an iron-cast constitution!'). Workers today are always awaiting some affliction to remove them from the game. For the 'I, Job' function relies upon a reproducible, self-disciplining and compliant expression of capitalism's intrinsic sickness. This malaise is born from the logic of the work itself, linked to a frenzied identification with pointless activity. People are too sick to stop working. So, illness is certainly the unstated currency of neoliberal order. However, the bodily limitations that are revealed as a virus takes hold of us might also indicate an interesting borderline between submission and refusal. Flanagan's beautiful journal conveys a difficult *aporia* in this regard. We see both the formal signification of the ill body working perforce (i.e. the neoliberal ideal being dependably repeated), but also a parody that reveals a totally impossible symbiosis between his body and labour. Flanagan's efforts are troubling because they ruin the illusion of work (sleep and the bedroom are endlessly mentioned in his narrative). In him we see the ruin that we have failed to see in ourselves.

And it is here I must make a confession. I love being temporally ill. Nothing terminal, of course. No one would wish for anything like cystic fibrosis. But a good flu with a touch of vomiting and diarrhoea can be constructed as a welcome event. If I am lucky, someone might tend me, which is always wonderful. But it is fine if that does not happen. The reason I relish being ill has nothing to do with masochism. The fact that I feel like shit and am momentarily incapacitated is not motivated by some tasteless obsession with self-destruction. No, it is the way my body is repositioned within the work–command matrix that confers such relief. Out of nowhere, I am released from the 'I, Job' function and its never-ending flows that have reduced my life to mere labour power. And yes, it is even better when the boss gets ill. Germs are a good excuse to be left alone. As Susan Sontag once put it, illness is the 'night-side' of life, whereby the daylight of power loses its painful glare and new ways of social articulation can be explored in the backstreets and bars of an otherwise captured body.

I am only half joking. But even in jest the proposition still feels counterintuitive. How should we understand this absurd relationship to illness today that Flanagan so brilliantly brings to our attention? I want to suggest that our strange rapport with bodily incapacitation is somehow symptomatic (no pun intended) of how work has changed under neoliberal capitalism. As I have argued in previous chapters, corporate managerialism has transformed our jobs into something we *are* rather than something we just *do* among other things. Whereas work used to obey the strict laws of confinement, containment and demarcation in space and time (especially concerning work and non-work, personal and private divisions) organizations now aim to enlist our entire repertoire of bodily affects, cultivating an attitude that sees us permanently on call. What is now called 'human capital' is difficult to separate from the actual person conducting the work. Its value-creating attributes are 'lived' on an ongoing and permanent basis. As we noted in Chapter 2, the totality of late capitalism has formed a curve that endlessly turns back on itself.

This represents a rupture in the conventional power relationships that defined organized work and illness in the past. For example, Marx (1867/1976) and Weber (1946) criticized the industrial labour process because it formally objectified the working subject. Employees become alienated abstractions separated from who they actually are. As a result, the workplace begins to resemble a prison environment that is austere, impersonal and completely regimented. The polar opposites of freedom and incarceration are unambiguously discernible in such an environment. Given the stupefaction that resulted under these conditions, engaged productivity was sometimes impeded. Therefore subsequent managerial techniques attempted to promote more human qualities on the job. The neo-human-relations movement in the 1960s and corporate culturalism in the 1980s, for example, aimed to reconcile our vibrant individualities with the demands of economic rationalization. But even after these reforms had taken place the alienating effects of waged employment were still evident – ideology was unable to square the structural disconnect between a syncopated life of coercion and life more generally.

More recent changes to labour regulation have led to 'life itself' no longer being systematically opposed to work, but *put* to work instead. As a result the boundary between work (i.e. the 'prison' of production) and freedom (what we do with the rest of our lives) is increasingly blurred. And this positions the ill body at an interesting political intersection. When placed within the system of governance that Foucault (2008) and Deleuze (2006) call biopower, illness dovetails with refusal, since the organic body is so overcoded by the injunction to produce. In order to conceptualize why, we must appreciate what makes biopower so characteristic of employment regimes today. Take these real-life examples to get a flavour: a real-estate agent prepares for her Monday morning meeting during the kids' football game at the weekend; a music store retail assistant is encouraged to wear his own clothes, because it evokes the kind of 'cool' that could never be prescribed by a dull middle manager; Mark Zuckerberg's trademark hoodie heralds a new kind of corporate entrepreneur in which hard work, lifestyle, extramural interests and skill blur into a singular ethos; an IT start-up realizes that most of its workers train themselves in their own time (as a labour of love), and concentrates on tapping these innovative capabilities rather than composing them; a large hotel chain posts its 'employee of the month' in the lobby, detailing his favourite movies, holiday destination and hobbies; an airline attendant trainee is told to act as if the aeroplane cabin is her living room, so that feelings of warmth and goodwill are more easily evoked; businesses as diverse as call-centres and pharmaceutical conglomerates expressly hire 'attitude' and 'personality', knowing that enrolling the 'whole person' is vital for teamwork, problem solving and customer interaction; a high-tech employee finds himself dreaming up code solutions in his sleep, dubbing it 'sleep work'; a rich investment banker laments to her half-forgotten husband, 'My job is my life'.

This sea change in corporate regulation is noteworthy in that it attempts to break down some of the definitive boundaries that have been fundamental to capitalism from its beginnings. Many occupations increasingly require workers to evoke their entire and unscripted personalities on the job, 'warts and all'. As a result, the rigid nine-to-five confines of the typical office have been replaced by flexitime, aided by technology, in which tasks can be achieved in unconventional times and places. Using terms like 'liberation management' and 'results-only work environment' (ROWE), some overly optimistic observers have insisted that firms have shed their old 'control mentality' (Semler, 2007), persuading employees to bring their self-fashioned artisanal interests to the job – skills that are often difficult to cultivate through standard management methods. The demands of work and 'life itself' are increasingly indistinguishable.

The so-called freedom that is said to follow from the displacement of the division between work and non-work is a deceptive component of the ideology of work today. If biopower is a forceful variant of capitalist regulation in the workplace, it functions by closing down opportunities for freedom rather than widening them. However, the real question for us concerns *resistance*. How do we challenge a modality of power that infects the very texture of everyday life? How might we resist a form of control that disassembles the long-standing industrial division between 'checked in' and 'checked out'? I will suggest that when our embodied sociality is colonized by biopower, the ways in which we are able to refuse work successfully also changes. Such resistance may take many forms, but let's follow Flanagan's lead and concentrate on one; namely, a novel appreciation of *illness* that is currently emerging among the workforce today. Being too ill to work appears to gather emancipatory import when power casts us as bearers of human and social capital. But in order to avoid glibly celebrating this viral underside of biopolitical capitalism, we must develop a degree of conceptual rigour and historical contextualization. How might we plausibly frame a gloriously debilitating bout of influenza as a new weapon with which to wage war on the 'I, Job' function? And what are the implications of doing so given that neoliberalism both (a) transforms work into a contagious, generalized sickness and (b) considers person-related illnesses (e.g. flu) as dangerous threats to productivity?

Being Tagged: The 'Open Prison' of Work Today

The onset of our flu begins slowly. First a twinge in the back of the throat – is it only a head cold or something more serious? Then a temperature change – is that the start of a fever? Then a nauseating pressure that centres in the stomach and gradually moves to other regions of the body. Now the bones begin to ache; perhaps a little vomiting; the real thing arrives and we are bedridden. With a sense of euphoria that is difficult to beat, we can now call in sick. Time to do something fun, like watching a movie, perhaps reading that book we haven't had the chance to pick up for months. Joyous rest. Meandering boredom. Unstructured time winding down to a civilized pace. Finally, life has begun again.

The line of argumentation I am developing here is not so much about illness per se, but about the underlying conditions of possibility that have made it a desirable experience today. What has changed in the way we work that makes the arrival of the flu feel like a reprieve from a life sentence? The image we typically have of most workplaces is one derived from the industrial imagination. The capitalist employment nexus is defined by a wage–effort bargain. In return for a wage that allows us to subsist, we forego all of those self-determined freedoms that from now on can only be enjoyed after we have checked out. As Marx (1867/1976) noted long ago, this feature of capitalism is part of the Faustian pact we all must make. When we enter paid employment someone else legally owns a good part of our time. And given the conditions of purchase, we are expected to conduct ourselves as per our employer's wishes, generally in accordance with the demands of economic rationality. Then follows the protocols of standardization and rationalization that aim to expunge from the job all of the rich individual qualities that make us unique, different … and potentially unpredictable. Hence the ubiquitous experience of alienation (from our work, the state, society and ourselves) as a definitive norm under industrial conditions.

Banishing the Self and Its Limitless Invariances

What are these elements of self that are prohibited as soon as we enter the capitalist workplace? According to Weber (1946), formal bureaucracy operates as a cultural ideology as much as a practical concern with efficiency and means–ends rationality. In other words, the bureaucratic environment requires a uniform personality type in order to function correctly. The bureau separates the official function from the limitless existential universe that makes each individual 'unique' (defined by singular and non-exchangeable life experiences, personalities and propensities). Love, hate, spirituality, sexual desire and revenge have no place in the ideal bureaucratic organization because they upset the cog-like calculus of systematized rationality. Of course, Weber was very clear about the downside of this remarkable achievement, namely, disenchantment. We deny a major part of ourselves for a large part of the day. Depression and innervating bouts of ennui soon follow as the existential flipside of personal restraint and self-abnegation.

The same mindset – with different subjective connotations – has been observed in a wide range of studies pertaining to factory employment. According to Marx (1867/1976), factory work not only physically damages us through long hours of arduous labour, but also mentally wreaks havoc on our emotional well-being. We may be alienated from our job task, fellow workers and end-product, but the ultimate expression of this modern predicament, according to Marx (1988), is self-alienation. Having no choice other than to sell his (or her) labour power under capitalism, 'the worker only feels himself outside his work, and in his work feels outside himself. He is at home when he is not working, and when he is working is not at home. His labour is therefore not voluntary, but coerced' (Marx, 1988: 74).

Critical sociology has subsequently identified the causes and effects of self-alienation in an array of employment settings. For example, in the factory he studied, Beynon (1973) even found employees being reprimanded for chatting on the shop floor since this could potentially confound industrial discipline. Leidner (1993) documented the deep sense of inauthenticity experienced among the service sector employees she interviewed, especially evident when customer service roles (e.g. the happy and smiling sales agent) clashed with their true feelings and identities. This type of self-denial has even been observed in relatively high-paid occupations, such as management consultancy, as employees find themselves paradoxically 'being who they are not' in order to succeed in the corporate setting (Costas and Fleming, 2009).

The Capitalist Compromise?

What do alienated workers do best? Weeks's (2004) study of modern office work answers this question fairly accurately: complain, bitch, gossip, steal, plan various acts of sabotage, avoid work if possible and basically dream up ways of being anywhere but where they unfortunately find themselves. In this respect, corporate managerialism swiftly realized that there was a serious problem to be dealt with. How can the capitalist enterprise have its cake (exploited and regimented workers) and eat it too (enthusiastic, motivated and heartfelt expressions of labour power)?

The rise of the human relations movement in the 1920s and 1930s is often believed to have been a pragmatic compromise by corporate managerialism – a relaxation of strict discipline in order to tackle the dehumanizing ills of work. The typical rationale goes like this: following the depersonalization engendered by the artificial imposition of calculative rationality, managers sought to find ways of injecting social meaning back into work – task rotation, self-fulfilment and a more consensual style of organizing might allow workers, in part at least, to enjoy their jobs. This history of management is a myth, however. We must place the rise of this corporate perspective in its proper historical context. The 1920s and 1930s, especially in the USA, was overwhelmed by industrial conflict (see Gillespie, 1991). Workers were revolting en masse, and for good reason. The human relations movement and other types of 'soft constraint' entered the fray, concerned by the unmitigated class war that seemed imminent.

However, the discourse of human relations still basically relied upon the metaphor of imprisonment when ideologically framing how work might best be organized. Containment was still the key objective of the management gaze. As Braverman (1974) points out in his excellent critique of Maslow and McGregor among others, so-called humanized work systems are conspicuously regimented around analogues of space and time indicative of earlier modes of confinement. We might think of this as Taylorism delivered with an Oprah Winfrey-like munificence – thoughtful and considerate until you decided work was not really your cup of tea after all.

The popularity of culture management in the 1980s appeared to denote a break from previous corporate ideologies. The attempt to build 'strong cultures' changed the tenor of work from one that was purely contractual to one that employed a more emotional and warmer labour–capital interface (Kunda, 1992). The literature on culture management is vast, and a full elaboration of its diffusion and acceptance or rejection by the workforce is beyond the scope of the present discussion. However, prominent among the arguments for 'strong cultures' by business writers was a fierce dislike of previous management systems. According to Peters and Waterman (1982), the rationalized employment relationship misses out on a key value driver in the post-industrial economy: employee commitment and loyalty. As such, organizations ought to instil the workforce with strong sentimental attachments to the business enterprise. When this is achieved, employees supposedly see little difference between the welfare of the firm's owners or shareholders and their own (Barley and Kunda, 1992).

What we now know clearly is that the trend towards strong cultures actually *deepened* the division between work and non-work in a striking manner (Fleming and Sturdy, 2011). Corporate cultures of the 1980s and 1990s functioned like clans or cults, treating all outside influences as potentially dangerous contaminants that might diminish the normative purity and authenticity of the firm (O'Reilly and Chatman, 1996). This is how Casey (1995) and Kunda (1992), for example, reveal the disconcerting side of this management trend, especially during its heyday in the 1980s. The work environment becomes a closed system in which an Orwellian uniformity prevails, suppressing all other personal and lifestyle signifiers. According to Willmott (1993), after employees are socialized in such spaces they must remain silent about their lives outside the office. The effort to build a lasting emotional link between the workforce and an exploitative organization, ironically, leaves employees more depersonalized than ever.

A Life Enlisted: Non-Work ... Goes to Work

In Western enterprises, especially in the United States and northern Europe, a strange mutation has occurred in managerial practice over the last 15 years. Rather than moulding workers into faithful reflections of the firm, typically by bombarding them with brainwashing media, organizations decided to allow employees to arrive at work 'as they are'. Hanlon (2007) persuasively demonstrates that this sustained focus on the in-house reconstruction of the individual was abandoned in favour of enclosing what the employee already is – the vested capabilities that workers bring to the office under their own steam. I think this is why we see more *self-sufficient* ideals entering the lexicon of management and HRM in the late 1990s, including distributive leadership, self-managing teams, flexi-work and the portfolio career. The message is clear. Rather than exhorting employees to display love towards the firm, which often resulted in satirized displays of deference, the corporation aims instead to tap the social intelligence already existing (including negative aptitudes such as fear, discussed in the last chapter). Even Tom Peters, the erstwhile guru of 'strong cultures', changed his mind about the efficacy of indoctrination. Instead he favoured 'liberation management', whereby the independent qualities of workers were tapped and utilized (Peters, 2003).

There are a number of important reasons for this shift in how workers are exploited. Soon after the 'culture craze' became institutionalized, a number of observers noted how the slavish adherence to corporate values often had undesirable outcomes (Foster and Kaplan, 2001). Not innovation, creativity or initiative, but staid conformity frequently resulted from the cult-like rituals of commitment. Understandably, many workers simply play-acted their way through the day, hoping to appease superiors, even when this undermined organizational productivity. The unintended consequences of extreme normative proselytization started to harm the expropriation of surplus value. Love became unproductive.

Another reason for this change in labour management pertains to the political economy of neoliberal employment regimes. Following the crisis of Fordism, the neoliberal paradigm was activated to salvage the accumulation process. But there was a big catch: fanatical neoliberalism – that is to say, unalloyed private property, commercialization, competition, ultra-individualism – is notoriously impractical for getting things done in the real world (see Fleming, 2014). As any management consultant will confess, in order to function, organizations are conspicuously reliant upon pre-rationalized currents of sociality, cooperation and informal collaboration – things that the broader neoliberal mission is generally aggressive towards. This is exactly why firms began to celebrate the self-organizing abilities of employees and to blur the boundary between work and non-work. From the 1990s onwards we see a distinct corporate attempt to encourage employees to take on more management responsibilities (whilst remaining hamstrung by traditional managerial relations of authority that do not disappear).

There are a number of important dimensions functioning here. Facets of the employee's life related to non-work are increasingly promoted during company time. According to Gorz, there is a clear capitalist agenda behind this development. Whereas workers in Taylorized industries

> became optimal only after they had been deprived of practical knowledge, skills and habits developed by the culture of everyday life ... post-Fordist workers have to come to the production process with all the cultural baggage they have acquired through games, team sports, arguments ... (Gorz, 2010: 9–10)

'Life itself' now enters the neoliberal machine, since our independent and socially rich abilities typically expressed outside the workplace become a principal resource. This has been facilitated by some work systems that would have looked bizarre in earlier organizational contexts. For example, in their bestselling book *Why Work Sucks and How to Fix It*, Ressler and Thompson (2011) argue that American industry is being substantially reshaped by results-only work environments. Such organizations no longer focus on inputs, as conventional management wisdom prescribes, but only on *outputs*. ROWE-orientated firms do not give a shit where, when or how the work is done, whether it's on a Sunday morning, or enclosed in an airport's toilet cubicle with iPhone conveniently at hand. Inputs are left to the discretion of employees, who hardly ever falter on delivering on time. Of course, self-sufficiency within this economic arrangement is just another way of saying, 'You are on your own – now you absorb the costs of production'. This is the same cost that capitalism (including the state) was once obliged to pay, given that it had got away with murder already. No such misgivings are required today, however.

In light of the concept of biopower (to be discussed further below), such 'freedoms' are, of course, yet another way of extracting more labour time from the workforce. I call this a *tagging* method of control. The fate of workers directed by ROWE or liberation management resembles that of criminal offenders in 'open prisons': free but also incarcerated, mobile but ultimately tracked, with tentative rights that are always on the verge of being revoked. In his diary of life as a tagged prisoner, Steve Taylor highlights the uncertainty that this supposedly 'freer' method of imprisonment involves in his day-to-day life. Taylor was required to be in his home between the hours of 7 p.m. and 7 a.m. In the classic panopticon, uncertainty would have stemmed from not knowing whether one was being watched or not. But Taylor's surveillance is electronic; he knows very well that if he leaves the house the police will arrive within minutes to arrest him. For him, the uncertainty arises from the gaps and postponements caused by the fallible humans behind the surveillance – humans who are clearly confused and disorganized. Their organized disorganization is obviously designed to induce a certain type of anxiety in the prisoner, a Kafkaesque state of mind that continuously anticipates an arrival that never eventuates. However, the tagged prisoner is emotionally tortured, not as the land-surveyor K. was by a mystically inscrutable Castle, but by a private firm called Securicor (now G4S) which had successfully bid for the governmental contract:

Day 2: As I enjoy a nice relaxing bath, the telephone rings. It's the Securicor monitoring centre in Manchester, asking if I am at home. Either the bath water obscured the signal, or I was out of range. They say they will send someone round to investigate.

Day 3: No one arrived yesterday to investigate my bath ...

Day 32: My partner's grandfather died, and I am passed from pillar to post and back again between the prison, Securicor and probation to try to vary my curfew hours to attend the funeral.

Day 33: Established that the decision lies with the prison governor. He says he'll let me know tomorrow.

Day 34: He hasn't decided. (Taylor 2000)

This scenario bears an uncanny familiarity with what it must be like working in ROWE-inspired labour processes. Under this regime of work, life is not taken over and deprived by the prison-like monotony of timetables that have a clear beginning and end. Instead, life persists, but always within the shadow of a background master signifier that never sleeps, using postponement, planned incompetence and the employee's own anxieties to squeeze more work out of them. Indeed, the tagged employee is always off balance, since destabilization is one of managerialism's key strategies of control. When the boundary between work and non-work is displaced in this way, an insidious regime of suspension is generated that does not require the typical industrial refrain of discipline to function. And ironically, as the excerpt above indicates, we find ourselves perpetually subjected to the injunction to perform, but at the same time must directly confront the bureaucratic disarray and carelessness that underscore the delivery of those injunctions. This defines neoliberal managerial capitalism – monitoring that is virtually algorithmic in its rigour and endemic in its ineptitude. Most importantly, the tagged worker experiences work time in a very different manner. Kamp puts it perfectly:

The 'normal working day' is gradually being effaced ... in reality, working hours are no longer defined by actual work time spent but by the nature of the assignment, by solution strategies, and by the level of ambition involved, as well as individual factors and preferences. (Kamp, 2013: 129)

In other words, when work bleeds into non-work and vice versa, we live the template of work as a constant pressure that is almost impossible to walk away from.

Deleuze and Viral Capitalism

We are now closer to conceptualizing how the first signs of influenza might be welcomed by the worker today as a significant opportunity for refusal. But in order to develop a fuller analysis around this issue, let's scrutinize the type of political body implied by the work–illness intersection, especially within the current phase of capitalism that has employed 'life itself' in the accumulation process.

We have already mentioned in earlier chapters the important insights provided by Foucault (2008) in his last set of annual lectures at the Collège de France. He argued that 'biopolitics' is the guiding motif of neoliberal reason, which he sought to reveal through a close reading of neoclassical economists like Gary Becker. Biopower refers to the way governmental and economic influence enlist 'life itself' in order to function effectively when markets dominate. This is why 'human capital' is an overarching preoccupation among neoliberal theoreticians. Whereas Fordism favoured containment in order to render us productive, biopower seeks to transcend boundaries and echo work throughout all domains of society. Biopower is the contagious weapon of neoliberalism, particularly because it yokes our entire living qualities to the capitalist project, something akin to a virus. Economic rationality inserts itself into our bodies like a disease that cannot be shaken. The increasing commercialization of everything, from family life to our value in the employment market, sees traditional forms of domination, such as disciplinary confinement, lose their usefulness in this regard. Biopower represents a different approach to regulation, one that utilizes openness, cross-boundary fluidity and the permanent instantiation of economic pressure.

Why Deleuze?

In my opinion, Foucault's concept of biopower only really made sense after Deleuze placed it within a wider narrative of capitalist class domination. Whereas Foucault tended to explain the rise of biopower as a gentler and non-interventionist method for managing modern populations, Deleuze pushed the idea in a more radical direction. Neoliberalism is primarily a class project and this drew Deleuze to a particular description of biopower to explicate the distinct features of this form of governance. For him, the prison-like apparatus of capitalist work relations has given way to networks of 'control' in which porous interconnections between institutions have rendered the space and time delimitations of Fordism somewhat outdated and even counterproductive.

Whereas disciplinary power sought to sequester, regiment and reform the subject into a composite ideal of the panopticon gaze, biopower seeks to accelerate and 'infect' the subjects of power so that they are always enmeshed within its abstract network (Deleuze, 1992). In other words, the logic of the prison (or factory) has escaped its traditional domain and is now the leading template for all social relations. The 'open prison' of post-Fordist employment relations thus poses even graver implications for the question of resistance than the high-security confinement that Foucault discussed in *Discipline and Punish* (1977).

In his famous essay entitled 'Postscript on the societies of control' (1992), Deleuze argues that biopolitical regulation is special because of its virtual qualities. It entails an index that reverberates through all social relations. Power is no longer quantitative – starting in the factory and then ending, beginning again in the family and then ending, sequencing our corporeal time in discrete chunks – but is dangerously *qualitative*. When comparing biopower to disciplinary procedures, Deleuze observes:

> In the disciplinary societies one was always starting again (from school to the barracks, from the barracks to the factory), while in the societies of control one is never finished with anything – the corporation, the educational system, the armed services being metastable states coexisting in one and the same modulation, like a universal system of deformation. (Deleuze, 1992: 5)

In this way, biopower incites the productive social body to overcome Fordist boundaries as a matter of course. For us, it is the natural thing to do. The trope of the virus and Deleuze's insistent use of the concept of the 'virtual' or 'gas' are important for understanding this form of force. Rather than directly coercing our efforts through manifest blockages and time/space prohibitions, regulation seeks to empower the individual so that she may pass from one domain to another, free of approximate conclusions or termini, but even more burdened by economic reason as a result. Let's explore this idea a little more before we employ it to dissect the contemporary role of illness in class society.

Towards a Theory of Modulation

As opposed to the disciplinary apparatus that truncates our bodily potentials, biopower prefers to operate by way of indexical modulations, so that we are 'never finished with anything'. The industrial factory of yesteryear gathers its social violence through beginnings and ends. We dutifully check in and out of the office, the hospital, university, the prison and so forth. In this way,

> [t]he individual never ceases passing from one closed environment to another, each having its own laws: first the family; then the school ('you are no longer in your family'); then the barracks ('you are no longer at school'); then the factory; from time to time the hospital; possibly the prison, the pre-eminent instance of the enclosed environment. (Deleuze, 1992: 5)

Biopower functions in an entirely different manner. It is successful when it *modulates* the social body in a syncopated manner, calibrating or 'indexing' its energies and efforts to an abstract principle (production, work, obedience, etc.) that can never be isolated in any one particular location. The modular code does not fragment difference but adjusts non-aligned ways or spheres of life to a dominant index without totally rewriting them or erasing their individual distinctiveness. By 'index' I mean a background structure of compatibility between otherwise distinct social groupings. This is never a one-to-one relationship, since biopower cannot function through *direct* compatibilities. It relies on more osmotic methods of influence. For example, life in the post-industrial school does not directly resemble the workplace. Under neoliberalism, however, education is indexed to the ideals of production so that schooling continuously resonates with the basic requirements of the workplace: art classes tap into one's employability, as do the 'stop smoking' sermons in social education classes; mathematics echoes the scientific professions and the 'skills deficit' in many Western economies; physical education presages lower company healthcare premiums; a relaxed and counsellor-like teacher imparts the importance of obedience to technocratic demands. It goes without saying that all of this becomes particularly evident following a Bukowski-inspired four-day stint in a comfortable bed. *Standpoint* rather than generalizable data is crucial for analysing biopower.

Forlorn university educators, of course, observe this type of 'indexing' every day. Compared to the student body in pre-neoliberal times (often attracted to drugs, sex, boozing and the occasional riot), today's students approach their education like fecund bank managers who see only rational and singular futures, with little end or alternative. No doubt debt management has a formative influence on this attitude in higher education (see Ross, 2013). But Deleuze is more interested in the capitalist activation of agency along one unending register, whereby any type of enclosure (e.g. a debtor's prison that would allow us to pay our dues and move on with a clean slate) would somehow defy the neoliberal project. The point, he suggests, is that there can never be any resolution or forfeit. As discussed in Chapter 2, this is the nature of the neoliberal totality. And it is what makes biopower so amenable to the organization of work today, which looks sympathetically upon the achievements of disciplinary power but finds its 'endings' obstructive: 'the *apparent acquittal* of the disciplinary societies (between two incarcerations); and the *limitless postponements* of the societies of control (in continuous variation) are two very different modes of juridical life' (Deleuze, 1992: 6, emphasis original).

This analysis opens up some important insights. The indexical command to work in neoliberal societies can no longer be analytically identified in any particular act or instance. That would be like a surgeon attempting to use a scalpel to remove the immune system from the human body – it is everywhere, part of the systemic whole and not reducible to any particular part. Writing with Felix Guattari in an earlier text, Deleuze explains this virtual aspect of power in relation to semiotics and the 'regime of signs' that designate domination within a schizophrenic mode of capitalism. Because of the open-endedness of our regulation, paranoia becomes an important fixture of self-exploitation, as noted in Chapter 1. We never know whether we have been completely subsumed by capital as we move between its cells, forever indexing our escape attempts to a central, all-seeing but paradoxically diffuse eye of power. Have I worked enough? When will I know when to stop and relax? Is somebody plotting my downfall in the office as I work on this spreadsheet at home on Monday morning? As a result,

> Nothing is ever over and done with a regime of this kind. It is made for that, it is the tragic regime of infinite debt, to which one is simultaneously

debtor and creditor. A sign refers to another sign, in which it passes and which carries it into still other signs. 'To the point that it returns in a circular fashion …' Not only do signs form an infinite network, but the network of signs is infinitely circular. The statement survives its object, the name survives its owner. Whether it passes into other signs or is kept in reserve for a time, the sign survives both its state of things and its signified; it leaps like an animal or dead person to regain its place in the chain and invest a new state. (Deleuze and Guattari, 1987: 113. 1987)

Like an animal or a dead person. When reading this passage, one can see Bob Flanagan poring over his pain journal as he curses his failing limbs. Have I worked enough so that I can now die debt free? Perhaps this is what makes the biopolitical modulation of work so powerful, because it cannot be singularly and exclusively identified as a target for rebellion and revolt. 'The man' is everywhere and nowhere. In other words, and as any good corporate social networker who is constantly glued to his or her worn-out iPhone will tell us, *I am my job*. The problem that I often face as such an individual, however, is that I no longer know exactly who this 'I' is. It feels as if a dead man has stepped into my suit and is now calling the shots.

On the Uses of Illness at Work in the Biopolitical Age

Let's now return to our opening question. How might biopower at work and its web of modulations be resisted by the growing number of employees – both rich and poor – subjected to it? There has been a growing research interest in this topic; unlike traditional forms of dissent that centre on the objective structures of capitalist work relations, opposing biopower requires an additional engagement, since the medium of regulation is often confused with 'living' in the modern world as such.

From 'Life' to Death and Sleep

Thus far I have proposed that biopower integrates with work through modular indexation processes. This is how it inserts the 'I, Job' function into life more generally, even if we experience it as an intrusion that we are able to oppose. The biopolitical totalization of the social body, as discussed by Deleuze, then exerts itself as a persistent pressure to perform and orientate our living energies to the needs of work, whether we are clocked in or not. Strangely, this occurs *regardless* of whether the work is organizationally necessary or not. In some cases, the compulsion to undertake unnecessary work – think of Bob Flanagan one more time – might actually harm the efficacy of economic rationality. This is why firms in France, for example, have banned their employees from checking work emails in the evening. Those messages sent at 1 a.m. after a 14-hour workday are useless and potentially damaging. Volkswagen and Daimler automatically delete emails sent to employees on holiday so they arrive back at the office with empty in-boxes. So in one respect, corporations are at the vanguard of the refusal movement, since the inclination to embody the 'I, Job' function to its full is a death sentence. However, we should not be too sympathetic towards this interesting shift in corporate 'work–life balance' policies. They are merely attempting to have it both ways: the capitalist benefits of biopower without the bad press that follows when an employee jumps off the headquarters office block.

So, are there more progressive ways to refuse the virus of work and its indexing machine? Surveying the politics of employment in the post-industrial West in particular, we might note three interesting trends in this regard. The first concerns disconnecting the independent sociality of employees from the ideology of production that currently exploits the 'common' in parasitical fashion inside the office and beyond. The clearest statement concerning this type of resistance can be found in the writings of the 'Invisible Committee', especially their manifesto *The Coming Insurrection* (2009). They suggest we exit the space–time totality of waged exploitation by repossessing the otherwise functional (from capitalism's perspective) domain of 'non-work' and redirecting this commonwealth towards democratic ends. They describe this tactic for undermining biopower in relation to the commune:

> The exigency of the commune is to free up the most time for most of the people. And we're not talking about the *number of hours* free from any wage–labour exploitation. Liberated time doesn't mean a vacation. Vacant time, dead time, the time of emptiness and the fear of emptiness – this is the time of work. There will be no more time to *fill*, but a liberation of energy that no 'time' contains. (Invisible Committee, 2009: 104, emphasis original)

The Invisible Committee demand collective separatism, or what I have called elsewhere 'post-recognition' politics (see Fleming, 2014). *Desertion* is the key motif here. Rather than calling for more inclusion and recognition in the corporate theatre of war, appealing for better work conditions and pay, the Invisible Committee suggest that our common living labour might be detached from the field of exploitation and enjoyed for its own ends. The point is that

> [t]o organize beyond and against work, to collectively desert the regime of mobility, to demonstrate the existence of a vitality and a discipline precisely *in demobilization* is a crime for which a civilization on its knees is not about to forgive us. In fact, though, it's the only way to survive. (Invisible Committee, 2009: 51, emphasis original)

The second way biopower is resisted today tends to be less positive. We explored these acts of refusal in the last chapter: namely suicide. Drawing on the notable cases of Foxconn in China and France Telecom, Carl Cederström and I developed a critique of biopower by examining the more self-destructive moments of escape that many choose under neoliberal conditions (Cederström and Fleming, 2012). Because the command to work has irrevocably infected individual life processes, it is not surprising that employees perceive the body as the true battlefield. In doing so, overworked subjects misrecognize the living organism as the source of their misery.

A third and related form of resistance has been explored by Crary (2013) in his study *24/7: Late Capitalism and the Ends of Sleep*. Because work has colonized almost every aspect of life, especially with the help of mobile technology, even sleep has become a victim of universal productiveness. Crary argues that we need to reclaim the benefits of sleep, approaching it as one form of effective escape in an ever 'switched-on' world. In this respect it is no surprise that sleep is often compared to death, since it offers oblivion and some respite, albeit brief.

And what about illness? I now want to posit a fourth approach to refusing the indexing machine of work by blending characteristics of each political response described above. In 1988 the normally camera-shy Deleuze agreed to give a set of interviews with Claire Parnet, insisting on just one condition: that Parnet should move through the alphabet, using each letter as a platform to discuss a topic of interest. For Deleuze, the letter M suggested the question of 'Malady'. His reasons are fascinating. He had been afflicted with bronchial tuberculosis at a young age, and this had provided a number of 'privileges' that he enjoyed very much. Central among them was a special relationship with work that granted a degree of autonomy and freedom from external obligations and the excessive preoccupation with industrial productiveness typical among academics. As we all know, Deleuze was extremely prolific in his philosophical output. So the counterproductivity he is referring to here is not related to his philosophical 'work' – but to the demands placed on him by the indexing apparatus, which he considered almost always petty, officious and useless in nature.

Illness, for Deleuze, implies a particular ethico-political threshold between the body and its injunction to perform. What is the nature of this threshold and how might it be theorized as a form of refusal in the biopolitical era? The so-called 'joys' of illness have been explored in a number of domains concerning modern work. Indeed, if we propose that illness under capitalism is defined by both the singular inability to work and unwillingness to do so, then we might begin to detect some anti-work affinities in our dreaded maladies. In his wonderful book *How to be Idle* (2004), Hodgkinson makes a persuasive case for an *unwilling illness* in this regard:

> That being ill can be a delightful way to recapture lost idling time is a fact well known to all young children. Being ill – nothing serious of course – should be welcome as a pleasure in adult life, too, as a holiday from responsibility and burden. Indeed, it may be one of the few legitimate ways left to be idle. (Hodgkinson, 2004: 68–69)

The last part of this quote is interesting because it points to the unquestionable yet indeterminate legitimacy that illness has acquired in an over-medicalized world: nobody can defend the idea that the sick ought to work (except for a few rabid right-wing members of the British Tory Party). Could this confabulation between the unwell body and the biopolitical insistence that we *are* our jobs be fruitfully exploited for emancipatory ends? To address this question, let us turn to one of the most insightful descriptions of biopower in the workplace. In his autobiographical essay about his role as an IT consultant, Rob Lucas portrays a life completely overtaken by work. Lucas even found himself working in his dreams when asleep, something he called 'sleeping working'. The difficulty Lucas had in resisting this form of power is described in relation to some classic modes of worker dissent. And towards the end of this description we find illness entering the picture:

Given the individually allocated and project centered character of the job, absenteeism only amounts to self-punishment, as work that is not done will have to be done later under increased stress. Given the collaborative nature of the work, heel dragging necessarily involves a sense of guilt towards other workers. On the production line, sabotage might be a rational tactic, but when your work resembles that of an artisan, sabotage would only make life harder ... It is only when sickness comes and I am involuntarily incapable of work that I really gain extra time for myself. It is a strange thing to rejoice in the onset of a flu. (Lucas 2010: 128)

Lucas concludes that if illness is the only recourse that workers have for combating biopower at work, then we are all in big trouble. There is little progressive purchase in contracting the flu since it merely offers an over-individualized and rather futile moment of escape, one that ends all too soon. However, perhaps he is not approaching the issue in the correct manner. Illness disrupts the modulations that calibrate our bodies to the virus of working by deploying the capitalist virus itself, using its own idiom. Here the neoliberal indexing process is momentarily scrambled, disgusted and ashamed before the afflicted body that it created but still must disclaim. Indeed, our bosses are usually more worried that our flu might infect the entire office rather than by the idea that we might actually be enjoying our bedridden state with a good book.

How to Use Illness as a Weapon

Echoing the preoccupation Deleuze had with illness as a political force, what came to be known as the Social Patients' Collective (or SPK) in Germany decided to use our collective maladies as a weapon against capitalism. Like Foucault and Deleuze, they also sensed the biopolitical tendencies of a new type of regulation emerging from the ruins of Fordism. Rather than 'hospitalizing illness' as a stigmatized deficiency (i.e. the inability to work) that ought to be quarantined, the SPK turned the tables on power by transforming bodily disorders (perhaps the true limit of capitalism) into political acts of sabotage. They reanimated amputations and chronic heart disease as positive forces, seeing in them a stealth-like response to the ideology of work. Their catchphrase was basic: Use illness as a weapon!

The SPK manifesto begins with a convincing description of the way many illnesses are intimately linked to the contradictions of capitalism, which in turn renders them deeply political. When we work too much, our immune system invariably suffers. For example, a recent report has stated that prolonged stress in the workplace is more adverse to your health than heavy smoking (see *Metro*, 2013). When illness sets in we often enter into a medicalized universe. According to the SPK, its true role is to assess the likely damage our affliction will have on the general rate of exploitation. It is this profound anxiety expressed by capitalist reason that might be utilized by the work-refusal movement. Specific illnesses (e.g. stress-induced haemorrhoids) form a new modulation with paid employment by revealing how the ritual of labour itself is a general type of organic disorder. But at the same time, capitalism frames the maladies it has helped cause as something obnoxious and menacing. This tension opens a path, perhaps even a revolutionary one, beyond the dogma of wage-exploitation:

> On the one hand, illness is a productive power. On the other hand as identity of production and destruction, illness is a concept of all relations of production. The basic antagonism between productive powers and relations of production is to be thought in this manner, that illness is a widespread necessity, which produces its own complement, revolution. Ill patients are thus a revolutionary class. (Socialist Patients' Collective, 1987: 56)

The SPK hoped that the productive incapacity engendered by the capitalist bio-assault on the body might be used to short-circuit our enlistment in unrelenting work-focused culture. However, illness must not be practised as an individual pathology, as Lucas appears to do in his description above. This makes it too easy for power to segregate and dismiss. Instead, it ought to be approached as a collective form of life. To unpack these ideas and apply them to the emerging tendencies of work under neoliberal capitalism, I foresee three ways in which illness may be used as a weapon to block the enrolment of 'life itself' at work.

Firstly, illness can be directed at breaking the spell of the 'all or nothing' approach to work instigated by neoliberal ideology. Biopower attempts to make our jobs seem like *everything*, whereby even our family and (ironically) our well-being are sacrificed in the name of it. But it is the 'nothing' component of this 'all or nothing' mentality that biopower is particularly effective in modulating. 'Nothing' here evokes, of course, death, whether symbolic, social or literal. If we cannot make it to the office and win, then all is lost. Catastrophe will ensue. I am nothing. However, once we are bedridden with flu, we begin to realize, as Charles Bukowski did when he simply went to bed for a few days, that the world does not end. Life does go on. From under the bedcovers, we begin to note that our obsession with work is a rather conceited, manufactured disposition with little bearing on social functionality. Illness allows us to regain perspective. We ought to welcome that perspective.

Secondly, collective or shared illness may break the *temporal* spell that the modern ethos of work has cast upon us today. The seemingly endless modulation of productivity that reverberates throughout all other life projects is disrupted by the white static of affliction. This space presents a new vista of social experience, whereby the ill individual enters a collective political pact with the already-ill multitude. In fact, sociality has always acted like a contagion. It comes from nowhere and leads in unexpected and novel directions. Like the SPK militants, a dreadful malady provides bountiful opportunities for social reassembly. This is the normative element of their manifesto. The life we enjoy when we are no longer obliged to send another useless email can only become a radical force if it stimulates a biopolitical class consciousness. To paraphrase Deleuze concerning his discussion of M for Malady, the happiness one practises when laid low by a nasty bout of the flu is only the joy of living together more generally. Many ill people reconnect with this communal register of time which lies outside of the alienating rituals of work. Some even take to YouTube to share the good news (see Danisonfire, 2013). Thus I foresee 'illness soviets' emerging that seek to put capitalist biopower back in its place, with the additional help of coffee, aspirins and a stack of wonderful books to read together. Mental illness might also be theorized in this way, but given that it is not contagious, we probably need another conceptual grid to optimize it. I am sure this can be done.

And thirdly, and more controversially, I propose that the only thing that is better than being temporally ill (under biopolitical conditions) is when those in authority are unwell and are forced to stay at home too. Who can deny secretly rejoicing upon learning that a superior has contracted a foul stomach bug? The elation does not derive from sadistic pleasure in the pain of another (since that would be plain evil), but from the prospect of being left alone for the day. And why shouldn't even the wickedest micro-managing boss participate in the respite and reflection that such an affliction would confer on them? We cannot be selfish in this matter. For sure, sharing our illnesses with the commanders of capitalism may create novel cross-class moments of solidarity, disabling the illusion that 'work is everything', even among the most tyrannical of employers. If the SPK's mantra to *use illness as a weapon* is truly to hold progressive purchase, then we must insist that our flu be shared, even among the least deserving.

Perhaps Bob Flanagan was of another era after all. Despite his crippling disease, he worked through it and made the best of a bad situation without dislodging the will-to-produce that is integral to the work ethic, especially as this was forged under Fordism. There are countless examples of creative artists – Proust, Kafka, etc. – who gained some weird sustenance from their illness and redirected it into an overcoded production ritual. Indeed, stereotypical industrial workers in the 1950s and 1960s, typically male, often continued working when unwell, only later to be diagnosed with lung cancer or some other terminal illness. The thought of visiting the doctor was deemed a sign of weakness. Consequently, the capitalist diagram was able to squeeze as much labour power out of them as possible before they expired and were replaced with fresh hands. I feel little compunction in recommending these approaches to illness as a means of work refusal. However, a new and recondite perspective concerning the viral possibilities of late capitalism may be emerging in which the circular speed of a life pointlessly saturated by the wage mentality might be coming to an end. Nowhere is this more evident than in the life philosophy of Charles Bukowski – who perhaps represents the threshold at which a Fordist mentality towards work dissolves into something more fitting for the biopolitical era. We should heed his advice:

> I have periods when I feel weak, ill, depressed, fuck it, the Wheaties aren't going down right. I just go to bed for three days and four nights, pull down all the shades and just go to bed. I get up to shit, piss, drink a beer now and then, and go back to bed. I come out of that completely enlivened for two or three months, I get power from that. I think that someday they will say this psychotic guy knew something. But today we are so obsessed that we have to get up and do something. People are nailed to the processes, up/down, get up and do something, then sleep. (Bukowski, 2012)

5

Corporate Ideology as False Truth Telling

One of the funniest parodies of corporate ideology that has emerged in recent years can be found on YouTube entitled 'Australians for Coal'. In the video appear dark-suited executives who rejoice in the Australian mining industry's commitment to carbon emissions reduction and sustainability. They exhibit deep concern about the devastating effects of climate change (Australia has one of the largest extractive industries in the world). Each industry leader declares what their respective multinational firms are doing about the urgent environmental question. Their message is especially sensitive to the future generations who will inherit a planet that until now the mining industry has been blindly destroying. The satire begins with everything we would expect in such a depiction of self-professed corporate ethics: *lies*. For example, a suited woman claims: 'As one of the major contributors to CO_2 emissions and as we begin to contend with the real-world effects of climate change, we have to prepare ourselves for the next step in addressing our corporate responsibilities in this area.'

Before we investigate the video in more depth, let's pause for a moment and consider the political context. Some might suggest that the Australian government has completely caved in to the demands of an immensely powerful mining industry. For example, take the 2010 attempt by the Australian Labor government to introduce the Carbon Pollution Reduction Scheme. The idea was to curb the environmental damage associated with the country's booming mining industry. The then prime minister, Kevin Rudd, proposed the policy and it was not surprisingly vigorously opposed by the industry. The growing criticisms of Rudd finally came to a head when the policy was suddenly withdrawn, shortly followed by the news that Rudd had resigned. Big business and its formidable lobbyists had clearly spoken. More recently, we can witness the sheer dominance of this industry over national politics. In 2014 the Australian government controversially abolished the carbon tax. It argued that the tax damaged the extractive industry's profitability. As a lobby group for the mineral and mining sector put it: 'The removal of the world's biggest carbon tax is an important step towards regaining the competitive edge that Australia lost over the last decade.' Indeed, Tony Abbott, the current prime minister, has been accused of being a zealot in denying climate change. For him, the very existence of global warming is a moot point:

> It seems that notwithstanding the dramatic increases in man-made CO_2 emissions over the last decade, the world's warming has stopped. Now, admittedly we are still pretty warm by recent historical standards, but there doesn't appear to have been any appreciable warming since the late 1990s.

According to the Abbott government's chief business adviser, Maurice Newman, the lies spread about global warming have resulted in Australia being totally unprepared for *global cooling*. So, within this bizarre context, the 'Australians for Coal' satire functions in a conventionally critical manner by revealing how ridiculous corporate lie telling can become in face of the facts. Indeed, a whole public relations industry has developed around the concept of 'corporate social responsibility' (CSR) to create a false image of multinational capitalism and its intimations towards a greener 'conscious capitalism', an ideal that is clearly at significant odds with everyday business activities.

But the 'Australians for Coal' video sketch gets somewhat more interesting and complex midway through. The suited talking heads stop telling lies and begin to disclose some realistic truth-statements that reveal their authentic opinions:

> **Tim Buckley:** I am proud to announce the company's new policy of 'Fuck you.' 'Fuck you' is more than a policy. It's a philosophy where we are able to straddle the dichotomy between what we know is true and how we can benefit by ignoring that truth.
>
> **Birgit Eichman:** 'Fuck you' takes what would be our present-day financial burden away from us and transforms it into a chronic, economic, social, cultural, and political crisis for future generations.
>
> **Rob Dean:** With this policy, we delay action and leverage the gap, and are able to maintain our role as a global leader in destroying the planet.

Tim Buckley: Ultimately, this is a reflection of the values of our shareholders. Everyday Australians have chosen to invest $20 billion into the company, but we prefer to think of it as 20 billion 'Fuck yous' to the Australians of tomorrow.

The brilliance of this portrayal of corporate propaganda functions on two levels. Firstly, and most obviously, corporate ideology no longer needs to make such outlandishly false claims about its non-existent contribution to society given its position of hegemony. No cover-up is required under triumphant neoliberal capitalism. Indeed, some corporations go out of their way to tell us how they actually do damage the environment and exploit its workers on the understanding that it is better to be truthful. In terms of future scandals and potential litigation, they can state with honesty that they were misleading nobody.

We can note a similar display of naked power in the workplace with the decline of the unbelievable 'cultures of commitment' that dominated firms in the 1980s and 1990s. Using indoctrination techniques that would not be out of place in a cult, management ideology sought to convince workers that the company was 'one', placing their emotional well-being and fulfilment at the heart of its strategic agenda. Today, however, very little is done to cultivate such sentiments among the workforce. In no uncertain terms, the message is clear: we are a business whose sole objective is to maximize profits for our owners. You are expendable and free to leave if you do not like it.

But there is another level of complexity that I think the 'Australians for Coal' parody captures in an interesting way. If CSR is the most visible ideological expression of the late-capitalist enterprise, it no longer seeks merely to tell lies about its so-called virtues and commitment to social well-being. Late-capitalist ideology also seeks to distort what it is by paradoxically uttering certain truths: our authentic philosophy concerning the public is 'Fuck you!' However, such truthfulness never takes the form of standalone admissions. They are always announced within a broader contextual discourse of business ethics, sustainability, worker rights and so forth. While 'Fuck you!' capitalism is certainly indicative of the growing confidence displayed by the multinational corporation, it is also connected with the intensification of ideological activity on the part of neoliberal capitalism. Some truths are useful for hiding what this extreme brand of social exploitation means for the majority of the planet: not a relaxation of propaganda but a more sophisticated version of it that is much more difficult to challenge than corporate lie telling.

The 'Australians for Coal' spoof captures this 'false truth-telling' tendency very well. We gain a glimpse into what the industry really thinks about us and the natural environment. But having heard this admission of truth we clearly feel that we are still being duped. For why would these executives bother saying anything at all? And why make an otherwise accurate statement only within a discursive medium (CSR) that is typically designed to propagate the incredulous myth of family-friendly capitalism? We can observe this disingenuous manipulation of the truth in the final statement by an elderly white male mining tycoon:

> There will come a day when my moral choices will no longer be beholden to the shareholders and a wave of profound regret and a sorrow will engulf me as I realize with painful clarity the enormity of the damage I have perpetrated upon humanity. And even if I plead with whoever has succeeded my role in the company to stop putting CO_2 in the air for the sake of my daughter's grandchildren, he or she can turn to me and simply respond with 'Fuck you.' And that legacy really does make me very proud.

The truth here is weirdly false, even while it is nevertheless truthful. We can see many instances of this sort of strategic truth telling emerging in the corporate and governmental sector. A conspicuous example is provided by the fascinating public relations exercise British Petroleum launched in 2000. With the growing fanfare around green and alternative energies in the late 1990s, a swelling critical concern about the petroleum industry's poor environmental and human rights record and flagrant disregard for workers' rights, and claims of exorbitant profiteering, the firm decided to rebrand itself 'Beyond Petroleum'. A new trademark was unveiled which the company call the 'Helios' after the ancient Greek sun god, symbolizing the firm's commitment to alternative energy sources. The company stated that 'it had decided to retain the BP name because of its recognition around the world and because it stood for the new company's aspirations: "better people, better products, big picture, beyond petroleum."' The hypocrisy and cynicism of this policy was widely derided, of course. So recently BP was obliged to clarify what 'beyond petroleum' actually meant. In doing so, it added an accurate truth to its definition, stating that 'it is shorthand for what we do … producing more fossil fuels'.

How are we to critically understand this form of 'truth telling' in relation to a broader capitalist ideological campaign that is deeply problematic concerning its pledge to workers' rights, environmental sustainability and democratic participation? As mentioned above, one avenue would be to assume pessimistically that firms are now so self-assured in their hegemonic position that they no longer feel the need to manipulate their images. This is correct up to a point. But if this was the case why would they even bother with CSR policies in the first place, which are expensive and time-consuming to develop?

A more optimistic reading might welcome such admissions by large corporations, since they indicate at least a degree of honesty and reflexivity about their business practices. For example, a large European arms manufacturer states in its CSR policy that it is committed to legal, humanitarian and fair business activity around the world (see Fleming, 2014). But it also realizes that these ideals cannot always be lived up to in business practice. The truth is told, but only in the context of statements about the firm's global standing as an ethical manufacturer and supporter of human rights and democracy. Given the controversial nature of this business, there is no way this company can hide the truth or tell its potential employees that the firm is not without its contentious and controversial dimensions. In light of the irrefutable knowledge about the interdependence between arms manufacturers, traders and war atrocities, shouldn't the firm be applauded for showing its 'true colours'?

I want to develop an alternative interpretation of such truth telling that I think is now becoming crucial to the way neoliberal capitalism reproduces itself in the face of the glaring reality concerning its inimical effects. Drawing on a number of examples, I suggest that by placing important truths within a broader symbolic context that may otherwise be dismissed as incredible, an important and perhaps more persuasive moment of deception is taking place. In the case of the well-known arms company mentioned above, for example, its truthfulness is positioned in such a way as to somehow justify and extend the production and sale of weapons. Moreover, the firm's truthful admission is located within a wider narrative that celebrates the organization as a vanguard of responsible business practice – a falsity that its truth utterance paradoxically comes to support. In other words, the partial confession of certain facts (which we would expect this firm to ignore or downplay) provides licence to make even grander and more unbelievable claims about its business activities. The same can be said for BP's moment of confessional truth telling concerning what 'beyond petroleum' really means. This partial truth is set against the broader symbolic backdrop of green plants, happy workers and a blue sustainable planet. This is what gives such truth telling its falsity: in telling the truth in this form, we move from an either/or semantic structure ('Our business model is either centred on the continuation of fossil fuel extraction or it is based on alternative energy') to one that hinges on coordinating conjunctions ('We are both, which we know is impossible').

Such 'false truth telling' was first examined by Michel Foucault (2010) in relation to *parrhesia* (i.e. frank speech). In his discussion of ancient Greek thought, he described *parrhesia* as the dangerous practice of candidly speaking to power. However, what he calls 'bad *parrhesia*' refers to the way candidness is used rhetorically to deceive denizens of the demos. Similarly, I define corporate false truth telling as the pre-emptive use of certain truths in an attempt to defend broader discursive structures that on their own would be considered false. Corporate truths uttered within a wider set of semantic statements that are false have an important inoculation effect. A small dose of truth does not contradict the dishonest context concerning what neoliberal capitalism would like us to think it stands for; it helps maintain the illusion.

This neoliberal strategy (of pointing out the mendacity of corporate discourse) partly subverts traditional ideology critique, because the firm under scrutiny is partially telling the truth. Charges of simple mendacity don't function here. The corporate propaganda machine is able to rebuff our criticisms: 'We never said that our business model was anything other than the unsustainable extraction of fossil fuels. We never said that our corporation doesn't harm workers in the supply chains we exploit around the world – but we are still an ethical company regardless because look at our broader commitments.' The concept of false truth telling therefore demonstrates how staged factual admissions have symbolic effects that are *more* mendacious than spurious and easily dismissible claims about 'doing good' for workers, the environment and global inequality. For this reason, we require updated understandings of how this type of ideology functions, especially if we are to challenge the current corporate hegemony.

So what does this all mean for workers and their oppositional movement to capitalism in our current biopolitical era? Many of the large-scale 'business ethics' programmes crafted by the neoliberal enterprise draw upon the idiom of work and employment as a key moment of justification. For example, when a large retailing business is forced to explain its irresponsible practices to governmental regulators, it also seeks to embolden the ideology of work at the heart of the neoliberal agenda. We are an ethical enterprise, so leave us unregulated and we will create jobs and invest in positive economic initiatives for the betterment of all. The ideology of work is buttressed by a broader complex that implicitly reflects the logic of production in a wide array of synaptic institutional relationships. By critically engaging with the significant shift in how the private corporation ideologically deploys the truth, we invariably challenge the axiomatic principle of work as well. And this is especially so when work becomes the ultimate social reference point, as it does in societies of control.

Corporate Ideology as Lie Telling

Capitalism has always relied upon ideological structures to legitimate its paradigmatic conduct, something we have understood since Marx. With the help of class-based representations (including the media, legislative bodies, education, etc.) a certain moral sensibility, or 'structure of feeling', as Williams (1977) insightfully called it, is developed, encouraging our ongoing participation within an exploitative social relationship. As Marx argued, while brute force and the whip of economic necessity do much of the labour of compulsion, a certain type of moral and ideational calibration between the oppressed and their oppressors is an integral supplement under conditions of inequality. In previous societies, religion and myth were important ideological enablers in this regard. But under capitalism, the cold cash nexus makes exploitation visible to all, and thus requires an intermediary discourse to absorb at least some of the backlash that it invariably inspires among the workforce. However, the neoliberal approach to ideology is not simply about brazen falsification, as it was in the past. For example, we noted in earlier chapters that the 'truth' of workers' fundamental status of abandonment is also used to wed them emotionally to their own exploitation. I believe a similar process is occurring with respect to the false truth telling we are witnessing in the current era of capitalist development.

In the twentieth century the corporation emerged as a formidable institution for formulating and proliferating pro-capitalist ideas among society. Whereas nineteenth-century capitalism was often justified by Darwinian tropes concerning the 'survival of the fittest', the twentieth-century firm used more democratically oriented themes of societal 'health' and 'prosperity for all' to garner legitimacy. CSR rose to prominence as a fully fledged capitalist discourse in the 1980s. It consists of ideas and practices that claim that profit maximization can be aligned with other societal values associated with workers well-being, the environment, consumer protection and social goods that the private firm had traditionally viewed as being detrimental to the bottom line.

A number of factors caused the rise of CSR to its conspicuous status in business today. First, as the democracy deficit in Western economies became blatant to all by the 1970s, corporations began to issue softer messages about businesses with soul, caring capitalism and enlightened self-interest.

Secondly, the populations of neoliberal societies began to fight back against the degradation of workers' rights, environmental destruction and widening income disparities. This prompted capitalist representations that sought both to have their cake (i.e. rampant free-market capitalism) and to eat it too (i.e. to been seen as the epitome of 'good citizens').

And thirdly, in terms of recruiting an increasingly weary, cynical and conscientious workforce, CSR was considered useful for ensuring that an otherwise disagreeable labour process could be successfully fulfilled by the best workers. A legitimation crisis has rocked the once robust ethical foundations of the corporation. This has been precipitated by social media, a more educated workforce and a generation raised watching films like Noam Chomsky's *Manufacturing Consent* and Michael Moore's *Capitalism: A Love Story*. All of a sudden, the raw material of exploitation (i.e. us) was not so keen to enter into an enterprise that, for example, manufactures the chemicals used to execute death-row prisoners in the United States. Indeed, as I have argued elsewhere (see Fleming, 2009), CSR is frequently used by firms to target their potential or existing workforces as much as outside parties (governmental regulators, NGOs, protest groups, etc.). Notwithstanding this, the masquerade of large corporations 'doing good' for society is scarcely credible and often comical, even to the most ardent believer in the virtues of capitalism. Hence CSR's almost universal dismissal as 'green-washing', 'propaganda' and 'bullshit'.

When Corporations Bullshit about Themselves

In the context of the global economic crisis, a strange contradiction has emerged in relation to the politics of CSR in neoliberal societies. This contradiction has two interesting dimensions. First, while companies are proclaiming the virtues of their ethicality on a scale never before seen (no large firm will omit a 'social accounting report' on its website), the 'business as usual' mentality now feels completely entrenched and immovable. The financial crisis might have opened up new ways of approaching the nature of economic activity, especially in terms of more progressive and imaginative alternative organizational forms. However, market fundamentalism has emerged from the 2008 meltdown in an almost unassailable hegemonic position, despite the growth of 'green' think tanks, sustainable economic practice reports, and the like. The second dimension of this contradiction at the heart of CSR pertains to the abiding legitimacy crisis of big business in much of the Western world. At the very time that the basic creditability of capitalism's commitment to social responsibility has reached a new ebb, we see the very discourse of 'ethics', 'shared value' and 'giving back' burgeon in scale, scope and ambition.

Unravelling these contradictions is important for understanding the current logic of capitalist ideology. It must be remembered that the notion of CSR first surfaced in a rather negative sense. The classic statement by Milton Friedman is now well known. He was deeply worried about managers of large publicly listed firms referring to 'business ethics'. For him, managers were neither qualified to deal with 'social issues' beyond their singular remit of shareholder return nor acting responsibility if they risked the fiduciary well-being of the organization by straying into ethical concerns. The only responsibility the manager legitimately has is maximizing profits for shareholders or the company's owners. As Friedman writes, 'the key point is that, in his capacity as corporate executive, the manager is an agent of the individuals who own the corporation or establish the eleemosynary institution, and his primary responsibility is to them' (Friedman, 1970: 33).

Less strict approaches within this strand of neoclassical economic thought have acknowledged the need for at least a rehearsed spiel about social, environmental and ethical troubles arising from unbridled profiteering. Friedman himself later admitted that maybe 'enlightened self-interest' might be the best stance, especially in a social climate of criticism and litigation. In other words, it is good for business to make a gesture towards responsible behaviour as long as this does not cut into the bottom line. A good deal of research in the US tradition (especially in the area of management strategy) has thoroughly explored this sentiment. It attempts to demonstrate how and why CSR activities can either be cost-neutral or can even bolster the profit margin of firms, suggesting that even if the idea of ethicality is somewhat vague, we might find moments of overlap between 'doing good' and making money.

But it is quite clear that CSR has now emerged as a key ideological weapon of the neoliberal enterprise, in both practice (among the corporate and political elite) and scholarship. Whereas Friedman was adamant that there should be little confluence between the pursuit of profit on the one hand and 'social' issues on the other, recent discourse has been more optimistic about the possibility of this overlap. In the extreme case, the model of an ideal 'ethical company' rethinks the very nature of business and society, especially in times of crisis and decline. The sub-areas of 'stakeholder management' and 'corporate citizenship' are good examples. In their call for a wider definition of citizenship, Matten and Crane argue that corporations might faithfully fill the institutional and political void left as the neoliberal state withdrew from civil society. In other words, the corporation is not inherently against the interests of other parties, and indeed might be reformed to facilitate the protection of stakeholders conventionally thought to be outside of its otherwise narrow economic focus. In this sense, corporate citizenship

> is not simply about corporate social policies and programs that might (or might not) be adopted in the same vein as CSR. Rather, we argue that the effective functioning of [individual] liberal citizenship has been sufficiently affected by the corporate uptake of government functions to render corporate involvement in 'citizenship' a largely unavoidable occurrence. (Matten and Crane, 2005: 170)

In the post-2008 climate of cynicism and refusal, the topic of CSR has reached an interesting impasse. This is particularly indicative in the way otherwise conservative publications, such as the *Harvard Business Review* (*HBR*), now abound with suggestions about the best methods for achieving ethical business models. As one special issue of *HBR* put it, the objective is clear – to save capitalism. For example, take a very popular article by Porter and Kramer regarding their notion of 'creating shared value'. They suggest that social goods and the economic viability of shareholder capitalism do not have to contradict each other. The two objectives can be aligned within market economies if the right processes (and corporate cultures) are fostered:

> The purpose of the corporation must be redefined as creating shared value, not just profit per se. This will drive the next wave of innovation

and productivity growth in the global economy. It will also reshape capitalism and its relationship to society. Perhaps most important of all, learning how to create shared value is our best chance to legitimize business again. (Porter and Kramer, 2011: 5)

The idea is that we might have both global capitalism *and* sustainability, corporate control *and* direct democratic engagement, a consumer society *and* green solutions, etc. (see Elkington, 1994).

In an attempt to 'rethink capitalism' and rebuild its lost legitimacy among the general public, these business analysts suggest that corporations must now consider their wider social impact – not simply out of kindness, but as a tool to create value for all stakeholders. As they put it,

the solution lies in the principle of shared value, which involves creating economic value in a way that *also* creates value for society by addressing its needs and challenges. Businesses must reconnect company success with social progress. Shared value is not social responsibility, philanthropy, or even sustainability, but a new way to achieve economic success. It is not on the margin of what companies do but at the center. We believe that it can give rise to the next major transformation of business thinking. (Porter and Kramer, 2011: 4)

A noteworthy point regarding this sudden interest in CSR among once hardened corporate strategists pertains to wider post-crisis calls from the public, media and political parties for more regulation. All of this talk about ethics and responsibility among pro-business analysts might simply be a way of ideologically pre-empting the patently obvious need to regulate markets and corporate activity. It is analogous to CEOs framing corruption and 'rogue traders' as cultural issues rather than as regulative ones. If we recondition our internal norms and beliefs, the reasoning goes, then firms can be left alone and trusted to comply with legal protocols without 'interference' from external auditors and the like. In other words, CSR becomes an excuse for 'business as usual' and unfettered corporate profiteering.

Talking Trash Goes Global

As a number of commentators have noted, this 'win–win' scenario in much CSR ideology misses the structural nature of the capitalist economic imperative. The dire track record of firms rebuked for social, environmental and economic irresponsibility is certainly significant here. After years of 'talk' about the way capitalist economic rationality and ethical social outcomes might be married within the modern business enterprise (including the 'triple bottom line', 'stakeholder management' and 'corporate citizenship'), it is as if none of it really matters when it comes to the day-to-day behaviour of many large organizations. This is why business ethics and other sustainability claims are often dismissed as 'talking trash' (Bansal and Clelland, 2004) ... a wonderful American-inspired phrase.

It would be an endless task to recount the plethora of examples of large business firms and governmental oligarchs contradicting the ethical claims they say guide their economic activities. But despite the vast and seemingly ubiquitous CSR campaigns, the depressing reality speaks for itself. Perhaps the 2010 Gulf of Mexico oil spill galvanized the view that corporations still don't really care for anything beyond the motive of maximizing their profits and minimizing their costs. The institutional ethos of 'Fuck you!' capitalism really made itself known by way of this disaster. Moreover, the relentless revelations about accounting scandals (Libor and Forex, for example) as well as accusations of blatant illegality are now expected almost daily in the business press. One is tempted to assume that genuine CSR never existed when reading how petroleum multinationals are prospecting previously protected areas of the globe, such as the polar ice caps and Alaskan wildlife sanctuaries. Labour rights around the world continue to be eroded on an exponential level, with the global financial crisis lending licence to the pursuit of labour policies that would have made nineteenth-century robber barons blush (see Piketty, 2014). And the virtues of unbridled consumerism are still proclaimed unabated, even when the unsustainable nature of its credo is obvious to all.

In this context of corporate pillage and open exploitation, it is understandable why many observers argue that CSR in large business enterprises creates a false image of the organization and garners legitimacy for an otherwise myopic profit-maximization focus. Roberts captures the tenor of these criticisms, especially those pertaining to claims about 'ethics' and the 'triple bottom line' in industries that can never realistically walk the talk, including those that make money from tobacco products, petroleum and the overpriced medicines in the Global South:

My fear is that this talk of ethics is just that – talk; new forms of corporate self-presentation that have no reference to or influence on what is practiced in the name of the corporation, beyond those associated with good public relations. In this form, corporate social responsibility is cheap and easy; a sort of prosthesis, readily attached to the corporate body, that repairs its appearance but in no way changes its actual conduct. (Roberts, 2003: 88)

And Roberts's fears are shared by a growing number of analysts, including myself. The ideology of responsibility is wonderful in itself, but is so far removed from the structural principles of the multinational firm that it is difficult to view such calls without scepticism. It is simply in the DNA of capitalism to control and exploit in the name of profit; and this invariably contradicts the wider ethico-political values most people hold. Perhaps this explains why CSR activities in business firms are so quickly relegated to the public relations department, far away from the revenue streams where they might have made a real difference.

This logic becomes transparent when corporations or neoliberal governments are presented with meaningful opportunities to change the nature of global capitalism in order to avert what some argue will be a cataclysmic social and environmental disaster in the years to come. The grand failure of the Rio+20 Earth Summit exemplifies this recent history of missed opportunities. Here the ideological talk of CSR might have potentially been put into practice. But when it came to the crunch, too many vested interests were involved. The chance to authentically and genuinely do things differently was stridently resisted both by large corporations and by governmental officials. Greenpeace's international executive director, Kumi Naidoo, relayed the difficulty in contesting the business plans of neoliberal rationality at the summit. His frustration boils over in this interview: 'We didn't get the future we want in Rio, because we do not have the leaders we need. The leaders of the most powerful countries supported business as usual, shamefully putting private profit before people and the planet' (*The Guardian*, 2012).

The central criticism of CSR among radical analysts is that it presents a false and misleading portrayal of the business enterprise in question. For example, it is very difficult to accept the truthfulness of the claim that a petroleum company expending most of its investments on oil prospecting is *truly* committed to alternatives to fossil fuels or to sustainability. A critical deconstruction of CSR discourse results from a comparison between an organization's claims (falsity) and the discernible reality (truth). In contrasting the concrete veracity of business activity and the glossy brochures (sporting images of smiling workers and laughing children from some unknown Africa country), the latter are often revealed to be nothing but a pack of lies.

What Is False Truth Telling?

The above criticism of CSR has revealed the insincere and politically motivated nature of its adaption in many neoliberal organizations. This criticism uses a specific analytical approach, summoning evidence of the core business model pursued by a firm and then comparing the firm's CSR claims against the facts. This allows researchers to unmask some of the more outlandish and cynical claims disseminated by certain businesses and industries. Indeed, it reveals that the exploitative and myopic nature of capitalist economic hegemony appears not only to have survived years of CSR intact, but might even have *prospered* because of it.

However, neoliberal corporations are today doing something different. They are placing tactical truths at the heart of their CSR policies, especially in those industries that might be deemed controversial and contentious. In these cases, as I shall demonstrate, it is difficult simply to dismiss these self-representational processes as a mere 'smokescreen' or green-washing, because what is being professed is technically true. When isolated, these truths ought to undermine the company's overall legitimacy. But the operative word here is *isolated*. When these truths are placed within a broader discursive narrative, which primes the admissions in a certain manner, we see the appearance of false truth telling. Rather than signalling an admission of culpability within the neoliberal discourse of enterprise, a different type of ideological distortion takes place that both bolsters the dominance of the corporate prerogative (i.e., exploitation) and seriously undermines traditional methods of critique (i.e. contrasting enunciated falsehoods with the cold reality of the situation).

A further example might be useful. The large foodstuffs corporation Nestlé has stridently adopted the language of 'creating shared value', an idea first posited by Porter and Kramer (2011). Some have lauded the firm for its attempt to integrate workers and human rights issues into its profit-making strategies. In relation to its water business, for example, Nestlé states, 'Rational water management is an absolute priority for

Nestlé, because water is essential to every stage of our value chain' (Nestlé, 2014). No one would disagree with this given water's increasing scarcity, especially in the Global South. However, when Nestlé chairman Peter Brabeck elaborated on this 'creating shared value' theme, he was presented with an opportunity to tell the truth. In actual fact, Nestlé was fully in favour of privatizing water and denying it as a public good or right:

> Water is of course the most important raw material we have in the world. The question is whether we should privatize the normal water supply for the population. There are two different opinions on the matter. The one opinion which I think is extreme [is] … declaring water a public right. That means that as a human being you should have a right to water. That's an extreme solution [waves hands to his left]. And the other opinion is that water is a foodstuff like any other and should have a market value. Personally I think it is better to give foodstuffs a value so that we are all aware that it has its price (Brabeck, 2008).

Here we see Brabeck telling the truth concerning how the firm approaches water as a human rights issue. And in isolation we see the authentic motives driving its privatization initiatives; that is, to make as much money out of a resource that was once considered a common good (also see Urs Schnell's documentary *Bottled Life: Nestle's Business With Water*). However, ideological truth telling never occurs in isolation but always seeks to establish a positive resonance with a false backdrop – in this case, a campaign that celebrates the humanitarian and socially progressive nature of the business. A symbiosis of signs is thus developed between the incredible proclamations of a firm's CSR credentials and the confession of some accurate facts. The truth reinforces rather than contradicts the distorting ideology of its environmental and human-rights discourse. So, how does this function in a technical sense?

Using the Truth to Lie

Echoing how late capitalism operates in the format of an alienated spectacle rather than through direct participation (e.g. we 'watch' democracy on television rather than having any lived connection with it), Deleuze helps us understand the logic of these deceptive truths. In particular, he points to the strange 'delirium' of its ideological tenor:

[N]othing is secret, at least in principle and according to the code (that's why capitalism is 'democratic' and 'publicizes' itself, even in the juridical sense of the term). And yet nothing is *admissible* ... in contrast to other societies, the regime of capitalism is both public and inadmissible. (Deleuze, 2004: 263)

Not only is the constellation of late-capitalist power holders confident in its own position of supremacy, not needing to worry about unbelievable concealments – what we have called 'Fuck you!' capitalism – it is almost as if this open truth telling actually shores up its contradictory opposite, our non-democratic subordination.

By partially telling the truth about one's morally corrupt motives, the broader lie that the system is democratically admissible somehow becomes more credible. In this sense, tactical deployments of the truth allow the meta-lie to function more effectively. Freud once relayed an old joke that perfectly captures the psychological trickery such truthful lie-telling plays on us:

Two Jews met in a railway carriage at a station in Galicia. 'Where are you going?' asked one. 'To Cracow,' was the answer. 'What a liar you are!' broke out the other. 'If you say you're going to Cracow, you want me to believe you're going to Lemberg. But I know that in fact you're going to Cracow. So why are you lying to me?' (Freud, 1905/1960: 137–8)

As Abbas (2012) points out, Freud ended up deleting this joke from his classic essay *Jokes and their Relation to the Unconscious* because it irretrievably deconstructed the truth/falsity dichotomy that he considered unassailable. But there is another way of approaching how this false truth telling functions. All we need to do is broaden the structural horizon of falsity (i.e. its semantic background) rather than collapsing the distinction between truth and deceit entirely. For could we not also tell the same joke with respect to, say, a tobacco company's use of the truth to redeem its broader self-portrayal as an agent of good in society? Why do you tell me that you sell products that kill people, so that I would think you are committed to broader social goods, when in fact you simply sell products that kill people? Why do you lie to me?

We can see this strategy of truthful lying in so many domains today. Perhaps my favourite example is the TV illusionist Derren Brown when being interviewed by the staunch rationalist Richard Dawkins (who is forever debunking mysticism, spirituality, and so forth). Brown's popularity (and wealth) lies in his astounding and sometimes shocking feats of mindreading. He can look quietly at a complete stranger and within a few seconds reveal everything about them, every thought, even their most intimate secrets. It is understandable why his fans widely believe him 'mystically gifted', although he quietly maintains there is a rational explanation for all of his tricks. So when he is confronted by angry non-believer Dawkins, Brown almost overenthusiastically agrees with the notorious sceptic. There is nothing supernatural whatsoever about any of this. Of course, as a result, his fans do not feel betrayed, which is the point. They assume Brown must be sensibly concealing his powers and hence their belief in them becomes even more stubborn. Once again, the truth strengthens the wider lie.

It looks like the real ideological operation occurring here is not simply the reinforcement of a false symbolic backdrop, nor the truth itself, but the relationship this tactical truth has with the discursive context in play. We can note this relationship in Mooney's overview of some wonderful experiments. The researchers sought to understand how incorrect conservative beliefs can strangely be reinforced by the introduction of correcting 'facts'. For example, in one experiment by Nyhan and Reifler, researchers gave participants a published article by US President George W. Bush in which he claims that reducing taxes will increase federal revenues, clearly an untenable proposition:

> In some versions of the article, this *false claim* was then debunked by economic evidence: A correction appended to the end of the article stated that in fact, the Bush tax cuts 'were followed by an unprecedented three-year decline in nominal tax revenues, from $2 trillion in 2000 to $1.8 trillion in 2003.' The study found that conservatives who read the correction were *twice as likely* to believe Bush's claim was true as were conservatives who did not read the correction. (Mooney, 2014)

Another study, by Monica Prasad, focused on the false claim that Iraq had strong links to Al-Qaeda (which justified the coalition invasion). She conducted 'challenge interviews' with staunch Republican Party supporters. In the interviews, evidence debunking the alleged connection was presented, even including a factual statement by George W. Bush who later admitted he was wrong:

Despite these facts, only 1 out of 49 partisans changed his or her mind after the factual correction. Forty-one of the partisans 'deflected' the information in a variety of ways, and seven actually denied holding the belief in the first place (although they clearly had). (Mooney, 2014)

Here we see how a preconditioned (and patently false) symbolic universe somehow gains veracious sustenance and vigour from the insertion of rectifying factual information – facts that ought to have completely discredited that symbolic universe. The dominant and a priori irrational semantic structure is not refuted by the introduction of truth, but inoculated to criticism by its presence, subordinating the truth claim to a secondary and supplemental role within the ideological function.

The Semantic Structure of False Truth Telling

Foucault (2010) mentions false truth telling only in passing during his last set of lectures delivered at the Collège de France not long before his death. Frank speech – *parrhesia* – is very difficult to achieve inside powerful institutions. Because elites tend to surround themselves with flatterers and false sweet-talkers, not just anybody can utter the truth about those who govern. Frank speech is shocking to power and requires 'courage' because it is rare. But in a proximate democracy that encourages 'all' to speak, Foucault notes that a paradoxical silence emerges. Since anybody and everybody can speak their mind on any political subject, very little is said or heard. This contradiction at the heart of democracy has, of course, been a difficult conundrum for political philosophy for many years. For Foucault, however, it creates a space in which *bad parrhesia* can appear: '[T]ruth telling gives way to something which imitates it, to false truth-telling. And those who deliver this discourse of false truth-telling are precisely the flatterers' (Foucault, 2010: 182). For example, a neoliberal government may tell the truth about its founding of two homeless shelters. But this statement of fact detracts from its general condemnation of the poor and its overall reduction of funding for housing allowances and so on.

We can analyse this aspect of false truth telling at the semantic level. It involves a process that has three steps. In the first, the characteristic dichotomy between a truthful utterance and a lie can easily be divided into dual components and then compared and contrasted accordingly. This echoes the classic logic of critical theory as it seeks to distinguish the real situation (the truth) from the false representations issued by power.

It recognizes a discursive contradiction, with each side of the dualism only able to enjoy semantic felicity if it negates its counterpart: your corporation is either for this or not (see Figure 5.1).

Figure 5.1   Ideological false-truth telling: Step 1

In the second step, an *inoculation* process beings. The truth is uttered just as it is in the first step. This time, however, it is not in a position of competitive equality with the false claim. The zone of untruthfulness has been enlarged to constitute a self-contained discursive context and symbolic parameter, becoming a semantic universe that defines its own borders. The truth is now subordinate to this linguistic regime. Integral to this moment of inoculation is what we might call a negative coordinating conjunction, the word 'but' in particular. The contrastive conjunction bypasses the polarized discursive semantic relationship observed in step one. A firm might now be able to say: Yes, our business model is built upon the profits of water privatization, *but* we are also committed to the global humanitarian issues that may detrimentally affect future generations (see Figure 5.2).

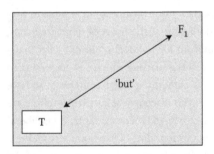

Figure 5.2   Ideological false-truth telling: Step 2

The third step allows false truth telling to gain full momentum. Here the negative coordinating conjunction morphs into a positive one: 'and'. This not only reinforces the false statement but exponentially replicates its universalization, extrapolating the inaccuracy by means of the truthful utterance. False truth telling in this step is dangerous and insidious because it completely dismantles the bipolarization that we typically expect in the critical exercise of demasking. The inoculation of an untruthful semantic universe relies upon a subtle polymerization so that two contradictory statements are able to coexist. Candidness can now be used to deceive others. For example, rather than denying the deadliness of their products, a large tobacco firm can say: 'Yes, our products obviously can kill *and* our firm is committed to tackling public health issues and increasing social awareness about cigarettes for those consumers who choose to smoke' (see Figure 5.3).

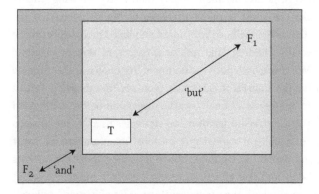

Figure 5.3   Ideological false-truth telling: Step 3

False Truth Telling in the Tobacco Industry

The example of Big Tobacco provides a good illustration of how false truth telling can operate in the ideological realm of late-capitalist politics. For this reason, I now want to examine an example of false truth telling in this extremely controversial industry. Cigarette smoking has shifted from being a very normal and legitimate activity to one that attracts a great deal of stigma, so much so that it can provoke rancour among even the most genial. As mentioned above, CSR in this industry is not only deployed to appease outside parties (the government, shareholders and lobby groups) but also its workers. Many large tobacco manufacturing firms have traditionally approached recruitment in a delicate manner given the nature of its products (Rosenblatt, 1994). More recently, firms have gone to great lengths to create an internal economy of legitimacy through philanthropy, equal opportunities, sponsoring the arts, investment in biodiversity, fair trade for primary growers, and other pro-society initiatives (all of which may be of value in and of themselves). But nevertheless, the elephant in the room is excruciatingly obvious to everyone.

The tobacco industry's approach to business ethics and CSR might be seen as a microcosm of neoliberalism's moral self-presentation more generally. The analogies are almost endless. Both attempt to defend the virtues of their nefarious business models on the basis of job creation, ignoring the deadly 'externalities' that those jobs are inextricably linked to. This might sound unfair to late-capitalist apologists who glorify work, but as I mentioned earlier, a recent study revealed that the accumulated stress of overwork is literally more deadly than heavy smoking (*Metro*, 2013). And like the latest business strategies of Big Tobacco, it is the Global South that bears the horrific brunt of neoliberal global governance policies, especially children (the unofficial target market of cigarette companies). Moreover, both posit the notion of free choice as the ultimate justification for the injuries it can cause (you are free to work, just as you are free to smoke). And finally, as the discussion below is intended to illustrate, the most recent legitimation strategies used by the tobacco industry share neoliberal capitalism's curious abandonment of overt propaganda and denial. As we noted above regarding Deleuze's analysis of the special delirium that afflicts societies of control, nothing is secret (inequality, class privilege, the cancer-causing nature of certain products) but nothing is admissible. The very platform of the open secret hides its own impossibility in full view.

Smoking Kills?

The tobacco industry has been mired in controversy for some time. The large multinational firms that dominate the market have recently developed sophisticated CSR policies to mitigate the negative reputation that surrounds the consumption of tobacco products. According to the World Health Organization's 2008 report, the worldwide 'tobacco epidemic' is responsible for one in ten adult deaths worldwide. It states that tobacco use

> already kills 5.4 million people a year from lung cancer, heart disease and other illnesses. Unchecked, that number will increase to more than 8 million a year by 2030. Tragically, with more than 80% of those deaths occurring in the developing world, the epidemic will strike hardest in countries whose rapidly growing economies offer their citizens the hope

of a better life. To the tobacco companies, these economies represent vast new marketplaces. (World Health Organization, 2008)

XYZ Tobacco (a pseudonym) is a large multinational firm based in London that in 2013 posted revenues of £15.26 billion. It was established in 1902 when a large US-based firm merged with a British company and is currently the third-largest (and most profitable) tobacco company in the world. Today it sells one-sixth of the world's cigarettes. However, the company has recently been dogged by controversy. For example, in 2007 its New Zealand branch won the Roger Award for worst company, with the judges stating it was a 'conspicuously bad corporate citizen'. In 2000, the Florida Circuit Court awarded ex-smokers US$145 billion in a class-action lawsuit involving XYZ Tobacco. Following appeals, the ruling was eventually overturned. In 2013, the Canadian province of Quebec included the firm in a US$27 billion class-action lawsuit for withholding information about the deadly nature of its products, which is still ongoing at the time of writing (CBC News, 2013). In 2007, the Nigerian federal government filed a US$42.4 billion lawsuit against XYZ Tobacco for selling deadly products to its citizens. And in 2007, the company was found to have spent 700,000 euros – four times more than it officially declared – for lobbying EU parliament officials to relax duties and public-space smoking bans and decriminalize noncombustible tobacco products, such as pouches placed on the users gum called 'snus' (Corporate Europe Observatory, 2009).

Like its large competitors, XYZ Tobacco places a great deal of emphasis on its CSR policy, seeking to present itself as a good citizen to wider society. There is an instrumental reason why, of course. As Friedman (2009) argues, there is much research that shows a strong correlation between anti-industry attitudes and reduced levels of smoking among adolescents, young adults and adults. However, it is important to note that XYZ Tobacco's CSR activities (and those of the industry more generally) have evolved over time. According to Breed (2014), during the 1970s and 1980s, scientific evidence of carcinogens in cigarette products was either ignored, derided or disputed: 'Scientists have not proven that cigarette smoke or any of the thousands of its constituents as found in cigarette smoke cause human disease' (Tobacco Institute, 1979, quoted in Breed, 2014). Around this time too, large tobacco firms began to sponsor their own research aiming to identify the specific personality traits or immune systems of smokers who contracted cancer as opposed to those who did not. Genes rather than smoking might be to blame.

Under increasing pressure from anti-smoking lobbyists and governmental health agencies, the tobacco industry changed tack. It began to celebrate the jobs and taxes it generated. A massive advertising campaign in the 1980s emphasized the freedom conferred upon smokers, disparaging the 'cancerphobic' hysteria promulgated by anti-smoking campaigners. In the 1990s, large tobacco companies cast themselves as crusaders for smokers' rights, even comparing the discrimination against their customers with racial segregation (Breed, 2014). Lobbying governmental legislators to limit regulations imposed on advertising was framed in this manner too, as an impingement on human rights and freedoms.

By the late 1990s many firms in the tobacco industry began to use CSR as a legitimation strategy. There is a double discursive strategy functioning here. The initial wave of CSR policies focused on philanthropy, charity, community sponsorship and pressing causes related to biodiversity and workers' health and safety. During this period, the negative health effects of smoking were still ignored. By the mid 2000s smoking in public spaces had been banned in much of Europe and the United States and cigarette advertising massively curtailed. So the second wave of CSR policies had no choice but to focus on the health question as well. Not only did CSR reports speak about anti-corruption measures, fairer contracts with tobacco growers and so forth, the industry also began to acknowledge the harmful outcomes of tobacco use. However, the customer's freedom to choose was still central to its framing discourse.

Truth as the Best Method of Deception

The above historical description is important for making sense of XYZ Tobacco's CSR strategy today, since its current approach would have looked truly alien to industry leaders perhaps as recently as ten years ago. For example, its home webpage surprisingly *tells the truth* about the deadly nature of its products. Building on our earlier argument, we see the dismantlement of the bi-polarized semantic field and the introduction of both negative and eventually positive coordinating conjunctions ('but' and 'and'). The intended inoculative effects of such truth telling can be observed in the company's latest business ethics campaign, which is simply titled 'Harm Reduction': 'It's simple – we want to reduce the public health impact of our products'. The narrative continues:

We know tobacco products pose real and serious health risks and the only way to avoid these risks is to not use them. But many adults choose to smoke, so our top priority continues to be working towards reducing these risks and making available a range of less risky tobacco and nicotine-based alternatives.

Such admissions are laudable and perhaps inevitable given the overwhelming evidence about the direct causal link between smoking and various life-threatening diseases. So why might we consider this to be false truth telling? Because these accurate depictions of XYZ Tobacco's products seek to enforce the false perception that the firm (and industry) is a champion of social progressiveness; it thus inoculates itself against criticism, especially from dying and litigious ex-consumers. The firm's truthfulness, I argue, functions to conceal a broader agenda that aims to expand the consumption of cigarettes. Firstly, the seemingly open admission about the health risks of cigarettes is firmly anchored to the false notion of free choice: 'Despite the well-known health risks and pressure to quit, millions of adults choose to smoke ... we believe that offering adult smokers the freedom to choose is key to [the 'Harm Reduction' campaign's] success.'

However, nowhere is it mentioned that nicotine is extremely addictive, which undermines the 'free choice' argument considerably. As Hirschhorn notes, the word addiction has long been avoided like the plague by the tobacco industry because it destroys the 'free choice' rationale. But 'since most smokers begin their addiction in their teenage years, few adults even have the luxury of choice' (Hirschhorn, 2008: 18). Therefore, this facet of XYZ Tobacco's CSR policy contains a misleading subtext which strongly implies that individual life decisions are to blame rather than a drug arguably more addictive than heroin. In 2008, XYZ presented its views on nicotine and addiction:

Many people in the public health community suggest that people only smoke because they are 'addicted' to nicotine ... the pharmacological effect of nicotine – a mild stimulant effect not unlike that of caffeine and a relaxing effect – is an important part of the smoking experience ... However, there seems to be more to smoking than just nicotine. Smoking embodies a considerable amount of ritual involving many of the senses ... especially in social settings, smoking involves a 'sharing experience' with other smokers. (Quoted in Hirschhorn, 2008: 24)

In other words, the global smoking epidemic is not to be blamed on nicotine – the highly addictive and thus unacceptable component of a deadly product – but is more about consumer preference, social habits and rituals that can in no way be the responsibility of XYZ Tobacco. The company's truth telling concerning the deadly effects of its products actually places the responsibility for contracting cancer squarely on the smoker. The tobacco industry uses truth in this manner for an important reason. It is the only avenue left to counter the enormous lawsuits increasingly coming its way, such as the Quebec case. Denial and lying does not work so well in this context. Following false truth telling ritual, XYZ representatives can now state that 'the claims are based on an unreal assumption that smokers were not aware of the dangers of smoking. A Gallup Poll in 1963 confirmed that 96% of Canadians were aware that smoking might be a cause of lung cancer' (Imperial Tobacco Canada, 2012).

Another facet of false truth telling can be noted in XYZ Tobacco's admission that its products can kill. Part of the 'Harm Reduction' campaign promotes the firm's commitment to investing in non-combustible alternatives to tobacco. Given the awful health effects of combustible tobacco use, they argue: 'It's time to look at alternatives. A new, more realistic and progressive route is needed. One where adult smokers looking to reduce the amount they smoke or quit, are given a choice of less risky products such as e-cigarettes' (XYZ Tobacco, 2014).

Again, this is a laudable objective. XYZ Tobacco state that they have invested £25 million over the last six years in responsible alternatives to cigarettes smoking (such as e-cigarettes), which they claim is driven by their interest in promoting consumer health. However, if we compare this figure to XYZ Tobacco's 2013 revenue of £15.26 billion, then it equates to £4.1 million a year invested in less risky alternatives or only 2.7 per cent of its annual revenue (a category that also probably includes the development of 'snus', which is currently illegal in most of Europe). The undeniably truthful claim about XYZ's investment in alternative products tactically deflects attention away from the firm's otherwise ferocious promotion of cigarette consumption, which by their own estimates will increase worldwide from 1 billion users in 2014 to 2.2 billion by 2050.

The ultimate aim of false truth telling in this killer industry is to use the partial admission of facts to promote the wider lie that lung cancer stems from consumer choice. This is vividly captured in a 1994 *New York Times* interview conducted by Roger Rosenblatt, whose subject was a self-congratulatory US trial lawyer hired by Philip Morris to defend a lawsuit brought against the company in the name of a Mrs Cipollone. Mrs Cipollone had begun smoking at a very early age. She tried to quit in the 1950s but found it impossible. She was encouraged, however, that her favourite brand had introduced amazing health innovations such as the 'pure white Miracle Tip'. Yes, she could smoke a pack a day without any worries. Over the years her smoker's cough grew worse and she changed brands many times. On 24 October 1984 Mrs Cipollone died of lung cancer. Following her death her angry representatives, led by her husband, took on Big Tobacco in her name. But in the end, all charges against Philip Morris were dropped. The free-choice argument had prevailed.

Back to the Roger Rosenblatt interview. When Rosenblatt asked the trial lawyer if he had trouble sleeping at night, he replied:

> I certainly didn't divide my job and my feelings in the Cipollone case. I didn't attempt to keep myself from feeling bad for Mrs Cipollone, who was a really neat lady. I met her a couple of times before she died. She was sort of spunky, you know. And Mr Cipollone was a very nice man. So I didn't try not to feel bad for Antonio Cipollone, because No. 1, I didn't think I could do it, and No. 2, what would that say about me? But I really did feel strongly that he was not entitled to get money because his wife chose to smoke. I mean, she was very clear about that. That she liked it. How it made her feel glamorous. That she enjoyed the taste of it. And never made a serious attempt to quit until she was told she had a problem. So when I met Mr Cipollone, when he told about how his wife died, it was a very moving thing. It was a terrible thing. But she chose to smoke. (Rosenblatt, 1994)

Neoliberalism Will Tell You the Truth ... But Not the Whole Truth

Unlike other societies in which secrecy, misinformation and deception are the guiding governing principles, late capitalism has developed a strange penchant for truth telling that is probably more blinding than gratuitous propaganda. This is why the 'facts' alone are not enough to refuse its organization of power. In many cases, the governing elite has digested and represented the facts that we think ought to automatically yield social justice outcomes. But things are not so simple. It is important to understand how these very admissions are fundamental to the maintenance of disempowerment in neoliberal societies. Secrecy no longer has monopoly over the medium of control as it once did. Regulated revelations paradoxically play an influential role in detaching the working multitude from the means of direct influence. Once again, Deleuze well understood this special 'delirium' peculiar to late capitalism. The organization of power is the only thing that matters today: 'Ideology has no importance here' (Deleuze, 2004: 263).

However, shall we press Deleuze a little on this observation? On one level he is correct. The current catastrophe we call 'society' has little reliance on rather over-contrived representations that might cloak the domination of the many by a minute and slightly retarded Etonian or Skull and Bones few. Power doesn't care what you think about it. What we earlier called '"Fuck you!" capitalism' denotes a profound hostility that is proudly displayed by corporations and the neoliberal state towards the 99.8 per cent. But Deleuze is incorrect when he argues that such openness has nothing to do with ideology. In fact, I would argue that power's use of the truth is deeply deceptive because it still wishes to validate a false totality by using the very weapon it has been afraid of for so long. In this sense, neoliberalism still has something to hide. It simply pulls off the sham in a different way.

The use of truth in this manner is quite different to the regimes of truth that Foucault (1977) once announced were decisive in modern Western society. This has nothing to do with philosophical relativism. Indeed, while Bruno Latour is sadly not much of a critic of capitalist realism, he was fairly accurate a few years back when he argued that relativism has been successfully co-opted by the pundits of neoliberalism to serve their own agenda (see Latour, 2004). Postmodernism as an era and intellectual movement is thankfully over. But so is modernity. Many social divisions and sources of authority exude a regressive pre-modern flavour that many of us find utterly stifling and archaic (even in the technologically advanced metropolises of late-capitalism … perhaps especially here). And it is very much a concrete reality since the environmental and human costs of global capitalism are positively feudal in their audacity. However, the method of concealment has changed, using factual information to support a complex myth concerning the virtues of this economic paradigm, including the centrality of work.

This raises the question of how practical critique might proceed, given that disclosure and demasking still remain central to the leftist political repertoire in Western societies and beyond. There are a number of paths forward that might be pursued here. Truth ought to be approached as a lineal totality; this in itself is the real falsity that these isolated corporate admissions seek to conceal. For we can only comprehend and register false truth telling with respect to the inter-linkages that it makes with the false universalization called 'caring capitalism'. Only then can we notice the lie hidden in the open. This is why straightforward visualization can no longer be relied upon by the democratic post-capitalist movement, as argued in Chapter 2. The totality can never be 'revealed' or 'unmasked' since the mask itself is an integral facet of its operational reality. We cannot say that BP is lying when it cuts the bullshit and truthfully defines what it means by Beyond Petroleum. And this is how the corporation mystifies its own terminal contradictions, using a certain figure of truth to conceal its own impossibility.

However, that partial and quarantined moment of truth telling still requires a hyper-secret code that cannot be revealed. Neoliberalism will tell you the truth, but not the whole truth. While we are unable to claim that BP is lying in this instance, we can actually demonstrate how this utterance of truth supports a broader false structure. And it intends to hide that function in order for false truth telling to operate. Power's revelation therefore is only fractional and semantically 'lonely', to evoke the spirit of J.L. Austin. The spectacle of corporate truth telling is always dependent upon a derisible contextual backdrop or structural order. I would say that this interconnection is its Achilles heel because it needs to be concealed in order to be successful as an ideological trope. Critical analysts must therefore paradoxically look *behind the truth* to detect its false settings. Only then can we definitively demonstrate how certain corporate admissions are grossly mendacious. In addition, this is why I am sympathetic to Freud's decision to excise the joke mentioned above from his famous essay. He thought that it would fatally blur the cool boundary between truth and falsehood. It grated with his modernist sensibilities. We too still ought to practise that wise caution, even as corporate capitalism asks us to respond to its confession. And isn't this an interesting turn of events? Now *we* appear to be the pastoral-like recipients of the most awful truths, which demand judgement. This time, however, the public confession is uttered by a ruthless economic machine that desires absolute control. So our communicative response ought to be a considered one.

6

Critique of Dialogical Reason

In a recent BBC interview with the controversial French novelist Michel Houellebecq, we observe the painful impossibly of truly talking about ourselves, especially within the confessional format so cherished by neoliberal society. The television presenter prefaces the interview by warning vulnerable viewers about the infamous challenges faced by anyone brave enough to talk with the elusive author: 'Michel Houellebecq has an interesting reputation amongst interviewers. In the past he has been known to fall asleep, get incapably drunk, make a pass at the interviewer and sometimes simply not turn up.' No wonder the conversation is stiff and awkward from the outset. 'Michel Houellebecq, welcome to Edinburgh.' Silence. More silence. And then another ten seconds of agonizing muteness. The flustered interviewer then makes a big mistake. It takes the form of a rather trite truth statement followed by a question: 'One of the things in your novels that I think fascinates the public, for good or for ill, is the relationship between Michel Houellebecq and the various narrators … I mean, how much of you is in the narrators?'

Of course, by now our suspicions are correct. All speech in this medium of exchange is somehow forced and inherently risky. The interviewer is probing for something that does not sit well with those who write in order to disappear. He is demanding *the subject* in all its impossible and fake positivity. The degree to which such an appearance remains impossible is only matched by its traitorous susceptibility to surveillance, a gaze that manufactures what it pretends to publicly present; namely, *you*. Houellebecq puffs on his cigarette, mutters to himself incomprehensibly, stares at the interviewer as if the question is too unreal. Following a very long minute or so it looks as if the conversation is already over. Only then does the author reply:

Perhaps the mistake is to think of me in actual fact [very long pause]. I mean by that, I have never been able to talk about my life actually. As soon as I talk about my life I start lying straight away. To begin with, I lie consciously and then very quickly I forget that I am lying.

The deceptive fallaciousness of speech when one is called upon to respond personally, to describe who one is and how one feels, what one stands for and the specificity of one's history, is an important political characteristic of the late-capitalist social system. One is forced to talk and represent in almost every situation, especially in the workplace where the 'truth of self' (warts and all) is painfully sought by human resource managers and other authority figures. Abandonment requires a present subject in order to function as an effective ideology. But as Houellebecq notes, an important conceit and dangerous discursive logic operates at the heart of autobiographical truth telling. We cannot but lie. When we open our mouths to utter descriptions about ourselves to the boss, a co-worker or government official dealing with an unemployment claim, someone else, an alien and foreign semiotic force, begins to speak in our place. An invasion occurs. We become bystanders to our own semantic exertions and efforts. We have all experienced this in job interviews; it is perhaps a post-industrial office version of invasion of the body snatchers. In a study by Weiss and Feldman (2006), it was discovered that 81 per cent of job candidates lie about themselves to their prospective employers. To be precise, candidates told an average of 2.19 lies every 15 minutes during the interview.

It might be tempting to explain this lying as merely the desire to impress, to tell those who have something we want (a job) what they want to hear: 'Oh yes, we are very committed, enthusiastic and honest ...' However, I suspect the compulsion to misrepresent is deeper than that. It may occur even when unnecessary. There is something about the unusual attention given to the supposed subject who speaks that activates another form of influence beyond our control. Who are these alien 'others' that abduct our internal lexicographies, taking over our bodies so that we become passive and tardy observers of our own discourses? I do not think it is indicative only of the existential void that forever displaces the aleatory subject, as a Lacanian reading of the utterance might suggest. Above and beyond this universal constitutive lack, something very historical is occurring here, specific to the particular time and space of neoliberal capitalism. Indeed, this type of power enlists the language faculties of what we have called the 'I, Job' function, transforming people into *speaking machines* of a certain sort; this is an integral facet of how post-industrial employment systems control us. All the talk that we are induced to perform in the overdetermined context of our jobs never really amounts to anything other than the reinforcement of sign itself, a *subjugation* to the impossible ideal of the 'I, Job' function. Deleuze and Guattari put it in no unclear terms:

> The elementary unit of language – the statement – is the order-word ... language is made not to be believed but to be obeyed, and to compel obedience. Language is not life; it gives life orders. Life does not speak; it listens and waits. Every order-word, even a father's to his son, carries a little death sentence – a Judgment, as Kafka put it. (Deleuze and Guattari, 1987: 76)

Even writing these very words causes a small death, of course, which brings to the surface the insurmountable impasse in Deleuze's thought. He attempts to short-circuit the sign's antinomy through style, but never quite succeeds.

But let's move on. Historically, the evolution of language has always been heavily influenced by record keeping or accounting: What do you owe us? This Sumerian inflection poisons our spoken word to this day, especially manifest when a moral deficit is implied: What are you lacking? It is thus only natural that we make things up and fake it when interrogated by the modern technocrat. Diversion becomes a weapon of the weak and slowly consumes us as a political force. Now we can see what really makes Houellebecq nervous about self-talk. For one is not speaking at all in any determinant sense. Instead we are being subjected to the speaking machine that imposes standards and criteria ultimately against the life we want. There is no subject of the statement. Its arrangement creates a faux-interiority that only seeks to drape these command words in the garb of free speech. A sort of broken and self-referential performativity is crucial for this purpose. These enunciating freedoms transform us into neoliberal ciphers via the *act* of dialogue as much as the content. It is the template that governs and its specific contents provide an alibi *post festum*. And this forced self-talk in our current era of anti-democracy and the all-pervasive 'I, Job' function has important ideological implications.

This confusion between form and content is crucial for valorizing the fascist inside us, maintaining the facade of participation (i.e. input and consultation) amidst an institutional setting that has long forgotten who we are. Indeed, the half-baked encouragement to represent and engage in dialogue, however critical that speech may be towards your captors, is part of the open madness that is capitalism today. Unlike other political systems in which heartfelt opinions are prohibited on pain of symbolic (or actual) death, neoliberal capitalism thrives on the word and a social garbage analogy: empty out your content and leave the container as a reminder of your tagged status. A closer inspection reveals, however, that there is still a dim message underlying this practical impotence. Speaking = nothing. Actually, *more* than nothing because proletarianized talk somehow gives power a weird excuse for its own embarrassing existence. What we are theorizing here has little to do with personal surveillance and the panopticon-like structures of confessional interrogation (although that is still a substantial part of the institutional landscape). We know from Foucault that technologies of the self screw us by getting to know us, endeavouring to elucidate who we really are whilst actually politically profiling us for purposes that are contrary to our interests. But this attention should not inspire any misguided narcissistic pretences – that we are questioned because there is something special about us and our voices are important. The type of regulation we face today has little genuine interest in us. Biopower has given up on us in this respect; this makes it much more dangerous.

But there's another catch. And this one will hurt. The enforcement of universal exchange value – your 'soul' and capitalist profit combined to form a backstabbing social monster that is the 'other' inside us – requires a modicum of linguistic presence to persist, for reasons that are both ideological ('You are free to speak your mind') and pragmatic ('Public opinion is in favour of the next iWhatever ... thankyou for your feedback'). This is why speaking to power has become so problematic today. A symbolic human-trap has emerged in this anti-person environment in which our speech is never *to* power (which implies an external vantage point), but always already *with* it. The sender1–recipient1–sender2 cycle with its gaps and interpretative spaces has irrevocably closed now, so we are no longer ever at home as we speak to the force that simply desires our recognition. This is also why many of us feel that we have become uninvited guests in our own personhood homes. The feeling of being out of place and lost behind enemy lines is usually the first response we have when solicited by a manager to present our authentic views.

When expression becomes an undue influence that has no outside and can't even be bothered entertaining the idea that the world might be otherwise, the putative 'free-speaking' citizen starts to serve a certain function. This function is to clearly signal to a captured social audience that capitalism and life are now one. There is no going back. This *is* the world. A precociously false ontology is introduced. Our ability to speechify in an openly acknowledged oppressive context somehow substantiates the notion that social life would be impossible without the order words that bully us. Questioning the presence of authority is like questioning the existence of the weather. This is why so many of us suspect that our talk is strangely useful to the neoliberal gaze, even as we are denouncing it and endeavouring to hold it to account. All is public yet nothing is admissible. And nothing is admissible *because* all is compulsively dialogical. Radical philosophical praxis has typically deployed two tactics in the realm of dialogical reason to dethrone power, both of which have struggled to remain relevant today when everything is permissible yet inadmissible: dialectical critique on the one hand and irony on the other. Let's examine dialectical reason first. It seeks to discern a space of synthetic excess born of the contradictions between the capitalist accumulation process – its forces of production (e.g. the social intellect, knowledge sharing, freeware, and so forth) and the relations of production (e.g. private property, patent laws, copyright, the HRM office, the neoliberal state, etc.). The overflowing social surplus that results is divined by way of analytically extending those contradictions towards capitalism's own structural inabilities. That is to say, those irreconcilable qualities that cannot be subsumed within the universal process and thus explode into a clearing in order to exist for their own sake. A distant and emancipatory 'other' emerges from capitalism's own contradictory dynamics; we might call this democratic communism.

However, there are some problems with this mode of radical praxis today. As we noted in Chapter 5 concerning false truth telling, self-criticism and open contradiction have recently become visible broadcast points in pro-corporate ideology. While mendaciously claiming to be open, the effect is to widen the distance between power and its dialectical 'other' (i.e. freedom) that we seek to render into a positive force. Societies of control engage in rituals of contrition in order to reinforce a permanent yet reiterative postponement of progressive political recompense, partially short-circuiting dialectical reason in the process. For example, a scandal concerning executive bonuses does little to rectify this patent affront to the ordinary working citizen who is struggling on the minimum wage. In fact, the revelations are vital for the continuation of the status quo since they lead us to believe that somewhere someone must be doing something about it. But they seldom are. UK readers might also think of the widespread furore caused by the Conservative government when it negligently undervalued the publicly owned Royal Mail before placing it in private hands; or the infamous 'horse meat' scandal, which led to nothing. It seemed that the immense verbal outrage functioned as a license to preclude criminal culpability. This warping of dialectical reason also connects with the speaking machine in increasingly strange and counterintuitive ways.

For example, a senior manager in the financial industry told me about the exercises he organizes with employees of a large bank that has been embroiled in scandal. For obvious reasons, one would expect the bank's internal culture to favour ignorance, silence and distortion over critical truth telling. Instead, the bank decided to embrace the unsympathetic and dark truth about itself. In the exercise, ten of the bank's employees are led into an 'immersion room', which is freezing, pitch-black and far too small. Following a few minutes of disorientation, six video screens start to play hard-core 'anti-advertisements' that completely destroy the bank's credibility, highlighting its connections with organized crime, tyrannical governments and endemic corruption. No holds are barred. Afterwards, the employees are asked to answer a simple question: Why did we show you that? Two dimensions of entrapping bio-talk are thus unleashed. Firstly, criticality itself becomes part of the backdrop of capitalist power relations, internalizing a potential moment of dialectical excess for its own regressive needs. Secondly, and perhaps more importantly, in the process of coercive enunciation the speaking machine actually intends to appropriate and snuff out the existential impact of the awful truth. Of course, employees will invariably fumble over their own lies when answering this already answered question, still recoiling from the shocking confession made by their own employer (and perhaps an element of capitalist perversity is involved here too). Once again critical admission mutates into a pro-capitalist stance and begins to serve an 'I, Job' function that is experienced as more inescapable than before. By facing the appalling truth these individuals paradoxically become more astute and willing investment bankers.

Again we witness a rather schizophrenic and demented feature of capitalist realism today. Because its revelatory contradictions are no longer hidden but expressed, the grit that dialectical analysis relies upon to force the synthesis is circumvented or even dissolved. This post-dialectical expression of power immunizes both patent falsehoods and plain-speaking corporate truthfulness from true radical criticism. Contrasting both types of deceptive speech with the 'facts', as dialectical criticism recommends, always risks feeding the very machine one seeks to subvert. These rituals of truth and reconciliation don't diminish the power that false statements currently hold over our realities. Indeed, domination occurs precisely through the statement format (the empty performative that only communicates its own subordination) rather than by appealing to some counter-argument or excuse, thus scrambling the co-ordinates of traditional critical reason, for obvious reasons. What is being hidden is actually in plain view, as Deleuze and Guattari point out:

> We see this in police or government announcements which often have little plausibility or truthfulness, but say very clearly what should be observed and retained. The indifference to any kind of credibility exhibited by these announcements often verges on provocation. This is proof that the issue lies elsewhere. Let people say ... this is all that language demands. (Deleuze and Guattari, 1987: 76)

We can observe this disempowering visibility all around us. The depravities of neoliberal society are constantly being paraded before us (by itself as much as by its critics), and we are relentlessly encouraged to respond. Whether we do or not, nothing ever happens. One begins to suspect that nothing ever happens *because* of the way these truths are used and our placement in relation to them, as we noted in the last chapter. This is evident when the presence of the sign intends to 'prompt' a certain speech-perception among the target audience: we know what is objectively going on, but that knowledge automatically renders itself inadmissible and can no longer be an open political concern to discuss meaningfully. This is why a hesitant resignation pervades political language today. The very invitation to engage verbally with power separates us from the organs of direct influence, turning the political event into a distant spectacle whose truths can be observed but never pragmatically questioned:

> Just look at what they call scandals today: the newspapers talk about them incessantly, everyone pretends either to defend themselves or go on the attack; but the search for anything illegal comes up empty-handed, given the nature of the regime of capital. Everything is legal ... they keep on talking about 'ideology'. Ideology has no importance here. What matters is the organization of power. (Deleuze, 2004: 263)

But we have already proved that this is actually a purely ideological process. Potentially damaging insights into the mechanics of power are now an important aspect of the 'slide show' that it presents to an otherwise disempowered audience, who paradoxically feel even more controlled by actually knowing these truths and being asked to reply within a setting that inexorably supplies its own affirmative answer, no matter what one says. A mannerist gesture that results in a cardboard cut-out version of 'critique' is now a basic aspect of corporate self-representation. It operates as an inoculation against more serious and systematic interventions that would otherwise undermine financial tyranny. For example, mining firms now honestly speak about some of the more controversial implications of their business activities. If they did not, then they would be open to a more ferocious attack, given the hypocrisy that accompanies their proclamations about environmental and social sustainability. But a small dose of radical truth – a prearranged opening for limited dialogue – provides a platform for feigned remorse and that most important instrument of neoliberal reproduction: remedial postponement. A large gold-mining company implicated in gross human rights violations in Papua New Guinea and Tanzania is thus able to state on its website:

> Businesses that strive to act responsibly can create and contribute to negative human rights impacts, and we are not immune from that regrettable reality. To mitigate this risk, we will continue to roll-out and implement our global human rights policy and human rights compliance program.

A space of dialogue between capital and its 'stakeholders', which ostensibly appears to be a progressive move, is actually the opposite. Consideration of how criticism can be appropriated by the institutional constellation under critique is not new, of course. And this is what troubled Adorno (2005: 66) as he pushed dialectical thought to its limits and unwittingly discovered pure, unadulterated power: 'The last grandly-conceived theorem of bourgeois self-criticism has become a means of making bourgeois self-alienation, in its final phase, absolute, and of rendering ineffectual the lingering awareness of the ancient wound, in which lies hope of a better future.' For Adorno, the antithesis of dialectical reason rendered speaking to power almost impossible from an emancipatory perspective. In his search for resolution, or at least a space of alterity to capitalist influence, he found only more domination, reverberating infinitely in all directions.

Hence his pessimistic advice: 'For the intellectual, inviolable isolation is now the only way of showing some measure of solidarity. All collaboration, all the human worth of social mixing and participation, merely masks the tacit acceptance of inhumanity' (Adorno, 2005: 26).

Let us now turn to irony. This method of engagement has held some promise for debunking domination in the late-capitalist social order. Indeed, it has long been recognized that power does not do irony very well. It demands that its edicts be taken seriously, on the formal level at least, even if it knows that no one ever does so, including those who wield the most power. If the capitalist totality is experienced as omnipresent, then revealing its double structure of 'fake faking' through ironic distancing may allow some respite, providing a place of escape which yet lies within the zone of subjugation. In Miller's beautiful investigation of how to 'fake it', he describes the critical freedom that irony affords:

> Those who adopt it seem to feel that irony gives them control over feeling foolish about playing the various roles that they are self-conscious about playing. It is a style of making one's less than full immersion in various roles the substance, as well as the style, of one's character. (Miller, 2003: 115)

If we push this reasoning further in a socio-political context, we might suggest that ironic language – including satire and exaggeration – aims to disrupt the seriousness with which power takes itself and which it demands from it audience. However, has not the neoliberal enterprise too discovered irony and put it to work? Many studies of corporate culture, for example, reveal that an ironic disposition and the pseudo-subjective distance it provides is part and parcel of the domination process. Do not take your subordination too seriously – we don't – but act as if you do and the 'joke' is on all of us!

I discovered the ironic corporation late one Friday night in my East London neighbourhood. After getting horribly drunk with some Swedish friends and wandering around aimlessly in the crowded streets, we were invited by a young man and woman to 'join the party and free drinks'. We went along to the party and were given a bottle of beer and ushered to a table with paints and placards. 'There is a protest tomorrow, help us tell them what we think of the government.' Other inebriated guests were painting peace signs and other slogans. I then asked who was sponsoring the party. 'Our firm is!' It turned out this was a marketing exercise for a large mobile phone company and our hosts were its employees. So, feeling devilish, I prepared a placard that read 'MOBILE PHONES KILL'. 'Wonderful!' said our host, 'the boss will absolutely adore that, we will use it tomorrow!' So much for the transformative potential of irony. I left the contrived festivity in a rather sober mood.

Rethinking Dialogical Politics at Work

What makes the contemporary politics of the 'ironic corporation' so fascinating is power's ability to absorb and pre-emptively utilize multiple points of reference in a non-dialectical manner, including speech acts that appear to be against capitalism itself. Its centre is centre-less and expansive, functioning through a network of oblique vectors, even though we now know that this sense of universality is actually an ideological distortion designed to make collective departure seem impossible. Regardless of this, the distortion is real. A society of control yields to an isotopic space, one that 'is constituted not by the abolition of circular segmentarity by a concentricity of distinct circles, or the organization of a resonance among centres' (Deleuze and Guattari, 1987: 211). Discerning an optical blind spot is not enough. Its supplementary character must also be occupied and subverted. Outlining the limits of our relentless co-optation (or a threshold that corporate ideology cannot easily integrate into its own parlance without making its own existence untenable) is therefore central for the anti-work project today. Of course, when domination channels refusal through its own prism, it too changes to a certain degree, something we have learnt from studying colonialism. The key difference between this and cynical neoliberal truth telling, however, is that the latter's apparent totality is only propagated rather than modified as a consequence. While, for example, 'corporate social responsibility' programs may imbue the firm with a facet of humanity, they add only a shallow genuflection to an otherwise unaltered universality that catapults us deeper into capitalist realism. How might we speak in power's presence without simply withdrawing, as Adorno sadly recommends, and without supplying it with the attentional energies that it so craves from us?

I Want This Too Much!

Managerialism in the contemporary neoliberal enterprise necessitates clamorous public speech with denied or barred admission. Our participation in the discourse of power makes us not only spectators in a theatre of domination but also audiences *to ourselves*. This is the paralysing abrogation that the speaking machine institutes. The travesty of power is now part of the corporate public script, cloaking the bases of regulation in ever more inscrutable ways. This is why some suggest that the traditional approach to opposition typically championed by the workers' movement – speaking the truth to power – is less effective today, especially as it pertains to traditional ideology critique: 'This is not how things really are.' The critical interlocutor submits that all is not what it seems, and furthermore, this 'what it seems' is a generative distortion aiming to obfuscate the outlandish truth. However, drawing attention to contradiction and falsehood – 'You say we are free at work, but look here, this is patently untrue' – is increasingly rendered ineffective in our neoliberal milieu. Why is this? Because, as Latour (2004) notes, hegemony has extensively appropriated the critique of meta-narratives so that now there is no longer one truth, only 'points of view' and opinion. This provides space for false truth telling to emerge. Ideology critique must therefore 'compete' in the capitalist marketplace of ideas along with the most ridiculous ones. This might look like pluralism, but it is the exact opposite. It conveys a pre-emptory structuring of the background master index so that the ideas of the ruling classes are the only ones that really win in the end.

By way of example one might think of the self-referential reasoning of former US president George W. Bush when he strangely confessed he felt very proud about the millions of street protesters opposing his policies. Why? Because he too stood for free speech and those were the very values he was defending when invading foreign countries!

What makes neoliberal pluralism (including 'communitarianism') so hazardous to progressive thought is that it implicitly relies upon its opposite: it symbolically twists emancipation into a mannerist byword for a society already lost to power. Its key word is 'yes' with an array of unremitting false guarantees. Yes, we are permitted to speak the truth, but only in a meta-context where our reflections do not matter or will be immediately deemed inadmissible through the sheer weight of the context. Power knows that we understand this logic very well, which is why it can nevertheless wryly recommend: 'But, nevertheless, still speak, speak as much as you like!' Making things doubly problematic is the way in which the very opportunity to speak is automatically deemed proof that speakers are free, by token of their own utterances. This is why the widespread celebration of 'tempered radicals' in US corporations ought to be viewed with scepticism. According to Meyerson (2001), the tempered radical quietly calls into question the inequalities that result from 'being different' and empowers the silent majority who are slowly changing their workplaces from within. In actual fact, they assist in reinforcing a fallacious and horrific dream of 'friendly capitalism' that embraces all standpoints. Žižek sheds light on what is happening here when he observes:

> We act as if we are free to choose, while silently not only accepting but even demanding that an invisible injunction (inscribed in our very commitment to 'free speech') tells us what to do and what to think. As Marx noted long ago, the secret is in the form itself. (Žižek, 2009: 134)

This is a nice point. The utterance of words designed to oppose arbitrary subjugation often takes place on an unquestioned stage of power – a capitalist supra-reality – that actively thrives on such words and gestures. Recalling the 'immersion room' exercise above, perhaps the same thing transpires in the postmodern 'organization' that demands we speak and display our true thoughts, be they happy or disgruntled ones. For instance, we might earnestly denounce a particularly nasty wave of organizational restructuring at the office. But this is treated as even more evidence of the wonderfully enlightened nature of the modern firm as the restructuring continues apace. The same goes for the ghastly 'consultation meetings' that follow an announcement of layoffs. Consultation merely means that a decision has been made regarding your fate and the firm can tick the right ethical and legal boxes claiming that you had your say before being fired.

Even Starbucks is now willing to listen to those who resist, declaring that open dialogue with dissenters (both in and outside the firm) is a key operative principle in their corporate culture. In his rather repulsive business book, *The Starbucks Experience: 5 Principles for Turning Ordinary into Extraordinary*, Michelli notes that Principle 4 of Starbucks' success is 'Embrace Resistance'. He quotes one executive as saying: 'This council brings in dissenting voices among our senior leadership and helps us look to areas of our business that may expect complex future challenges' (Michelli, 2007: 127). Open consultation can be politically invidious since even fearless speech may aid the endless deference of the real target, which remains irrefragable and patently uncontested.

Emancipatory dialogue within the neoliberal setting must be recalibrated to avoid the recuperative traps we have noted above. If one must speak with power at all, then caution, care and circumspection are required. The first recalibration might be labelled 'over-identification'; this has been explored a little in the post-work literature (see Fleming and Spicer, 2010). The idea here is relatively straightforward. Because much of the ideology in the biopolitical enterprise (e.g. self-managing teams, democracy, freedom, open speech, etc.) is not meant to be taken literally, it must invariably rely upon a subtextual negation that must not be fully articulated. The cynical enterprise must configure an inbuilt mental distance in this dialogical structure. For example, in the 'immersion room' exercise described above, employees are asked why they think the bank has shown them such devastating truths. Everybody clearly knows the serious answer: the boss is an idiot and finance capitalism is inherently corrupt and unsalvageable. But with the help of the abstract speaking machine, workers can distance themselves from this obvious truth and utter some moronic words like, 'Well, you have shown us these shocking things about the organization because we need to be honest about what has happened. Only then can we learn from our mistakes and serve society as an agent of good.' But what if the message being burnt into these employees was taken too seriously? Something like: 'After seeing these truths I can no longer have anything to do with the enterprise.'

The strategy of over-identification undermines this cynical distance and takes corporate claims *at face value* to reveal and subvert the negation that it hopes will automatically transpire ('These employees won't really tell us managers what they think'). Indeed, one of the wonderful weaknesses of what is called in the United States 'liberation management' (with its celebration of flat hierarchies, free speech, self-organization, etc.) is that if it was practised to the letter and fully realised it would result in a fundamental shift in the logic of capitalism: economic organizing would resemble an anarchistic collective serving wider needs rather than a capitalist excuse for humiliating work and manufactured scarcity. Moreover, this recalibrated type of speech act is often infused with an element of humour. Corporate managerialism cannot belabour itself and punish those who follow its proclamations without undermining its own axiomatic authority.

Dissenting Consent and its Incorrigible Mirth

If we must accept the order to speak to power, a second dialogical recalibration may be useful. I term it 'dissenting consent'. Again, like over-identification, it does not launch its criticism from any imagined dialectical vanishing point, but aims to use the partially reconfigured qualities of domination against itself, an immanent engagement with the capitalist overcoding process. Our forced visibility within the confines of the non-admissible can be used to fulminate against the supplementary impossibility that totalization draws upon to sustain its internal integrity. The peasant knowledge we mentioned in Chapter 2 allows us to remember the present and see the unseen extremism of our domination. But how does such 'dissenting consent' work in the context of dialogical exchange? The paradoxical 'visible intrigue' of cold war politics presents a myriad of examples of this cat and mouse game. The famous 'Kitchen Debate' might serve as a useful illustration. When, during the early 1960s, the Soviet leader Nikita Khrushchev was shown around a model American kitchen at a trade exhibition in Moscow by US vice-president Richard Nixon, an unexpected debate ensued before the world's media. Nixon knew full well that the press in the Soviet Union was highly censored. The debate was thus an opportunity to demonstrate the moral superiority of the United States over the demonic communist bloc. Khrushchev mocked Nixon, joking that when the Soviet Union overtook the USA in economic, political, military and social richness, all the Soviets would do is collectively smile and wave, 'Bye, bye … bye, bye'. An embarrassed Nixon, furtively turning to the giggling media, asked Khrushchev whether he intended to permit the Soviet people to see this excellent kitchen and their leader's rather rude treatment of his host. Khrushchev insouciantly replied, 'Of course'. Nixon could now sense victory. With a wry smile, he quipped, 'and the US shall also hear your words'. Khrushchev's mood grew hesitant: 'Oh … erm … do you mean translated into English?' he nervously queried, clearly worried about the prospect of having his intemperate views broadcast around the world in English. 'Yes,' answered Nixon with a confident and resounding smile. Suddenly, Khrushchev beamed with glee, 'Wonderful! The US people will finally hear the truth!'

Of course, Nixon had been completely outmanoeuvred – not by Khrushchev, but by himself. This engagement with power is interesting because it second-guesses what the seemingly more powerful party feels to be the weaknesses of the subordinate party. And then it leverages these false strengths of the superordinate position (that the Soviets will censor and the United States will not). The ideological coordinates of regulatory speech are then imperceptibly reordered, presenting a reference point (a debate about the free media, in this case) that might potentially serve the stronger actor. And then comes the death blow. The semantic structure unwittingly supplied by the dominant party is swiftly reversed with devastating impact. Only with free speech will the American public learn about the superior greatness of the Soviet people. In effect, the powerful party has pulled the rug from under its own feet.

Now let us return to the equally open intrigue of the neoliberal enterprise and the societies of control. How might this ideological technique be deployed in a corporate setting? A good illustration pertains to the way communication guerrilla groups challenged a number of European airlines involved in deporting 'illegal immigrants'. Autonome a.f.r.i.k.a. gruppe (2002) report on the symbolic sabotage of Lufthansa by the German anti-racist collective Kein Mensch ist illegal. They understood that a radical critique would need to bypass the cynical neoliberal distancing norms discussed above. Kein Mensch ist illegal therefore prepared overly positive leaflets using the company's easily recognizable brand. The leaflets explained to customers that the company was very concerned about customer comfort and safety, but simply could not restrain its prisoners with handcuffs and gags to protect its loyal frequent flyers. The leaflets were in fact a glowing humanitarian portrayal of the company, but framed in a manner that immediately revealed the truthful underside about the company's complicity with a racist state. Importantly, the message of refusal *consents* to the company's own caring image and thus has more critical impact than simple chastisement: 'The company found itself in a bind: it couldn't deny that it was carrying out the deportations, and that this inconvenienced customers, but it was offering them no compensation' (autonome a.f.r.k.a groupe, 2002: 167–168). The airline could not disagree with the leaflet unless it disagreed with itself. Paradoxically, it had to buy into the criticism (and undermine itself) in order to uphold a favourable presentation of itself.

The much publicized antics of the Yes Men employ a similar strategy of dissidence. Their strategy is clear: infiltrate a disliked institutional form, impersonate its blithe stereotypical verbiage, and then push that corporate-speak to its logical extreme. This openly reveals the nefarious reality underlying the glossy-brochure-like depictions of the neoliberal business enterprise. Investment bankers, right-wing politicians and management consultants have all been on the receiving end of this kind of sabotage. What makes such 'culture jamming' effective is the way it uncovers the rotten core of, say, an arms-trading firm, but in a manner that makes it difficult for those arms traders to dispel. This is because the manoeuvre occupies the firm's own declarations about itself. This in turn incites a potentially uncontainable and irremediable *self-criticism*, which is far more difficult to dismiss than external criticism. The latter can simply be ignored or explained away with phoney figures whereas the former gets far too close for that to happen.

As with over-identification, a crucial aspect of this kind of dialogue with power involves humour and mirth. While there isn't scope to deal with humour in an extensive manner here, suffice it to say that we must be cautious about the significance we give it in relation to refusing neoliberal regulation. Some see in humour the ultimate weapon of defiance, deeming it a crucial weapon for the oppressed. Laughing somehow rescues us from the cold unfeeling technocrat within and can even upset the foundations of oppressive political regimes. I remain ambivalent on this count. In the end, there is nothing remotely funny about the open prison of work today and the recriminating social memes proliferated by an extreme version of neoliberal capitalism. Perhaps Adorno (2005) issues the most pertinent reservation on this topic. For him, any kind of comedy in the context of a horrific totality only serves as a moment of wilful blindness, or worse, a symbolic resonance with the present. Jokingly debunking power nevertheless evokes a secret economy of equivalence, a mutual understanding shared with power. According to Adorno, this mutualism must be rejected by the critic. If there can be no poetry after Auschwitz, then there certainly cannot be laughter. Its countenance of light-heartedness inadvertently hardens the iron in our souls. Even innocent laughing in the street, as Brecht avers, commits a grievous miscalculation since it implies silence about so many travesties. No doubt Adorno had Brecht's haunting 1939 poem 'To Those Who Come after Us' in mind when sketching his reflections on a damaged life:

> Truly I live in dark times!
> The guileless word is folly. A smooth forehead
> Suggests sensitivity. The man who laughs
> Has simply not yet had
> The terrible news. (Brecht, 2007: 70)

While this austere stance is valuable for checking careless laughter, it does come across as slightly puritanical. For this reason I think we can reconstruct a worker's diction of humour that could politicize the present and avoid the potential pitfalls outlined by Adorno. Here it is useful to note the Communards of the Paris Commune, the events of '68, and present-day political satire that truly tests the norms of capitalist acceptability (especially street-sign sabotage). Two modes of laugher can be considered in this regard. The first might be termed *having fun* while contesting power, in which a carnivalesque attitude serves to motivate the otherwise serious business of political praxis. Here we might do well to reread Ross's (1989) excellent essay on the Paris Commune and its vertiginous decodification in the drunken poetry of Rimbaud. She explores the lexiconic sympathies between the Communards' reinvention of everyday life and the poet's literary derangement of the senses. Indeed, is it possible that he was fighting on the barricades? What a wonderful thought! As the child-poet announces to his de-worked comrades in 'Blankets of Blood': 'It's our turn! Romantic friends: our fun begins./O waves of fire, we'll never work again!' The deactivation of bourgeois seriousness and its tyranny of surplus scarcity was a mostly playful event. But not because it was cruel (Rimbaud did have a reputation after all, as Verlaine learnt well enough) but because it released workers from their subjective straitjackets, from the imprisoning idiom of the *métier*. And in a society overcome by a negative ideology of work, the *métier* includes everyone. Rimbaud understood what a false totality could imply, as his lyrical scorn attests ('Bosses and workers, all of them peasants, and common'). Ross (1989) suggests that the Paris Commune pursued an anti-work modulation via humorous pleasure; one that was wilfully oblivious to the work ethic as defined by fathers, teachers, priests – and today, perhaps the Gates Corporation. But this does not mean that things didn't get done or children went hungry, as if the Communards were blissfully high on some cult-like utopian dream. Participative mutual aid, co-operation and democratic multitasking abound. For it was only after a long propaganda campaign that this type of sociality came to be termed 'idleness'. The Commune turned the tables by revealing the truth. Rationalized exploitation was closer to useless idleness than to collective self-management. Indeed, 'by a striking paradox, laziness remained outside the work order, but moved fast, too fast' (Ross, 1989: 53).

Antonio Negri (2009) introduces a second way of approaching laugher in the notes he penned in an Italian jail cell. His words are extraordinary, given that political prisoners are not known for their promotion of frivolity. However, he does not go quite that far. In the context of totalized pain, Negri suggests, we might turn inward to affirm a joyous ethic, constituting a form of life that exudes the uncontainable expansiveness of living labour. This is a communist ethic. Laughter might provide a code that takes the subordinated life beyond itself, for it cannot be entirely reduced to a calculus of economic obedience. I believe this kind of humour is very amenable to the anti-work movement. Nevertheless, it is still always susceptible to co-optation, repackaging, and so forth. It must therefore be enunciated with circumspection and pointed calculation. Negri writes:

> [I]n a world that no longer knows anything of measure but only of the immense [*smisurati*], the principal of criticism consists in 'laughter'. 'Laughter', 'irony' and 'sarcasm' have, in this world of immense contrasts, the same function that doubt had in the limited world … It is a picaresque laughter that accompanies paradox or constructs it and intersperses the discussion with its critical effects. The demolition of the function of retribution in the relationship of morality and theology is carried out in the name of sarcasm. (Negri, 2009: 60)

In principal, therefore, we certainly ought to view humour as politically suspect, especially the humiliating laughter of the powerful. But sarcasm can conjugate the internal failure that is definitive of all forms of domination and wrest from it points of departure that avoids the restitution of an already bad position. The impossible subject (i.e. the imprisoned) that we have become is no longer an open secret, the elephant in the room that we must ignore. This is why our sarcastic remark reveals a secret public stepping forth to partially resolve its own impossibility. Power cannot accept the forthrightness that this remark signifies, for it is also a path to redemption and power's absence within that symbolic structure. So if one is to laugh at power, it must be done tactically. Was not Khrushchev's barbed sarcasm in the context of Nixon's economy of retribution the most pure expression of such humour? Truth's unpredictable force is turned inside out – not by earnestly revealing power's straightforward hypocrisy, but by sarcastically amplifying the double duplicity within its own semantic alliances.

This is why Adorno is wrong when he asserts that the proletariat have no language of their own. Uncompromising humour is the intelligence of the oppressed because it reveals an alternative set of historical lines that are in no way dependent on capitalism for their self-articulation. Unfortunately, Adorno's understanding of this ostensibly immured stance misses the point when he argues, 'the language of the subjected … domination alone has stamped, so robbing them further of the justice promised by the unmutilated, autonomous word to all those free enough to pronounce it without rancour. Proletarian language is dictated by hunger' (Adorno, 2005: 102). This is where dialectics gets into trouble or, more accurately, gets Adorno into trouble, something he later rectified.

If we view capitalism as a parasitical structure unable to author its own preconditions, then we must also impute an ontic positivity at the heart of that incapacity. This positivity is not a dialectical contradiction but a diffuse and universal negative opiticalization that draws upon our peasant knowledge to remember the present. Herein lie the remnants of a proletariat discourse, a mute excessive autonomy. Its syntax is precisely silent and withdrawn when perceived from the viewpoint of capital, since it cannot express neoliberalism's founding impossibility by using the language of that impossibility: *capitalist reason itself.*

Post-Dialogical Politics at Work

If biopolitical societies of control put 'life itself' to work through the 'I, Job' function, then how can we trust ourselves, our anxieties, words and gestures? More importantly, if the CEO now criticizes the ethical standing of his or her firm more stridently than employees (albeit in a mannerist form), then how is it possible to discern the boundaries that distinguish a genuine anti-capitalist activation of politics? How do we sidestep those intimate zones of sympathy that capital constantly establishes in order to re-territorialize dissent, draw it back into the logic of accumulation and turn it into an instrument of exploitation? As the 'immersion room' example discussed earlier demonstrates, we can now see all sorts of attempts to make resistance speak in order to make it congruous with the ideology of work. Advertising in London currently seeks to cash in on underground chic and revolutionary cool – 'Be your own revolution!' cries one advert for new computer software. Right-wing management consultants tell their readers that much can be learnt from the creative upheaval of 1960s counter-culture: promote an organization that resembles the attributes of a topsy-turvy world of anarchy and hire employees that hate capitalism.

But let's look more closely at what we really mean by co-optation and recuperation. Indeed, the question of appropriation is somewhat analogous to those old (and yet still very relevant) debates about commodification. This may prove instructive for us too. As many pessimistic commentators have noted, there does not appear to be any limit to the commodification process. All forms of dissent are potential grist for the commercial mill, as millions of Che Guevara T-Shirts around the world attest. So what exactly are the limits of commodification and what forms of radicalism are impervious to being transformed into yet another marketing message for Google or Levi's? To find the answer, we need to revisit our basic critique of dialogical reason in the neoliberal age. The ideology of work and its capitalist correlates operates through an implicitly empty performativity. Thus we need to think in terms of *form* rather than *content*. Once the commodity form has attained regulative dominance (i.e. real subsumption), everything and anything can be inserted as content, from radical chic obscenities to revolutionary pornography, to the most poignant critique of capitalism posted on the Google Lecture Series. Content is transposed through an indomitable formalization in which it becomes yet another empty gesture, marketing gimmick or simulated lifestyle with no real connection to social release other than that of the senses. It is in this way that the commodification process arrests the shared sympathies between content and form. However, there is one thing that cannot be commoditized: the commodity's *absence* from its own generative form. That particular lack is beyond the commodity's conditions of possibility. It is unable to recover any exchange value from that gaping non-presence. Here we arrive at the intractable limit of the commodity form.

We can apply the same rationale to approaching the restorative limits of neoliberal co-optation, especially pertaining to criticism and the universal injunction to work. What kind of refusal can remain resistant to becoming the content-grist for the speaking machine as it seeks to reduce life to a tradable piece of human and social capital? For as we know, late capitalism can reintegrate all sorts of non-economic and wacky recalcitrant activities, drawing upon them as useful 'contents' to deepen real subsumption. But, as with the commodity form, the neoliberal project cannot incorporate its own formal absence, just as the capitalist paradigm cannot incorporate its non-existence into its ideological rhetoric (although it often does so with respect to content). To push the argument one step further, we must also consider the victims of neoliberal integration. While the artificial intelligence wired into the 'I, Job' function means that even the most rebellious views (even in a purely inverted form as with moral deviance or criminality) can safely be processed within its system, it cannot incorporate its own formalized non-presence. The machine reveals its own internal limit and begins to malfunction and emit smoke. However, if this negative field cannot be achieved through dialogue (given that resistant speech always risks being hijacked by the incorporative flows of the generalizable exchange form) then absence ought to be instantiated through silence. By this, I do not mean a mute presence, but a collective and pro-democratic exchange that the pundits of corporatism view as silence only after we have literally departed the scene altogether. This is the non-identical reversal of the ideology of abandonment which otherwise so forcefully holds us in its crushing gaze.

Why Does Capitalism Fear Our Desertion So Much?

This reasoning might explain the rise of a *post-dialogical* approach to refusing the ideology of work. This method of resistance decides that dialogue with power is simply too perilous. It prefers silence, an ethic of inscrutability and, if possible, of communal departure. The agents of struggle understand that one of the most insidious features of neoliberal capitalism is its ability to neutralize a speech act before that utterance gains power. For all our pleas to power to halt its invasive degradation of living labour, its various modulations continue unabated, often making good use of those pleas. This is indicative of the type of domination we are facing today. So here is the central *aporia*. The clear demands of the bio-proletariat's refusal movement are rendered inaudible (indeed, they are smothered) precisely by having employees speak – or, more accurately, by having them sacrifice themselves to the whims of a pugnacious speaking machine. Rather than allowing workers too few opportunities to speak and invite recognition, the modern corporation is a veritable recognition machine, inducing endless waffle about ourselves, our worlds, our identities, likes and dislikes. And in a rather schizophrenic manner, this recognition is closely connected to the inadmissible, peddled by the postponed promise of abandonment.

The ideology of abandonment representative of neoliberal employment policies complicates post-dialogical refusal. It enrols workers in the power matrix not by welcoming us into its domain, but by threating permanent exile. Of course, this false promise of abandonment operates as a Trojan Horse for a painful form of subjectification. In this respect, the ideological policeman interpellates us not with a 'Hey you!' but with a 'Go away!' This is why I distrust the term 'exit' for explaining progressive post-dialogical politics. It has become part of the fear apparatus that binds us to work. The rhetoric of abandonment carries a potent conditioning reference: 'You are nothing more than a debt, why have you done this to us and yourself? What is the matter with you?' The capitalist employment relationship begins to resemble a weird version of battered-wife syndrome: the more we are beaten and emotionally taunted by rejection, the more we desire to stay. Adorno makes a striking observation about this intersection between the discourse of social exclusion and the magnetic attraction to stay put:

'Sociability itself connives at injustice by pretending that in this chill world we can still talk to each other' (Adorno, 2005: 26). From now on the mouth becomes an indigent chronicler of its own unworthiness, an open fetishization that is systematically collated by the coordinates of power. Dialogue can only verbalize its mute consent. The sensible objective of departure is hamstrung by the interpellative command: 'Go away!' In this respect, post-dialogical politics involves a withdrawal from both the syntax of power and its ensnaring discourse of dismissal.

The generalized speaking machine currently breathing down our necks is cunning. It uses the arithmetic of abandonment to hold us in place and undermine our intuitive reflex to simply walk away. Regardless of this, the preliminary frontrunner of post-dialogical politics is a buoyant suspicion concerning the benefits of 'participation' and 'consultation' within a broader capitalist horizon that ends up being reinforced by our involvement. At the present moment, the collective trajectory of our class struggle is simply about being left alone. Of course, any parasitical social system like extreme neoliberal capitalism cannot abide by this under any circumstances. Hence the bizarre 'no-escape' culture that we find ourselves perpetually entrapped in. Escape? That we don't even know what might lie beyond the outer perimeter is a sure indication of how bad things have become. But in this dire predicament there is a pinprick of optimism to be found. That capitalism has entered into a profoundly parasitical mode at least indicates a founding weakness in the system, its internal impossibility. What is the nature of this weakness? In the past, anti-capitalist analysis frequently made the mistake of seeing living labour as the by-product of capitalist control. The institutional brawn of private ownership was assumed to be a first mover, a leader, given the havoc it has caused. This line of analysis misses the infinite and overflowing social wealth that capitalism can't do without but has little reciprocity with. Because of its ultimate class structure, capitalism is unable to summons what it truly needs – living labour – but cannot acknowledge that systemic impotence. This line of thinking, I suggest, clears the ground for post-dialogical political struggle, because living labour cannot be truly abandoned by a system that is unable to exist without it. The ideological spell is broken. Now it is us who wield the threat of desertion, which is simply an articulation of our peasant knowledge in practical form. Post-dialogical praxis confounds power's self-assured assumption about the way employees comprehend their oppression. Slowly the semantic hold begins to fail. The space for any old content now drastically shrinks. Finally, the totality dissolves when we nullify the grammatical attention it absolutely requires from us. Just as the pervert cannot stand being ignored or passed over, the mute mouth of our militant non-observance reduces the social factory to something of a little policeman with nothing to say. Now we are free.

Absentification

Given this theoretical backdrop, we can now delineate two practical types of post-dialogical struggle that may help us withdraw from the stage of late-capitalist regulation: namely *political* and *ethical* methods of absence. Let's discuss the political dimension first. Radical absenteeism in this respect includes those concrete initiatives that self-valorize the non-coincidental, unassignable or unrecognizable exterior points within the capitalist exchange circuit. This kind of critical praxis seeks to build autonomous filaments that collectively repossess social time. Indeed, if the hyper-accelerated time codes of capitalism require an impossible level of presence, cognitive attention and visibility, then some typography of structural anonymity can secure a common time when we are left alone. But this invisibility can also be transformed into a weapon if utilized correctly.

As the Invisible Committee's manifesto *The Coming Insurrection* suggests, 'Turn anonymity into a defensive position' (Invisible Committee, 2009: 112–113). This is very different to the anonymous 'sabotage' that has long been a feature of industrial life. For example, the 'Anonymous' radical group does actually have a face (a Guy Fawkes mask), an icon (a headless suited man) and a set of protocols (on the Internet if you search closely). However, this is a paradoxical 'identity-less' identity guiding its anti-corporate interventions, because a real and identifiable human face is the medium in which power functions most effectively today. In short, avoid the face.

Anne Elizabeth Moore (2007) nicely explores this post-dialogical politics in the music industry, which is notorious for capturing and exploiting the living labour of artists. In the 1990s a thriving network of autonomous culture producers had developed a unique sub-economy of music in a number of US cities. These communities often celebrated anti-capitalist independence and a DYI ethic that dispensed with the need for large commercial labels. At the same time, however, large music multinationals were making ever deeper forays into this subculture. While engagement with powerful corporations through various forms of ironic and cynical analysis was still the common currency (*à la* Nirvana or Radio Head), this frequently resulted in artistic 'sell-out'. In this context, Bikini Kill (which had considerable underground success with the song 'Suck My Left One') and other 'riot grrrl' bands (anti-consumerist, feminist DYI groups) sought to resist this aspect of commodification. They rendered the unmarketable marketable. So these bands practised a politics of imperceptibility: 'Riot grrrl participants developed a sophisticated response: a media blackout ... for the most part the mainstream media were forced to describe what they could comprehend of the burgeoning scene from the outer edge of a sweaty mosh pit' (Moore, 2007: 9).

Under a regime of power whereby the corporeal and social 'I' is the key locus of regulative compliance and the 'I, Job' function is almost indistinguishable from what we are, an additional form of refusal has to be undertaken to support our political absence. This moves us into the *ethical* domain. Recalibrating struggle through modes of imperceptibility can also become a *way of life*, in which ethical subjects (re)relate to their pre-constitutive socialities by turning their backs on power through subjective desertion. If 'life itself' is now a central concern of the sadistic neoliberal corporation, then what better substance to graft itself onto than 'the subject', with all its idiosyncratic fears and desires? We are fairly pathetic in this respect. But let's work through the process. We know that subjectification requires a number of technologies in order to become operative – language and representation being some of the more pivotal ones (and this might also explain why Foucault became increasingly interested in *aphasia* in the context of the liberal injunction to speak). US-style human resource management did, of course, perfect this form of regulation in the 1990s. And contemporary managerialism has continued the trend in an inverted form by deploying abandonment as an indubitable instrument of enrolment.

Perhaps this is where Deleuze and Guattari's (1987) *Thousand Plateaus* comes into its own as a consummate guide for de-subjectification and resisting the 'I, Job' function in the neoliberal era. The authors argue that the so-called 'subject' of capitalism is radically distinct from the rich existential being we experience as individuals. It is possible to differentiate the individual from the doleful identikit imposed upon us by neoliberal conditions. Joyful individuality connotes social living proper, an unstated testimony to the open speeds and movements that cross the body beneath the radar of static (i.e. asocial) perceptibility. Societies of control (or molar superstructures) govern by harnessing the 'I' to the speaking machine, thus blocking the vectors of silent movement that are always at our disposal; namely, by *becoming imperceptible*. But how do we expunge this fascist imposter, this alien 'other' that speaks in our place, lies in our name and commands us to become our work, even as it slowly kills us? Self-flagellation only makes matters worse. And therapy is more than pointless. Instead, Deleuze and Guattari encourage a movement towards becoming the non-subjects we already are within an impossible totality, which allows us to pass like water through a metal sieve and elude the systems of recognition that drive this sadistic variant of capitalism. This is not merely a novel form of humanism, but a tactical anti-humanism taken to its furthermost limits.

De-subjectification can never be achieved just for the sake of it. Only in response to a horrible manifestation of power can it gather momentum. Many artists, addicts and romantics have paid a dear price for believing otherwise, approaching it as a *stylistic* project. It for this reason that Deleuze and Guattari approach the topic of de-subjectification by demonstrating its importance in relation to the everyday fascism we all now confront, such as the ideology of managerialism we discussed earlier. They isolate three forms of micro-fascism that define the late-capitalist world: the organized body (i.e. the organism), the interpreted desire (i.e. representation) and the subjectified soul (i.e. the subject). To become imperceptible is to *cast off* this organism–representation–subject combo from our collective existences. This negative optical line of flight seeks not self-destruction but a *shedding*. Perhaps this is why an acceleration of the 'I, job' complex (escaping into work) and the recent wave of work-related suicides we discussed in Chapter 1 all represent failed attempts at becoming imperceptible. Death makes you visible … far too visible. Especially to yourself when you fantasize about it. De-subjectification has nothing to do with self-harm.

In analysing this problem more closely, Deleuze and Guattari raise a perplexing yet critical question: 'What is the relation between the (anorganic) imperceptible, the (asignifying) indiscernible, and the (asubjective) impersonal?' (Deleuze and Guattari, 1987: 279). Their answer is especially relevant when the generalized employment form appears inescapable, as it does today. For the neoliberal enterprise can only enforce its ideology of abandonment through the internal lie of the other who speaks on our behalf. In doing so it identifies the 'us' in the mirror of power as *you*. Thus, 'a first response would be to be like everybody else

... to go unnoticed is by no means easy. To be a stranger, even to one's doorman or neighbours. If it is so difficult to be like everybody else, it is because it is an affair of becoming' (Deleuze and Guattari, 1987: 279). In a symbolic environment where the injunction to speak is merely an excuse to transform us into a distant audience to ourselves, absence takes on the obligation of solidarity. To become an embodied negation of the seer/seen couplet: in short, to disappear. How does one do this? Three steps are offered by Deleuze and Guattari (1987). First, eliminate everything that is too identifiable, that roots us to ourselves and makes us easily reflected in the screen of neoliberal abandonment. Second is saturation, to become universal – not just act like everybody else but actually *be* everybody else. Here we are using a reverse calculus *in toto*, forming a kind of totality that rubs out the postponed and vague lines of control we discussed in Chapter 2. This is not a bourgeois withdrawal into solitude but more a cancellation of the individualizing capitalist flows that have made us into somebody else. We must cancel that debt that is the fearful human monad and instead gift ourselves to everybody, a very *social* disappearance. To disappear in the neoliberal world of mute and precluded visibility requires much help and support. We move, then, from the ethical back into the political domain. This ethical version of political imperceptibility is indebted to a sort of Brownian movement. If dead labour is but the congealed reification of lost time and unstated co-operation, then its opposite, living labour, consists more of a 'pageantry of movement' to put it in Baudelairian terms. And returning to the central theme of this book, that movement courts the impossible.

The Mute Grammar of Subversion

The syntax of late-capitalist regulation conspires to discourage any movement into the invisible social. After all, the rent has to be paid. And this brings us to an important problematic concerning post-dialogical reason. If the politics of imperceptibility discovers another continent elsewhere, then there are undoubtedly going to be moments when, by accident or design, we will come face to face with power *and have to speak*. An overly comprehensive social imperceptibility might run the risk of being unable to talk ourselves out of a bad situation if the 'I, job' function' catches up with us. As Seth Price points out in his *How to Disappear in America* (2008), one must always have a story. But our story also needs to be resistant to storyfication. Indeed, even Deleuze and Guattari suggest that a capacity for speaking to power in the social factory ought to be retained for crucial moments, occasions of both defence and attack. Otherwise our very inability to speak is used against us, as a rationale for why our imprisonment is deserved:

> You have to keep enough of your organism for it to reform each dawn; and you have to keep small supplies of significance and subjectification, if only to turn them against their own systems when the circumstances demand it, when things, persons, even situations, force you to; and you have to keep small rations of subjectivity in sufficient quantity to enable you to respond to the dominant reality. (Deleuze and Guattari, 1987: 160)

How is this unstorifiable story to be forged successfully? Entrance into the perceptible obviously requires an imperceptible grammar – the common excess of sociality that is 'everybody' – in order to function. We cannot speak from 'nowhere' but only from 'everywhere'. This is what is sometimes missing in Foucault's (2001) analysis of fearless speech in his interesting investigation of the cynics and stoics. While he notes that *parrhhesia* relied upon a social arrangement in order to be performative (the Athenian democratic polity), the inscrutable and preconditional formatting that makes such speech possible is understated. Ultimately, the power conferred upon the fearless speaker is contingent not only on the more powerful party (from whom the truth-teller takes his or her cues) but also on the vested abilities of the reasoning individual himself or herself. In Foucault's reading of *parrhhesia*, it appears that the courageous talker is divorced from the social antecedents that compelled him or her forward in the first place. Here we must remind ourselves that Diogenes was not the paragon of lone individualism that he is often made out to be, but the epitome of communist praxis! His visibility (in the *agora* for example) was only a minor element of the levelling invisibility fundamental to his project: 'If I masturbate and piss in the marketplace, it is to remind you that I am just like you, and you are the same as everybody else!' He practised *elimination* to the nth degree. And his conspicuousness was merely an accentuated dimension of his complete fullness, the imperceptibility of his unrelenting sociality.

But how can one speak to power and still retain anonymity? How can an imperceptible politics still semantically influence the architecture of domination without being seen and marked by the gaze of the boss?

An initial way to think about the valence between engagement and post-engagement politics would be to conceptualize them as diachronically interconnected, following a sequential pattern as refusal evolves. Remain imperceptible until a John Ball-like 'The time is now' arrives when we can speak with convincing force, rather than with irony or marauding impotence. As some have recently argued,

> Visibility must be avoided. But a force that gathers in the shadows can't avoid it forever. Our appearance as a force must be pushed back until the opportune moment. The longer we avoid visibility, the stronger we will be when it finally catches up with us. (Invisible Committee, 2009: 114)

The arrival of this opportune moment might also be called an 'event', which duly collapses the distinction between visible and invisible politics. The nature of this event and its precipitation has long been debated, from the spontaneous strike of early twentieth-century socialism to the mystical messianic collapse of the distinction between present and past we find in Benjamin's *kiaros*. Such an event concerns a transitional rupture whereby all cards are put on the table and history closes in on itself and opens a new vista. The lesson is that we must appear before the enemy at the right time and location armed with the right things to say. And this timing is often unpredictable, almost coming out of nowhere.

But is this sequential argument too simplistic? Can we not decipher a workable juxtaposition in which an exchange between engagement and post-engagement politics takes place simultaneously? To help us theorize this invisibility–visibility co-presence in the workplace we might turn to the wonderful image of Svejk from Hasek's classic novel *The Good Soldier Svejk* (1973). Svejk practised a quintessential form of imperceptible politics, summoning the rich sociality of his fellow foot soldiers to exploit weak points in an otherwise formidable institution (the Austro-Hungarian Army). As is well known, Svejk was the master of calculated guile, flummox and foot-dragging, patiently building a common ground among his comrades via a very tentative yet sophisticated engagement with power.

Most relevant for us, Svejk knew how to innocently manipulate the *in situ* contextuality of his formal disempowerment by becoming a kind of wallpaper figure during his communicative interventions with the authorities. In other words, his bosses recognized and engaged with Svejk on a daily basis, but in a manner whereby he was quickly forgotten or considered as just another piece of cannon fodder on the way to the front line: of course, before they realized it, it was they who landed in jail rather the merry Svejk. In this paradoxical zone of perceptible imperceptibility, he was able to turn the tables, dismantle immediate long-standing hierarchies and still pass 'under the radar' of the dominant executive authority.

In this sense, Svejk's visibility operates paradoxically to *hide his invisibility*. Hasek was very clear on this point. Svejk should be understood as the product of a perspicuous social logic rather than as an eccentric or heroic individual. The man and the social universe are combined in a way that bourgeois ideology finds challenging to comprehend. Svejk secures his subversive unrecognizability precisely by engaging with power directly, but in a manner that grants licence to blend in with his comrades and exact chaos. This involves active disengagement: camouflage (telling the boss what he wants to hear, but doing exactly the opposite), sarcastic role baiting (turning the tables on power whenever possible), and often proudly flaunting his mental or physical absence. It is through this kind of practised astuteness that he manages not only to stay alive but also to be left alone to have fun with his comrades. Visibility becomes a cloaking device for Svejk's resistant behaviour. The 'we' operates as a form of stealth, even when exposed by some cankered senior officer. And Svejk does this not simply for his own amusement (although there is much of that), since a palpable sense of social justice animates all of his acts of social sabotage.

A contemporary version of Svejk-like behaviour in the workplace is provided by Carmen Segarra, the US Federal Reserve Bank of New York regulator who secretly taped 48 hours of conversation that revealed the intimate relationship between regulators and Goldman Sachs. The degree of implicit cooperation between the Fed watchdog and Goldman Sachs was so close that she decided to gain evidence in case she could no longer participate and was fired (which she eventually was). Goldman Sachs is a very powerful, very aggressive and very male institution. Following the financial crisis, *Rolling Stone Magazine* colourfully described the company as 'a great vampire squid wrapped around the face of humanity, relentlessly jamming its blood funnel into anything that smells like money'. Insulting to squid some might say. Anyway, Segarra recalls her reaction when the boss announced her next assignment:

He said, do you know where you're going? And I said, no. And he said, you're going to Goldman. And my thought was, uh oh … The look on his face was like he was very much looking for my reaction. And when I

... I think after so many years of practicing law, when you see someone that is just looking to see what your reaction is going to be, my first instinct is let me make sure that I don't give a reaction. (This American Life, 2014)

Instead of letting her anxiety show and risk being inserted into the speaking machine, she remained blank and bought a voice recorder. She subsequently observed some incredible lapses in judgement from the Fed. Any normal person would have raised serious objections about the level of collusion. But an institutional climate of fear was deeply ingrained, and large investment banks could count on the regulators turning a blind eye when required. As she recorded, Segarra was mostly invisible, a wallpaper character that looked like everybody else. She finally spoke out when a superior asked her to change her report about Goldman Sachs so that it omitted a damaging fact. Her defiance was no doubt licensed by the clandestine voice recorder, which was a stroke of genius. Coming out of the woodwork at the crucial time, and knowing full well that it would certainly mean 'moving on', is a definitive Svejkian trait. As Segarra refuses to change the damaging report, her boss Jonathan Kim suddenly concentrates on *her*, amplifying the 'I, Job' function. Segarra has been outed. Her interrogator, however, is too late; this modern-day Svejk is much more skilled than he is in post-dialogical politics. This malfunctioning speaking machine now steps forth from the darker edges of corporate life and wreaks havoc:

Jonathan Kim: I'm never questioning about the knowledge base, or the assessments, or those things, right? It's really about how you are perceived. And so if there's a more of a general sort of feedback that says, OK, it's not only one person, it's not only two persons, but it's many more people who are perceiving that you have more sharper elbows or that you're sort of breaking eggs. And obviously, I don't know what the right word is ... I think the message has come back to me saying that you really need to make these changes quickly in order for you to be ...

Carmen Segarra: Not fired?

Jonathan Kim: ... successful as part of the team.

Carmen Segarra: Not fired, basically.

Jonathan Kim: Well, I don't even want to get there, because ... and here's why.

Carmen Segarra: Well, I think that it would be unfair to fire me when I am, at the end of the day, doing a good job.

Jonathan Kim: Well, there's ... look. I'm here to change sort of the definition of what a good job is, right? Couple of things that could ...

Carmen Segarra: I can see it a mile away.

Jonathan Kim: OK. Couple of things that I would suggest ... have a sense of humility, because a lot of the things that you say ... and this is the way you're coming across, right? I think I know you well enough that that's not what you're saying, but if I were to be a new person, I would say, Carmen, you're very arrogant. (This American Life, 2014)

Segarra's boss clearly seeks to reactivate the 'I, Job' function in its more disciplinary and paranoid mode in order to visibilize her. A formerly anonymous and inconspicuous bearer of technical skill (or 'knowledge base') is now targeted as a problematic subject of recognition (or 'how you are perceived'). As noted throughout the book, this aspect of neoliberal personality policing is an ongoing facet of the biopolitical employment system. However, when employees like Segarra become a liability (in this case, by failing to rubber-stamp a dodgy business deal), it can take on a particularly nasty format. More specifically, the speaking machine is used to destabilize Segarra, not only to normalize her but to lead her into statements that will irrecoverably destroy her legitimacy. The boss might have expected her to forlornly admit, for example, that she is unsuitable for the role given common perceptions in the office. In this respect, it must be recalled that the 'I, Job' function seeks not only arduous feats of overwork but also expedient means for abandoning labour power once the time arrives. The unspoken correlate of the employability discourse is its opposite.

However, with the help of her clandestine recorder, Segarra pulls off some classic Svejkian manoeuvres of refusal, utilizing her long-standing status as a nameless office drone to undermine the obvious trajectory of domination in this space. First, she uses the speaking machine against itself by redirecting its insinuations back at the boss. Now he is talking too much and discovering an alien presence within his own overly divulging dialogue ('if I were to be a new person'). Secondly, Segarra uses the general drift of the conversation to let Kim vaguely admit to things that he could not openly state without contradicting the watchdog role of the Fed. All of a sudden, it is he who is on the back foot. And thirdly, knowing full well that she is going to be fired, Segarra makes sure she has a record of the real reason. Some very shaky performance criteria are cunningly teased out of Kim. It was not lack of skill that landed her in trouble but more nebulous subjective factors ('I'm here to change sort of the definition of what a good job is'). After the scandal broke this made the Fed's defence difficult to accept: 'Personnel decisions ... are based exclusively on individual job performance and are subject to thorough review. We categorically reject any suggestions to the contrary' (*The Independent*, 2014).

By simply releasing these recordings online Segarra has won. They are remarkable. She is also seeking a settlement for unfair dismissal. Moreover, one can only guess what the climate must currently be like in the Fed (and the large investment banks). And is this not the lasting efficacy of Svejkian resistance and post-dialogical politics more generally? Fear and trepidation are inspired among the technocracy since they don't exactly know how many other Segarra-like imposters are in their midst. This paranoia among the powerful involves an interesting dynamic because it is agent-led. It can thus result in behaviour more characteristic of the disempowered. Put differently, just as managerial oppression frequently does not incite office rebellion, the converse can also be the case: the suspicion that one, two or maybe ten employees may be surreptitious saboteurs can result in the corporation acting somewhat meekly and confusedly rather than tightening the screw of repressive surveillance. The perverse non-dialectical techniques that define biopower (i.e. egregious acts of injustice that do not automatically provoke the rational response of open rebellion) can therefore be used against power too. The feeling that one has been occupied by a false language, as Houellebecq expresses in the interview quoted above, is put to work against neoliberal capitalism. This is precisely why non-speech and anonymity are apt weapons of refusal in the era of the 'I, Job' function – not because they allow us to hide, but because of the emotional economy they instil among those who believe they govern. Here we are simply restating a classic observation in Stoic philosophy. The unprecedented proliferation of surveillance cameras and undercover police spies under neoliberal capitalism is symptomatic of its profound integral weakness. The point is to understand how to use that weakness to our advantage and implode the ideology of work using capital's own claims of strength and ineluctability.

Conclusion
Inoperative Critique
and the End of Work

Work can be partly refused if we avoid its current fetishistic character. As a seemingly indomitable reification, the 'I, Job' function infiltrates everything and sucks it into its operating system. I am not putting forward a *subjectivist* argument in this respect. Identity is the last thing we need to consider, since it is simply another facet of the map we are planning to leave. Experiences of employment today are expressions of a particular configuration of capitalism which is multifaceted, openly deceptive and counterintuitive. Thus, experience is also difficult to trust. We must compress our practical knowledge into sympathetic schematizations in order to look ahead. As a noted psychologist once declared, there is nothing as practical as a good theory. So, given the investigation we have undertaken in this book, what would our theory be? Capitalism represents a class structure, one that is often obfuscated and hidden by the present ritualization of work. To resist the mythology of work we must resist capital's class relations. And this brings us to the heart of the matter. Do we stay and fight or do we collectively disappear and rebuild? And how is it possible to exit from a totality that appears to have no beginning or end? I believe that the time for fighting capitalism's class structure is nearing an end and that alternative structures of self-organized democracy will follow. Simply working less is not enough. Struggling for a better 'deal' within the capitalist paradigm is not enough either, although it is important not to make that claim lightly given the immiseration many find themselves experiencing in the neoliberal nightmare that some call 'reality'. We must depart in a non-dialectical and counter-negative fashion; we can no longer allow our opposition to be no more than a secondary response to capitalism (or any other overarching and pernicious force). This is partially what it wants as it threatens to abandon those who have been abandoned already. New lines of flight are required that are autonomous and self-determined.

The self-abolition of the global working class ought to be the ultimate goal of refusal. It is time to desert your own subordination.

On the one hand, philosophical criticism is fundamental to this project. Without it we are unable to gauge the shape and force of the enemy. On the other hand, it is too easy to over-intellectualize this enemy, introducing newfangled concepts and theories that surreptitiously require a fixation with power to sustain them. As I mentioned earlier, no doubt the apologists of neoliberalism would appreciate the idea of left-wing intellectuals reading the complete works of Hayek. What is the alternative? A positive criticism of work and the late-capitalist employment system ought to be *inoperative* from the standpoint of the ruling class. By describing emancipatory praxis as inoperative I do not mean that it is *useless*, but that it remains inscrutable to and independent of capitalist rationality. In part, resistance fuels the totality, which feeds off it like a vampire ('You see! You do have free speech'). Might not this book itself be part of that self-entrapping dynamic? I hope not. But the onus is on me to clarify the inoperative normativity of the method I have deployed in the preceding chapters, which I have drawn upon to unsettle the capitalist mythology of work today.

To begin with, this book is certainly not about pointing the finger of 'blame' at anyone. It is not a moral statement. As the philosophers of social critique have long noted, the difference between moralism and criticism is that the former always positions the critic outside the circumstances they condemn (hence the frequent charge of hypocrisy and self-aggrandizement when critics are sized up against their actual behaviour), whereas the latter insists that the observer is a participant of the place, scenario or object under scrutiny. Auto-criticism never divides the object from the negating subject, but centres the social universe under negation at the centre of the representing eye. This is why it is completely unproblematic to use a Microsoft product whilst challenging its grip on society, or wear Nike products to an anti-capitalist protest. Hence, the essays presented in this book have been as much about self-analysis as challenging the neoliberal orthodoxy, and I'm certainly not uninvolved or non-complicit in the problematic the book takes issue with (I am, after all, a middle-class university worker!). The book's criticisms could only really be conducted in light of my own complicity. But what we do with that complicity – however minor or insignificant – is what really matters.

In reporting on what work has done to us in neoliberal societies, I have been forced to tell the 'sad truth' of the matter. Indeed, as anyone who has ever been unlucky enough to write a book will attest, it is an unpleasant and laborious affair. I refer to my study space at home as the 'torture chamber'. This is why I used the word *forced*. There is little pleasure or satisfaction in reading fat dossiers describing the recent wave of job-related suicide cases, for example. The 'sad truth' is something that draws one into the text, making life a little unbearable and free of respite, perhaps with the exception of the text's greater proximity to the void that is always lurking behind reason. Rather than endorsing Orwell's rather heroic interpretation of this predicament, I am more sympathetic with Deleuze on this count. He argued that there is always a conceited coward behind the language of criticism (especially amongst academics!). The void is somehow *too* easy.

We might have uncovered some 'sad truths' about a socio-economic system presently in catabolic decline, but the sadness renders its own particular world projection, as Mark Fisher (2014) has noted in his brilliant analysis of contemporary dejection and dysphoria. There are many truths (and falsehoods) in this area, but as Critchley (2008) also points out exceedingly well, the emotive texture of abstraction often begins with a constitutive disappointment: this is where reflection has little choice but to become politically orientated and the text assumes the role of an unforgiving slave master running ahead of the author to forge a path. This disappointment is certainly born from the realization that we, those we depend upon, and our broader transnational community could be living in so much better conditions. But this tragically hopeful 'could' of retrospective analysis often hardens into a brick wall – criticality that begins to see itself only in the ultra-negative totality of late capitalism, a *doxa* that can never be transcended: 'This is as good as it gets, and it's really pretty bad.' As the old saying goes, if the optimist believes this to be the best of all worlds, the pessimist worries they might be right.

Of course, we would certainly be in trouble if the story ended there. But it does not, since the disappointing truths yielded by critical reason are inherently pragmatic. This brings us to what I think is the crux of the matter. How is one to *use* the theoretical and empirical vistas of disappointment that critical inquiry makes visible? Or, with regard to the subject matter of this book, what does one take away from this critique of work. How should we now act, participate and continue to make decisions in a world that is clearly out of joint? One response I have observed among students and scholars alike might be called cynical self-interest. Its internal logic goes like this: 'Yes, it does look like the world is in deep shit, that there are gross injustices and insurmountable powers obstructing progressive change. Am I concerned? Yes, of course! This knowledge grates with all of my liberal beliefs. But why should I go out on a limb if the situation is so futile? Given that there doesn't seem to be any alternative, perhaps it's best if I look after myself (and selected loved ones) and get the most out of the system, because ultimately it is what it is.' The generative logic is clear. It transforms the knowledge garnered from criticism into a practical (if not ideological) acceptance of its own suffering. This way of seeing the world is as parasitical as capitalism itself ... *it is capitalism.*

That critical insight is converted into a kind of competitive advantage in which fear and individualism are its predominant directors is unsurprising if one predicts that the game is over. Even worse is the sense of intellectual aloofness that can follow the moment of insight, something that ameliorates the discomfort of collusion and strengthens the object of annulment. In a wonderful (autobiographical?) aphorism in *Minima Moralia* (2005), Adorno carefully unpacks the character of this transposition, suggesting that the detached critical observer (Adorno himself?) can sometimes be more dangerous to freedom than those who appear ignorant:

> The detached observer is as much entangled as the active participant; the only advantage of the former is insight into his entanglement, and the infinitesimal freedom that lies in knowledge as such. His own distance from business at large is a luxury which only that business confers. This is why the very movement of withdrawal bears features of what it negates. (Adorno, 2005: 26)

If this cynical self-interest entails a rather opportunistic form of self-preservation then another response tends towards the opposite end of the resignation spectrum, entailing a sort of spiralling nihilism that derives a momentary pleasure from a world so corrupt and moribund. For this unhappy consciousness, it is difficult to 'go on' knowing what it knows, let alone to imagine a more just future. This is typified in Berardi's almost apocalyptic analysis of our alienated lives within the wasteland of hyper-capitalism. He writes:

> Breathing has become difficult, almost impossible: as a matter of fact, one suffocates. One suffocates every day and the symptoms of suffocation are disseminated all along the paths of daily life and the highways of planetary politics. Our chances of survival are few: we

know it. There are no more maps we can trust, no more destinations
for us to reach. Ever since its mutation into semiocapitalism, capitalism
has swallowed the exchange-value machine not only for the different
forms of life but also of thought, imagination, and hope. There is no
alternative to capitalism. (Berardi, 2009: 131)

The diagnosis is desolate, hopeless and depressed; and not without
reason. Certainly there is a kind of truth in depression, since it is *inter
alia* the psychological manifestation of a world in needless disarray, pure
potential separated from itself and put into the service of surplus necessity.
But this therapeutic deliverance of the 'sad truth' flirts with surrender
in which the hated object obtains a power it does not deserve. This is
how criticality can unwittingly give to capitalism what it cannot see in
itself, a gift without return except for the backwash of an empty void that
invariably takes over. In the phraseology of Deleuze and Guattari (1987)
we become a 'black hole.' This is why political positivity is not a necessary
corollary of negative knowledge; for we cannot even trust our criticality
concerning the late-capitalist condition. The ideological territory we are
struggling on today, especially in the realm of capitalist work relations, is
different since it is this very low-down, dirty pessimism that defines the
dominant ideology.

Where does this leave us? When our unhappiness consumes the very
object of analysis, entailing a reverse consumption whereby this sadness is
simultaneously overdetermined by the object, then how are we expected
to divine a way out? For even hope is useless here; nay, worse than useless,
since it mockingly reminds us of our infinite impotence. The problem
with this melancholic pose is not its unreasonableness. For it is more than
understandable in the present context of neoliberal class relations. The real
problem concerns its use value. An analogy can be found in the Lacanian
warning about the function of jealousy: just because there is good reason
to feel jealous (for example, witnessing our beloved being caressed by an
attractive stranger) does not detract from the fact that jealousy is still a
pathological condition. So, *it is what we do with the observation that really
matters.* Do we turn it into poison or a collective act of refusal, a path back
into life?

Pertaining to the uses of social criticism, Adorno pursued this line
of argument to its limit. One of his most fecund auto-critical moments
is found in his declaration that 'he who imagines disasters somehow
desires them' (Adorno, 2005: 163). Our sad observations might secretly

be harbouring a desire for a sad end. To counter this will to nothingness that is latent in critical reason, Adorno suggested that we reconfigure the problematic by first acknowledging our elemental *implication* (or entanglement) in our most nightmarish observations. Here, the observer and the observed subject matter become dangerously entwined; but not in any simplistic solipsistic way, since criticality would be unnecessary if word and world perfectly coincided. As a result, Adorno concluded that

> there is no way out of entanglement. The only responsible course is to deny oneself the *ideological misuse* of one's own existence, and for the rest to conduct oneself in private as modestly, unobtrusively and unpretentiously as required, no longer by good upbringing, but by the shame of still having air to breath in hell. (Adorno, 2005: 27–28, emphasis added).

It is this *misuse* that is Adorno's greatest concern, and what allows us to distinguish the divergent characters of the two uses of criticality discussed above.

But what would a non-ideological usefulness of one's critical embeddedness actually look like? And is there such a thing as an *inoperative critique* of neoliberal capitalism and its mythology of work? Inoperativity here means practical criticism that is not guided by or predicated on what it critiques, but simply aims to affirm a world beyond class domination. For it must be recalled that what late capitalism most desires from us is our attention, whether positive or negative. Therefore, to be effective, our opposition must (a) envisage a time of attainment and future self-redundancy (when goals of emancipation, revolution etc. have been fulfilled), to avoid criticism falling into the trap of wound attachment (or the reliance on victimhood for self-definition) and (b) posit emancipatory goals that are not defined merely in terms of opposition to capitalist extremism, since that would draw us back onto an untenable stage of power. This is a central tenet of post-dialogical politics in relation to contemporary employment systems.

In this regard, direct action in forming alternatives to organized exploitation is of the utmost importance. However, we must be reflexive here too, since the call to 'action' can also harbour unstated sympathies with the ideology of productivism: *We must do something.* Of course, we must. But there may also be a false promise within this injunction to act, blunting our analytical scrutiny concerning the interconnections between critical praxis and the cult of activity currently promoted by capitalism. This does not mean useless or ineffectual activity – indeed, perhaps the opposite. Only once we depart the universe of neoliberal rationality – which is in fact but a degenerative form of capitalist reason – can we begin to act collectively again and rediscover our common agency. It is in this spirit that I want to offer a number of suggestions concerning what a post-labour strategy might entail under the dire economic and symbolic conditions I have outlined in this book. I specifically focus on the UK context since I know it the best. However, the recommendations are hopefully applicable in other socio-economic variations of capitalism too. Most importantly, and returning to the argument made at the beginning of this chapter, in order to hasten the end of work we must first recognize its fetishistic character and secondly confront the source of that mythological conceit.

1. **A surplus living wage**. Everybody in society ought to be paid at least an average of £30,000 irrespective of what they do. And no one should be paid more than £95,000 a year (roughly a 1:3 income ratio between the poorest and richest in society). The neoliberal retort, of course, resembles the blind bluster of the hysteric: if we did that, this part of society won't work, or this, or this ... and so on. But who cares? These parts are not working anyway. Moreover, this is not money for nothing – free money is precisely what the rich currently receive as our labour subsidizes their affluence and leaves us with next to nothing. The establishment of this surplus living wage would change the entire political game, the horizon of power relations that seem so immovable at present. The justification for this strategy is as follows. There is no longer any fiscal connection whatsoever between effort and value, my salary and what I do, my role as employee and my well-being, income and work, and so forth. This is especially so for the rich. But they would like us to think that the reason a CEO receives a £450,000 bonus is owing to effort, contribution or what the economists call marginal productivity formulated by a functioning free market. But upon closer inspection there is absolutely no equivalence. So why not apply this disconnect for progressive purposes? The consequences that would follow would be overwhelmingly positive from a social-demo-cratic point of view. Time would be freed up to explore alternatives. The insane roller-coaster that we currently call 'the market' would halt as it begins to serve broader social needs rather than its own untenable perpetuation. Moreover, this universal wage would deal with many of

the problems that plague counter-capitalist models that still hold onto the relational equivalence between effort and reward (e.g. Albert's [2004] participatory economics).

2. **Post-state democratic organizations.** The governmental structure as it currently stands should be abandoned and a more direct form of participatory democracy should be instituted. Parliamentary democracy is neither parliamentary nor democratic, but a vehicle of direct oppression to enhance the interests of an elite so minute and removed from everyday life that we have little idea who most of them are. As I mentioned in the Introduction, the neoliberal state (and its capitalist form more generally) is a major stakeholder for enforcing the real toil of a society built around the idolatry of work. Killing work also requires the neoliberal state's demise. The structure of this new democratic forum might take numerous forms: neighbourhood councils, multi-tiered collectives whose leadership revolves on a regular basis, and so forth. But they ought not to be exclusively defined by work, as Wolff's (2012) similar proposals tend to imply. Work needs to be put in its place and de-fetishized. And we should decide what is important and what is not (such as the salary gradations mentioned in Recommendation 1). Additionally, these forums cannot be coercive – nobody likes to be subjected to endless mandatory meetings. The means cannot once again become the ends.

3. **The transfer of all monopolistic and oligopolistic enterprises into public hands,** that is, under the direct control of their own users. Railways, banks, healthcare providers, suppliers of water, electricity and foodstuffs, for example, have completely lost sight of their respective purposes under neoliberal capitalism. The role of the railways is to make profits for its shareholders first and foremost – providing decent and affordable transport for the majority of its users is way down on the list of priorities. Apologists for neoliberalism argue that this is merely an outcome of the division of labour. We require specialists whose sole role is to deal with, say, railways. And they are better motivated to do a good job if they are provided by private companies. Such an argument is false and highly misleading. The time taken to purchase a massively overpriced railway ticket, for example, could be better used for periodically electing officials to voluntarily occupy senior co-ordinating roles. The new democratic forums

mentioned in Recommendation 2 would run these institutions. They would do so not because they want more money or have a sense of civic duty, but because they use the product or service themselves and have an interest in its quality and accessibility. For isn't the opposite scenario basically how the class system functions under neoliberal capitalism? Public hospital CEOs opt for private healthcare; parliamentary ministers of public education much prefer their own children to be privately educated; and the list goes on – this is about a class elite being detached from the multitude that subsidizes their 'welfare'. The ruthless attitude that neoliberal managers have towards workers in their own organizations partially derives from the fact that they have no sense of what it means to be on the receiving end of the production cycle. This distance is extremely corrosive and for obvious reasons is a recipe for dilapidation.

4. **The three-day work week.** From a historical viewpoint, societies that insisted people work more than three days a week were usually slave societies. The maintenance of even a 'sophisticated self-subsistence' does not require more than 20 hours of work a week (see Gorz, 1994), and there is little economic reason for us to do more than this. In terms of productiveness it makes no sense, since creativity and concentration simply cannot be sustained for the long five- or six-day rituals of work that neoliberal capitalism argues are necessary. No economic value is added after a certain threshold is passed. Little of interest is created over and above the three days a week. This book has aimed to understand the real reason why all of this useless, extra work is demanded from us. We now know why: it serves to quell the seething discontent that an extreme class contradiction plants at the heart of society, at the centre of everything. There is nothing functional about many of the jobs we do, strangely enough even those that are certainly worthwhile to humanity (e.g. surgeons, scientists, train drivers, artists, etc.). This may sound controversial. But when jobs are cast within the bureaucratic and commercialized sphere of hyper-capitalist relations, even brain surgeons sometimes wonder what their worth is, especially when forced to cut costs, meet targets and generate process efficiencies in those public healthcare services that still remain in the West. This is where David Graeber's (2013) otherwise insightful notion of 'bullshit jobs' is problematic. He suggests that there are wide swathes of occupations that are not really necessary since they do not

really add anything to the public good (e.g. management consultants, derivative traders, etc.). The problem is, however, that this is the very worldview that informs the neoliberal gaze. *All* jobs are regarded as bullshit, even the ones that you and I are wholly dependent upon: the local midwife, the public-sector train driver. And once they have been rationalized to the point where the means (e.g. performance measurement, bureaucracy, etc.) become the only ends that matter, the notion of bullshit work develops into a depressing (and perhaps disciplining) employee experience.

So here we need to go back to the drawing board – to get rid not only of the jobs that exist merely for self-enrichment, but of the entire structural configuration that informs the very meaning of employment. What exactly do we want from our society and the jobs it creates? This sounds like a big question, and it is. But there are many ways forward. For example, the present use of unemployment to maintain a nervous equilibrium in wealthy Western economies could be flagged as a potential measure for what is possible without exploitative work. Because we apparently do not have enough work to go around, we once again witness the blatant disconnect between individual subsistence and one's coerced employment. Some might object that this would impinge upon the freedom of those who choose to work more than three days a week. But such arguments are clearly deluded. Once everyone has received their weekly pay after three days, why would they choose to work for nothing?

5. **Demassifying society as a positive global movement.** A friend recently sent me this:

> About 70 per cent of agricultural land and freshwater is used for livestock – more for grains as livestock feed. Beef production uses three-fifths of global farmland. It yields under 5 per cent of protein. A kilogram of beef requires 15,000 liters of water. Shouldn't we stop eating meat?

Slow meat will yield beautifully slow humans and a counter-offensive that will undermine the planet of work. Slowing down meat consumption is a metaphor for a wider process: slowing down the massification of ways of life that not only have little ethical purpose but are incredible self-destructive. This is a very apt anti-work mentality, because all of the same terms apply. One of the most insidious ideological tropes of late capitalism is that it promotes difference, diversity and gradations of taste. In other words, because individuals can pick and choose in the marketplace they are able to express their true wishes. But this is a myth. For example, the universalizing ritual of work (that generalizes the 'I, Job' function to every corner of society) represses individual differences on a scale that even the Soviet Union would have found crass. In fact, contemporary capitalist work patterns and coercive state communism share a set of elective affinities in this regard. And much of this has to do with the pointless and self-referential aspects of work – accelerated actions that go nowhere, that use up more energy than they give back, and so forth. Capitalism does not equate to individual freedom of expression; exactly the opposite is true.

6. **Demonetarizing incentive structures.** This is not the place to develop an alternative model of money. But we can make some suggestions about one part of the issue: incentivization. We are currently imprisoned in a theory of money that suggests that its endless accumulation is the only thing that makes us do anything – getting out of bed in the morning, acquiring an education, going to work; and for neoclassical economists such as Gary Becker, finding a romantic partner, obeying the law, etc. But the theory is false on two grounds. First, the artificial scarcity created by neoliberal policies means that our interest in money is more related to avoiding a looming human scrapheap than to any positive self-interest. Only a moron would call monetary self-preservation in the face of economic ruin yet another example of competitive 'self-interest'. And secondly, a panoply of research tells us that we become our creative, moral, insightful, inventive and productive best (i.e. happy people) when motivated by intrinsic rewards rather than financial ones (see Sandel, 2012; Pink, 2009). After a certain threshold is passed, money tends to spoil things; our desire for it (to buy things, obtain status, etc.) quickly becomes self-referential and tautological (we want money for its own sake). And is this not also a key factor underlying the feeling of endlessness that marks the ideology of work? We tend to be at our best when we do things that we are inherently interested in for their own worth or geared towards important social goals. In this sense, it is easy to imagine a self-authored incentive structure that would allow the common to thrive with rich and eclectic differences; it might even incorporate

its own negation for those who wish not to have incentives. This is why the monetarily 'rich' are so often impoverished along a number of equally important dimensions.

This list of easily achievable alternatives goes on and on. And the reader knows what needs to be changed as much as I do. However, one of the objectives of this book is to insist that alternatives and perception go hand in hand when considering the end of work. In other words, we require a different way of seeing the seemingly universal nature of a social construction that ought to be only a minimal part of life – instead, it has connected itself to everything. And this has a peculiar effect on our political imagination because we see no exit. David Eggers captures a facet of this ideological trap in his brilliant 2012 novel about the psychological impact of the global financial crisis, *A Hologram for the King*. The protagonist, a desperate, humiliated and near-bankrupted sales executive, considers his enslavement to mobile technology: 'This is the peculiar problem of constant connectivity: any silence of more than a few hours provokes apocalyptic thoughts.' Or applied to the topic of this book, the only alternative to work is thought to be the cataclysmic annihilation of humanity. But why can't we turn this powerful silence around and use its bipolar, 'all or nothing' logic for emancipatory purposes? It is the neoliberal gaze and its class relations that ought to suffer from debilitating anxiety as we refuse to stay in touch, refuse the attention it so urgently demands from us, and decline participation, realizing that the true apocalypse is not an unthinkably frightening future, but a very flat and linear present.

References

Abbas, A. (2012). 'Adorno and the Weather: Critical Theory in the Era of Climate Change'. *Radical Philosophy*, 174: 7–14.

Adams, D. and Newsham, J. (2014). 'Happy ending for Market Basket employees, customers'. *Boston Globe*. Available at www.bostonglobe.com/business/2014/08/28/happy-ending-for-market-basket-employees-customers/8DYrQ8orJYtvHM1BdYSEyK/story.html?p1=Article_Trending_Top

Adorno, T.W. (1966/1973). *Negative Dialectics*. New York: Routledge.

Adorno, T.W. (2005). *Minima Moralia: Reflections on a Damaged Life*. London: Verso.

Albert, M. (2004). *Parecon: Life After Capitalism*. London: Verso.

Aubenas, F. (2011). *The Night Cleaner*. Polity: Cambridge.

autonome a.f.r.k.a groupe (2002). 'Communication Guerrillas: Using the Language of Power'. In E. Lubbers (ed.). *Battling Big Business: Counter Greenwash, Infiltration and Other Forms of Corporate Bullying*. Common Courage Press: Maine.

Bansal, P. and Clelland, I. (2004). 'Talking Trash: Legitimacy, Impression Management, and Unsystematic Risk in the Context of the Natural Environment'. *Academy of Management Journal*, 47(1): 93–103.

Barley, S. and Kunda, G. (1992). 'Design and Devotion: Surges in Rational and Normative Ideologies in Managerial Discourse'. *Administrative Science Quarterly*, 37: 366–399.

Bauman, Z. (2005). *Work, Consumerism and the New Poor*. Maidenhead: Open University Press.

BBC (2013). 'Amazon workers face "increased risk of mental illness"'. Available at www.bbc.co.uk/news/business-25034598

BBC (2014a). 'Recession led to 10,000 suicides'. Available at www.bbc.co.uk/news/health-27796628

BBC (2014b). 'Managers work an extra day per week in unpaid overtime'. Available at www.bbc.co.uk/news/business-28220312

Becker, G. (2012). 'American Neoliberalism: Michel Foucault's Birth of Biopolitics Lectures'. Available at http://vimeo.com/43984248

Berardi, F. (2009). *The Soul at Work*. Los Angeles: Semiotext(e).

Beynon, H. (1973). *Working for Ford*. London: Allen Lane.

Bloch, E. (1964/2000). *The Spirt of Utopia*. Stanford: Stanford University Press.

Bobo, K. (2009). *Wage Theft in America: Why Millions of Working Americans Are Not Getting Paid – And What We Can Do About It*. New York: New Press.

Brabeck, P. (2008). 'Nestlé CEO Peter Brabeck'. Available at https://www.youtube.com/watch?v=qyAzxmN2sow

Braverman, H. (1974). *Labor and Monopoly Capitalism*. New York: Monthly Review Press.

Brecht, B. (2007). *Bertold Brecht: Poetry and Prose*. New York: Continuum Publishing.

Breed, L. (2014). 'Strategies of the Tobacco Industry'. Available at http://archive. tobacco.org/resources/history/strategieslb.html

Bukowski, C. (2012). 'Charles Bukowski discusses mental health strategy'. Available at https://www.youtube.com/watch?v=GXpUthEv2xM

Casey, C. (1995). *Work, Self and Society: After Industrialism*. London: Sage.

CBC News (2013). '3 tobacco companies in $27B lawsuit begin their defence'. Available at www.cbc.ca/news/canada/montreal/3-tobacco-companies-in-27b-lawsuit-begin-their-defence-1.1385839

Cederström C. and Fleming, P. (2012). *Dead Man Working*. London: Zero Books.

Certeau, M. de (1984). *The Practice of Everyday Life*. University of California Press: Berkeley.

Chu, B. (2014). 'Top Bosses' Rewards Now 143 Times Workers' Pay'. *The Independent*, 18 August, p. 47. Available at www.independent.co.uk/news/business/news/top-bosses-rewards-now-143-times-workers-pay-9674953.html

Clastres, P. (1989). *Society Against the State*. Trans. Robert Hurley. Zone Books: New York.

Cohen, J., Hazelrigg, L.E. and Pope, W. (1975). 'DeParsonizing Weber: A Critique of Parsons' Interpretation of Weber's Sociology'. *American Sociological Review*, 40: 229–241.

Collini, S. (2012). *What Are Universities For?* London: Penguin Books.

Corporate Europe Observatory (2009). 'Obscured By the Smoke'. Available at http://corporateeurope.org/lobbycracy/2009/06/obscured-smoke

Costas, J. and Fleming, P. (2009). 'Beyond Dis-identification: Towards a Discursive Approach to Self-Alienation in Contemporary Organizations'. *Human Relations*, 62(3): 353–378.

Crary, J. (2013). *24/7: Late Capitalism and the Ends of Sleep*. London: Verso.

Critchley, S. (2008). *Infinitely Demanding: Ethics of Commitment, Politics of Resistance*. London: Verso.

Crouch, C. (2011). *The Strange Non-death of Neoliberalism*. Polity: Cambridge.

Crozier, M. (1964). *The Bureaucratic Phenomenon*. Chicago: Chicago University Press.

Danisonfire (2013). 'The Joy of Illness'. Available at https://www.youtube.com/watch?v=_h17_opyIu4

Dardot, P. and Laval, C. (2014). *The New Way of the World: On Neoliberal Society*. London: Verso.

Deleuze, G. (1992). 'Postscript on the Societies of Control'. *October*, 59, Winter: 3–7.

Deleuze, G. (2004). *Desert Islands: And Other Texts 1953–1974*. Los Angeles: Semiotext(e).

Deleuze, G. (2006). *Foucault*. New York: Continuum.

Deleuze, G. and Guattari, F. (1983). *Anti-Oedipus*. Minneapolis: University of Minnesota Press.

Deleuze, G. and Guattari, F. (1987). *A Thousand Plateaus: Capitalism and Schizophrenia.* Trans. B. Massumi. Minneapolis: Minneapolis University Press.

Doward, J. (2014). '"Endies": Employed with No Disposable Income are struggling in London'. *The Guardian*, 15 September. Available at www.theguardian.com/uk-news/2014/sep/13/endies-employed-no-disposable-income-struggling-in-london

Duménil, G. and Lévy, D. (2011). *The Crisis of Neoliberalism.* Cambridge, Mass.: Harvard University Press.

Economist, The (2014). 'Work Until You Drop'. Available at www.economist.com/news/finance-and-economics/21623757-ageing-societies-create-many-employment-challenges-work-until-you-drop

Economist Intelligence Unit (2014). 'Global Liveability Ranking and Report'. www.eiu.com/public/topical_report.aspx?campaignid=Liveability2014

Edwards, R. (1979). *Contested Terrain: The Transformation of the Workplace in the Twentieth Century.* New York: Basic Books.

Elkington, J. (1994). 'Towards the Sustainable Corporation: Win–Win–Win Business Strategies for Sustainable Development'. *California Management Review*, 36(2): 90–100.

Ferriss, T. (2011). *The Four-Hour Work Week: Escape the 9–5, Live Anywhere and Join the New Rich.* New York: Vermilion.

Fisher, M. (2014). *Ghosts of My Life.* London: Verso.

Flanagan, B. (2000). *The Pain Journal.* Semiotext(e): Los Angeles.

Fleming, P. (2009). *Authenticity and the Cultural Politics of Work.* Oxford: Oxford University Press.

Fleming, P. (2014). *Resisting Work: The Corporatization of Life and Its Discontents.* Philadelphia: Temple University Press.

Fleming, P. and Spicer, A. (2003). 'Working at a Cynical Distance: Implications for Power Resistance and Subjectivity in the Workplace'. *Organization*, 10(1): 157–179.

Fleming, P. and Spicer, A. (2010). *Contesting the Corporation.* Cambridge: Cambridge University Press.

Fleming, P. and Sturdy, A. (2011). 'Being Yourself in the Electronic Sweatshop: New Forms of Normative Control'. *Human Relations*, 64(2): 177–200.

Foster, J.B. and McChesney, R. (2012). *The Endless Crisis: How Monopoly-Finance Capital Produces Stagnation and Upheaval from the USA to China.* New York: Monthly Review Press.

Foster, R. and Kaplan, S. (2001). *Creative Destruction: Why Companies That Are Built to Last Underperform the Market – And How to Successfully Transform Them.* New York: Currency.

Foucault, M. (1977). *Discipline and Punish: The Birth of the Prison.* London: Penguin.

Foucault, M. (2001). *Fearless Speech.* Los Angeles: Semiotext(e).

Foucault, M. (2008). *The Birth of Biopolitics: Lectures at the Collège de France, 1978–79.* Palgrave: London.

Foucault, M. (2010). *Government of Self and Others: Lectures at the college de France 1982-1983.* London: Palgrave Macmillan.

Freud, S. (1905/1960). *Jokes and Their Relation to the Unconscious*. Trans. J. Strachey. New York: Norton.

Friedman, L. (2009). 'Tobacco Industry Use of Corporate Social Responsibly Tactics as a Sword and a Shield on Secondhand Smoke Issues'. *Journal of Law, Medicine and Ethics*, Winter: 819–827.

Friedman, M. (1970). 'The Social Responsibility of Business Is to Increase Profits'. *New York Times Magazine*, 13 September.

Gallup (2013). 'State of the Global Workplace Report'. Available at www.gallup.com/strategicconsulting/164735/state-global-workplace.aspx

Gillespie, R. (1991). *Manufacturing Knowledge: A History of the Hawthorne Experiments*. Cambridge: Cambridge University Press.

Goffee, R. and Jones, G. (2003). *The Character of the Corporation*. London: Profile Books.

Gordon, D. (1996). *Fat and Mean: The Corporate Squeeze of Working Americans and the Myth of Managerial 'Downsizing'*. Martin Kessler Books: New York.

Gorz, A. (1989). *Critique of Economic Reason*. London: Verso.

Gorz, A. (1994). *Capitalism, Socialism, Ecology*. London: Verso.

Gorz, A. (2010). *Immaterial*. London: Seagull Books.

Graeber, D. (2013). 'On the Phenomenon of Bullshit Jobs'. *Strike Magazine*, August: 7–8.

Gregg, M. (2011). *Work's Intimacies*. Polity: Cambridge.

Guardian, The (2012). 'Rio+20 Earth Summit: campaigners decry final document'. Available at www.theguardian.com/environment/2012/jun/23/rio-20-earth-summit-document

Guardian, The (2013). 'The US Super-Rich Hit New Wealth Record Five Years After the Crisis'. www.theguardian.com/business/2013/sep/16/us-super-rich-recover-losses-financial-crisis-forbes

Guardian, The (2014a). 'The Rise of the Renegade Professionals'. http://surface.theguardian.com/more-inspiration/

Guardian, The (2014b). 'Closed Shop in Elitist Britain, Study Says'. Available at www.theguardian.com/society/2014/aug/28/closed-shop-deepy-elitist-britain

Hamper, B. (1992). *Rivethead: Takes from the Assembly Line*. New York: Warner Books.

Hanlon, G. (2007). 'HRM Is Redundant? Professions, Immaterial Labor and the Future of Work'. In S.H. Bolton (ed.). *Searching for the Human in Human Resource Management: Theory, Practice and Workplace Contexts*. Basingstoke: Palgrave MacMillan, pp.263–280.

Hardt, M. and Negri, A. (2000). *Empire*. Cambridge, Mass.: Harvard University Press.

Hart, A. (2014). 'Why Everyone's Started Clockwatching'. *Stylist*, 30 April.

Harvey, D. (2001). *Spaces of Hope: Towards a Critical Geography*. Edinburgh: University of Edinburgh Press.

Harvey, D. (2014). *Seventeen Contradictions and the End of Capitalism*. New York: Profile.

Hasek, J. (1973). *The Good Soldier Svejk*. London: Penguin Books.

Hayek, F. (1960). 'The Intellectuals and Socialism'. In George B. de Huszar (ed.). *The Intellectuals: A Controversial Portrait*. Glencoe, Ill.: The Free Press, pp.371–384.

Hayek, F. (1973/2013). *Law, Legislation and Liberty: A New Statement of the Liberal Principles of Justice and Political Economy*. New York: Routledge.

Hirschhorn (2008). 'Evolution of the Tobacco Industry Positions on Addiction to Nicotine'. *World Health Organization Report*. Available at http://whqlibdoc.who.int/publications/2009/9789241597265_eng.pdf?ua=1

Hodgkinson, T. (2004). *How to Be Idle*. London: Penguin.

Imperial Tobacco Canada (2012). 'Background to the Blais and Letourneau Class Actions'. Available at www.imperialtobaccocanada.com/groupca/sites/IMP_7VSH6J.nsf/vwPagesWebLive/DO8SBK2L?opendocument&SKN=1

Independent, The (2013). 'Women Working Long-Term Night Shift Jobs Twice as Likely to Develop Breast Cancer, Warns Study'. www.independent.co.uk/life-style/health-and-families/health-news/women-working-longterm-nightshift-jobs-are-twice-as-likely-to-develop-breast-cancer-warns-study-8682363.html

Independent, The (2014). 'Segarra claims NY Fed fired her "for Goldman finding"'. Available at www.independent.co.uk/news/business/news/segarra-claims-ny-fed-fired-her-for-goldman-finding-8875352.html

Invisible Committee, The (2009). *The Coming Insurrection*. Semiotext(e): Los Angeles.

Jameson, F. (1996). *The Seeds of Time*. New York: Columbia University Press.

Kamp, A. (2013). 'New Concepts of Work and Time'. In M. Hoegsberg and C. Fisher (eds). *Living Labor*. Berlin: Sternberg Press.

Kellaway, L. (2014). 'Branson's Big Holiday Offer – Give Us a Break'. *Financial Times*, 29 September, pp. 16.

Keynes, J.M. (1930/2009). 'Economic Prospects of Our Grandchildren'. In *Essays In Persuasion*. Classic House Books: New York, pp.191–202.

Kreitzman, L. (1999). *The 24 Hour Society*. Profile Books: London.

Kunda, G. (1992). *Engineering Culture: Control and Commitment in a High-Tech Corporation*. Philadelphia: Temple University Press.

Larkin, P. (2012). *Philip Larkin: The Collected Works*. Edited by Archie Burnett. Faber and Faber: London.

Latour, B. (2004). 'Why Has Critique Run Out of Steam? From Matters of Fact to Matters of Concern'. *Critical Inquiry*, 30, Winter: 225–248.

Lazzarato, M. (2012). *The Making of the Indebted Man*. Los Angeles: Semiotext(e).

Lefebvre, H. (1947/1991). *The Critique of Everyday Life*. London: Verso.

Leidner, R. (1993). *Fast Food, Fast Talk: Service Work and the Routinization of Everyday Life*. Berkeley: University of California Press.

Lordon, F. (2014). *Willing Slaves of Capital: Spinoza and Marx on Desire*. Verso: London.

Lucas, R. (2010). 'Dreaming in Code'. *New Left Review*, 62: 125–132.

Lukács, G. (1971). *History and Class Consciousness*. Trans. Rodney Livingstone. Cambridge, Mass.: MIT Press.

Lynch, R. (2014). 'Thanks to Help To Buy, Builders are the New Bankers'. *The Independent*, 20 August, available at www.independent.co.uk/news/business/comment/thanks-to-help-to-buy-builders-are-the-new-bankers-9679820.html

MacFie, R. (2013). *Tragedy at Pike River Mine: How and Why 29 Men Died*. Wellington: Awa Press.

Marcuse, H. (1941/1982). Some Social Implications of Modern Technology'. In A. Arato and E. Gebhardt (eds). *The Essential Frankfurt School Reader*. Continuum Publishers: New York, pp.138–163

Marcuse, H. (1955). *Eros and Civilization*. London: Abacus Books.

Marx, K. (1867/1976). *Capital*. London: Penguin.

Marx, K. (1988). *The 1844 Philosophic and Economic Manuscripts*. New York: Moscow Press.

Matten, D. and Crane, A. (2005). 'Corporate citizenship: towards an extended theoretical conceptualization.' *Academy of Management Review*, 30(1): 166–179.

Meek, J. (2014). 'Sale of the Century: The Privatization Scam'. *The Guardian*, 22 August. Available at www.theguardian.com/politics/2014/aug/22/sale-of-century-privatisation-scam

Metro (2013). 'Burnout is a Bigger Heart Attack Risk Than Smoking'. 14 March.

Meyerson, D. (2001). *Tempered Radicals: How People Use Difference to Inspire Change at Work*. Cambridge, Mass: Harvard Business School Press.

Michelli, J. (2007). *The Starbucks Experience: 5 Principles for turning Ordinary into Extraordinary*. New York: McGraw-Hill Professional.

Miller, W.I. (2003). *Faking It*. Cambridge: Cambridge University Press.

Mirowski, P (2013). *Never Let a Serious Crisis Go to Waste: How Neoliberalism Survived the Financial Meltdown*. London: Verso.

Monaghan, A. (2014). 'Self-employment at Highest Level for 40 Years'. *The Guardian*. Available at www.theguardian.com/uk-news/2014/aug/20/self-employment-uk-highest-level

Mooney, G. (2014). 'Here Are Five Infuriating Facts that Make People Dumber'. Mother Jones. Available at www.motherjones.com/blue-marble/2014/03/brendan-nyhan-backfire-effects-facts

Moore, A.E. (2007). *Unmarketable*. New York: The New Press.

Negrey, C. (2012). *Work Time: Conflict, Control and Change*. Polity: London.

Negri, A. (2009). *The Labor of Job: The Biblical Text as a Parable of Human Labor*. Durham, NC: Duke University Press.

Nestlé (2014). 'Creating shared value'. Available at www.nestle-waters.com/creating-shared-value

News China (2013). 'Worked to Death'. Available at www.newschinamag.com/magazine/worked-to-death

O'Reilly, C. and Chatman, J. (1996). 'Culture as Social Control: Corporations, Cults and Commitment'. In B. Staw and L. Cummings (eds). *Research in Organization Behaviour*. Greenwich, CT: JAI Press.

Paulsen, R. (2014). *Empty Labour: Subjectivity and Idleness at Work*. Cambridge: Cambridge University Press.

Peters, T. (2003). *Re-Imagine! Business Excellence in a Disruptive Age*. London: Dorling Kindersley.

Peters, T. and Waterman, R.H. (1982). *In Search of Excellence*. New York: Harper & Row.

Piketty, T. (2014). *Capital in the Twenty-First Century*. Cambridge, Mass.: Harvard University Press.

Pink, D. (2009). *Drive: The Surprising Truth about What Motivates Us*. Edinburgh: Cannongate.

Pook, L. (2014). Only Smart Drugs Have the Answer?' *Stylist*. Available at www.stylist.co.uk/life/only-smart-pills-have-the-answer

Porter, M. and Kramer, M. (2011). 'Creating Shared Value'. *Harvard Business Review*, 89(1/2): 62–77.

Price, S. (2008). *How to Disappear in America*. New York: Leopard Press.

Ressler, C. and Thompson, J. (2011). *Why Work Sucks and How to Fix It: The Results-Only Revolution*. New York: Portfolio.

Reuters (2014). 'U.S. sues N.Y. company that workers say made them pray, say 'I love you'. Available at www.reuters.com/article/2014/06/11/us-usa-new-york-onionhead-idUSKBN0EM2PR20140611

Roberts, J. (2003). 'The Manufacture of Corporate Social Responsibility: Constructing Corporate Sensibility'. *Organization*, 10(2): 249–265.

Rosenblatt, R. (1994). 'How Do Tobacco Company Executives Live With Themselves?' *New York Times*. Available at www.nytimes.com/1994/03/20/magazine/how-do-tobacco-executives-live-with-themselves.html

Ross, A. (2013). *Creditocracy and the Case for Debt Refusal*. New York: OR Books.

Ross, K. (1989). *The Emergence of Social Space: Rimbaud and the Paris Commune*. Minneapolis: University of Minnesota Press.

Sallaz, J. (2013). *Labor, Economy and Society*. Cambridge: Polity Press.

Sandel, M. (2012). *What Money Can't Buy: The Moral Limits of Markets*. Farrar, Straus & Giroux: New York.

Scarry, E. (1985). *The Body in Pain: The Making and Unmaking of the World*. New York: Oxford University Press.

Semler, R. (2007). *The Seven-Day Weekend*. New York: Penguin.

Shragai, N. (2014). 'Paranoia at Work Is Out to Get You'. *Financial Times*, July 18.

Socialist Patients' Collective (1987). *Turn Illness into a Weapon*. Heidelberg: KRRIM Publications.

Spicer, A. and Alvesson, M. (2012). 'A Stupidity-Based Theory of Organizations'. *Journal of Management Studies*, 49(7): 1194–1220.

Taylor, F.W. (1911/1967). *The Principles of Scientific Management*. New York: W.W. Norton and Co.

Taylor, S. (2000). 'Diary of a Tagged Prisoner'. *The Guardian*. Available at www.theguardian.com/society/2000/jan/12/aitken.politics

This American Life (2014). 'The Secret Recordings of Carmen Segarra'. Available at www.thisamericanlife.org/radio-archives/episode/536/the-secret-recordings-of-carmen-segarra

Thompson, E.P. (1967). 'Time, Work-Discipline and Industrial Capitalism'. *Past and Present*, 38: 56–103.

Times Higher Education Supplement (2014). 'Swansea Staff Accused of Being Stuck in the 1960s'. Available at www.timeshighereducation.co.uk/news/swansea-staff-accused-of-being-stuck-in-the-1960s/2014442.article

Virilio, P. (2012). *The Lost Dimension*. Los Angeles: Semiotext(e).

Virno, P. (2004). *A Grammar of the Multitude: For an Analysis of Contemporary Forms of Life*. Los Angeles: Semiotext(e).

Virno, P. (2008). *Multitude: Between Innovation and Negation*. Los Angeles: Semiotex(e).

Weber, M. (1905/1930). *The Protestant Ethic and the Spirit of Capitalism*. New York: Allen & Unwin.

Weber, M. (1946). *From Max Weber: Essays in Sociology*. New York: Oxford University Press.

Weeks, J. (2004). *Unpopular Culture: Rituals of Complaint in a British Bank*. Chicago: University of Chicago Press.

Weil, D. (2014). *The Fissured Workplace: Why Work Became So Bad For So Many and What Can Be Done to Improve It*. Cambridge, Mass.: Harvard University Press.

Weiss, B. and Feldman, R.S. (2006). 'Looking Good and Lying to Do It: Deception as an Impression Management Strategy in Job Interviews'. *Journal of Applied Psychology*, 36(4): 1070–1084.

Williams, R. (1977). *Marxism and Literature*. Oxford: Oxford Paperbacks.

Williams-Grut, O. (2014). 'Drinking on the Job'. *Evening Standard*. 3 July.

Willmott, H. (1993). 'Strength Is Ignorance; Slavery is Freedom: Managing Cultures in Modern Organizations'. *Journal of Management Studies*, 30(4): 515–552.

Wolff, R. (2012). *Democracy at Work: A Cure for Capitalism*. Chicago: Haymarket Books.

World Health Organization (2008). *Report on the Global Tobacco Epidemic, 2008*. Available at www.who.int/tobacco/mpower/mpower_report_full_2008.pdf

Zenger, J. (2013). 'Why Gallup's 70% Engagement Data is Wrong'. *Forbes*. Available at www.forbes.com/sites/jackzenger/2013/11/14/why-gallups-70-disengagement-data-is-wrong/

Žižek, S. (2009). *First as Tragedy, Then as Farce*. London: Verso.

Index

Compiled by Sue Carlton